SOCCER

THE RECO

SOCCER
THE RECORDS

Jack Rollin

GUINNESS BOOKS

Editor: Beatrice Frei
Design and Layout: David Roberts and D P Press Ltd, Sevenoaks, Kent

Published in Great Britain by Guinness Superlatives Ltd, 2 Cecil Court, London Road, Enfield, Middlesex

Phototypeset in 11/12pt Times and 8pt Helvetica by Input Typesetting Ltd, London SW19 8DR
Printed and bound in Great Britain by
Hazell Watson & Viney Ltd, Member of the BPCC Group, Aylesbury, Buckinghamshire.

British Library Cataloguing in Publication Data

Rollin, Jack
Guinness soccer: the records.
1. Soccer
I. Title
796.334 GV943

ISBN 0–85112–436–4
ISBN 0–85112–449–6 Pbk

Introduction

Soccer – The Records represents a new treatment of the facts and figures of the game featuring the best of the all-time records at various levels, plus in-depth illustrated stories of some of the world's most famous players past and present.

Moreover, the book highlights the most exciting aspect of soccer – goalscoring – and features interesting details of domestic football not previously referred to in record presentation.

All major tournaments including the World Cup, European Championships and the three leading European club competitions are given extensive coverage, and the analysis of Football League and Scottish League as well as their respective cup competitions is also well documented.

The author would like to acknowledge the assistance and contribution of John Byrne, Maurice Golesworthy, Christine Phillips and C. R. Williamson.

Contents

Index to special features

Major British records

Highest scores

First class match
Arbroath 36 Bon Accord 0, Scottish Cup 1st rd 5.9.1885
International
England 13 Northern Ireland 0, 18.2.82
FA Cup
Preston North End 26 Hyde 0, 1st rd, 15.10.1897
League Cup
West Ham United 10 Bury 0, 2nd rd, 2nd leg, 25.10.83

Football League

Division 1
home West Bromwich Albion 12 Darwen 0, 4.4.1892; Nottingham Forest 12 Leicester Fosse 0, 21.4.09; **away** Newcastle United 1 Sunderland 9, 5.12.08; Cardiff City 1 Wolverhampton Wanderers 9, 3.9.55

Division 2
home Newcastle United 13 Newport County 0, 5.10.46; **away** Burslem Port Vale 0 Sheffield United 10, 10.12.1892

Division 3
home Tranmere Rovers 9 Accrington Stanley 0, 18.4.59; Brentford 9 Wrexham 0, 15.10.63; **away** Halifax Town 0 Fulham 8, 16.9.69; Brighton & Hove Albion 2 Bristol Rovers 8, 1.12.73

Division 3 Southern
home Luton Town 12 Bristol Rovers 0, 13.4.36; **away** Northampton Town 0 Walsall 8, 2.2.47

Division 3 Northern
home Stockport County 13 Halifax Town 0, 6.1.34; **away** Accrington Stanley 0 Barnsley 9, 3.2.34

Division 4
home Oldham Athletic 11 Southport 0, 26.12.62; **away** Crewe Alexandra 1 Rotherham United 8, 8.9.73

Scottish League
Premier Division
home Aberdeen 8 Motherwell 0, 26.3.79; **away** Kilmarnock 1 Rangers 8, 20.9.80

Division 1
home Celtic 11 Dundee 0, 26.10.1895; **away** Airdrieonians 1 Hibernian 11, 24.10.50

Division 2
home East Fife 13 Edinburgh City 2, 11.12.37; **away** Alloa Athletic 0 Dundee 10, 8.3.47

Football League

Most wins in a season

	Team	Division	Season
31	Tottenham Hotspur	1	1960–61
32	Tottenham Hotspur	2	1919–20
30	Plymouth Argyle	3S	1929–30
30	Millwall	3S	1927–28
30	Cardiff City	3S	1946–47
30	Nottingham Forest	3S	1950–51
30	Bristol City	3S	1954–55
33	Doncaster Rovers	3N	1946–47
32	Aston Villa	3	1971–72
32	Lincoln City	4	1975–76

Most drawn games in a season

23	Norwich City	1	1978–79

Most defeats in a season

31	Stoke City	1	1984–85
31	Tranmere Rovers	2	1938–39
31	Newport County	3	1961–62
29	Merthyr Town	3S	1924–25
33	Rochdale	3N	1931–32
32	Workington	4	1975–76

Fewest wins in a season

3	Stoke	1	1889–90
3	Woolwich Arsenal	1	1912–13
3	Stoke City	1	1984–85
1	Loughborough Town	2	1899–1900
6	Merthyr Town	3S	1929–30
4	Rochdale	3N	1931–32
2	Rochdale	3	1973–74
3	Southport	4	1976–77

Fewest defeats in a season

0	Preston North End	1	1888–89
2	Leeds United	1	1968–69
0	Liverpool	2	1893–94
2	Burnley	2	1897–98
2	Bristol City	2	1905–06
3	Leeds United	2	1963–64
5	Queen's Park Rangers	3	1966–67
4	Southampton	3S	1921–22
4	Plymouth Argyle	3S	1929–30
3	Port Vale	3N	1953–54
3	Doncaster Rovers	3N	1946–47
3	Wolverhampton Wanderers	3N	1923–24
4	Lincoln City	4	1975–76

Longest winning sequence

14	Manchester United	2	1904–05
14	Bristol City	2	1905–06
14	Preston North End	2	1950–51

Longest unbeaten sequence

42	Nottingham Forest	1	Nov. 1977–Dec. 1978

Most goals scored in a season

128	Aston Villa	1	1930–31
122	Middlesbrough	2	1926–27
127	Millwall	3S	1927–28
128	Bradford City	3N	1928–29
111	Queen's Park Rangers	3	1961–62
134	Peterborough United	4	1960–61

Most goals conceded in a season

125	Blackpool	1	1930–31
141	Darwen	2	1898–99
135	Merthyr Town	3S	1929–30
136	Nelson	3N	1927–28
123	Accrington Stanley	3	1959–60
109	Hartlepool United	4	1959–60

Fewest goals scored in a season

24	Stoke City	1	1984–85
24	Watford	2	1971–72
33	Crystal Palace	3S	1950–51
32	Crewe Alexandra	3N	1923–24
27	Stockport County	3	1969–70
29	Crewe Alexandra	4	1981–82

Fewest goals conceded in a season

16	Liverpool	1	1978–79
23	Manchester United	2	1924–25
21	Southampton	3S	1921–22
21	Port Vale	3N	1953–54
32	Rotherham United	3	1980–81
25	Lincoln City	4	1980–81

Longest sequence without a win in a season

31	Cambridge United	2	1983–84

Longest sequence of consecutive defeats in a season

17	Rochdale	3N	1931–32

Scottish League

Most wins in a season

27	Aberdeen	Pr Div	1984–85
35	Rangers	1	1920–21
33	Morton	2	1966–67

Most drawn games in a season

18	Hibernian	Pr Div	1976–77

Most defeats in a season

29	Morton	Pr Div	1984–85
31	St Mirren	1	1920–21
30	Brechin City	2	1962–63

Fewest wins in a season

3	St Johnstone	Pr Div	1975–76
0	Vale of Leven	1	1891–92
1	East Stirlingshire	2	1905–06
1	Forfar Athletic	2	1974–75

Fewest defeats in a season

4	Aberdeen	Pr Div	1983–84
4	Aberdeen	Pr Div	1984–85
4	Celtic	Pr Div	1976–77
1	Rangers	1	1920–21
1	Clyde	2	1956–57
1	Morton	2	1962–63

Longest winning sequence in a season

23	Morton	2	1963–64

Most goals scored in a season

90	Dundee United	Pr Div	1982–83
90	Celtic	Pr Div	1982–83
132	Heart of Midlothian	1	1957–58
142	Raith Rovers	2	1937–38

Fewest goals scored in a season

23	Clydebank	Pr Div	1977–78
23	Kilmarnock	Pr Div	1980–81
18	Stirling Albion	1	1980–81
20	Lochgelly United	2	1923–24

Fewest goals conceded in a season

21	Aberdeen	Pr Div	1983–84
14	Celtic	1	1913–14
20	Morton	2	1966–67

Individual British goalscoring records

Football League
10 goals, Joe Payne, Luton Town v Bristol Rovers, Division 3S, 13.4.36

Division I
7 goals, Ted Drake, Arsenal v Aston Villa, 14.12.35; and James Ross, Preston North End v Stoke City, 6.10.1888

FA Cup
9 goals, Ted MacDougall, Bournemouth v Margate, 20.11.71

FA Cup (preliminary rounds)
10 goals, Chris Marron, South Shields v Radcliffe, 20.9.47

Scottish League
8 goals, Jimmy McGrory, Celtic v Dunfermline Athletic, 14.1.28

Scottish Cup
13 goals, John Petrie, Arbroath v Bon Accord, 5.9.1885

British International Championship
6 goals, Joe Bambrick, Ireland v Wales, 1.2.30

Career totals

Football League
434 goals, Arthur Rowley, West Bromwich Albion, Fulham, Leicester City and Shrewsbury Town, 1946–1965

Scottish League
410 goals, Jimmy McGrory, Celtic and Clydebank, 1922–1938

Quickest goals
6 seconds, Albert Mundy, Aldershot v Hartlepool United, Division 4, 25.10.58; 6 seconds, Barrie Jones, Notts County v Torquay United, Division 3, 31.3.62; 6 seconds, Keith Smith, Crystal Palace v Derby County, Division 2, 12.12.64; 6 seconds, Tommy Langley, Queen's Park Rangers v Bolton Wanderers, Division 2, 11.10.80

Fastest hat-trick
3 goals in 2½ minutes, Ephraim 'Jock' Dodds, Blackpool v Tranmere Rovers, Wartime Regional League, 28.2.43 and Jimmy Scarth, Gillingham v Leyton Orient, Divison 3S, 1.11.52
4 goals in 5 minutes, John McIntyre, Blackburn Rovers v Everton, 16.9.22; Ginger Richardson, West Bromwich Albion v West Ham United, 7.11.31 (from the start of the game)
6 goals in 21 minutes, Lincoln City v Halifax Town, Division 3N, 16.1.32

Fastest International hat-trick
3 goals in 3½ minutes, Willie Hall, England v Ireland, 16.11.38

Fastest own goal
6 seconds, Pat Kruse, Torquay United v Cambridge United, 3.1.77

International goalscoring records

For club
16 goals, Stephan Stanis (Stanikowski and sometimes known as Dembicki), Racing Club Lens v Aubry-Asturies, French Cup, 13.12.42

International Matches
10 goals, Sofus Nielsen, Denmark v France, 1908 Olympics; and Gottfried Fuchs, Germany v USSR (as Russia), 1912 Olympics

World career records
1329 goals, Artur Friedenreich, in Brazilian football, 1910–1930
1216 goals, Edson Arantes do Nascimento (Pelé) 1956–1974, in Brazilian football and later in USA for New York Cosmos taking total to 1281

Goalscoring in European competitions

European Cup individual aggregate
49, Alfredo di Stefano (Real Madrid) 1955–56 to 1963–64; 46, Eusebio (Benfica) 1961–62 to 1973–74; and 36, Gerd Muller (Bayern Munich) 1969–70 to 1976–77

European Cup in one season
14, José Altafini (AC Milan) 1962–63

Cup Winners' Cup
14, Lothar Emmerich (Borussia Dortmund), 1965–66

Highest scores
12–2 Feyenoord v KR Reykjavik, European Cup 1st rd, 17.9.69
11–0 Dynamo Bucharest v Crusaders, European Cup 1st rd, 3.10.73
16–1, Sporting Lisbon v Apoel Nicosia, Cup Winners' Cup 1st rd, 13.11.63
13–0 Cologne v Union Luxembourg, Fairs Cup 1st rd, 5.10.65

Highest scores involving British clubs
13–0 Chelsea v Jeunesse Hautcharage, Cup-Winners' Cup, 29.9.71
12–0 Derby County v Finn Harps, UEFA Cup, 15.9.76
10–0 Ipswich Town v Floriana, European Cup, 25.9.62
10–0 Leeds United v Lyn Oslo, European Cup, 17.9.69
11–0 Liverpool v Stromsgodset, Cup Winners' Cup, 17.9.74
10–0 Liverpool v Dundalk, Fairs Cup, 16.9.69
10–1 Liverpool v Oulun Palloseura, European Cup, 1.10.80
10–0 Manchester United v Anderlecht, European Cup, 26.9.56
10–1 Aberdeen v KR Reykjavik, Cup Winners' Cup, 6.9.67
10–1 Dunfermline Athletic v Apoel Nicosia, Cup Winners' Cup, 18.9.68
10–0 Rangers v Valetta, Cup Winners' Cup, 28.9.83
12–0 Swansea City v Sliema Wanderers, Cup Winners' Cup, 15.9.82

Top British marksmen in European competitions

Leading scorers
30 goals Peter Lorimer (Leeds United) 1965–66 to 1976–77; 28 goals Denis Law (Manchester United) 1963–64 to 1968–69; 20 goals Kenny Dalglish (Celtic and Liverpool) 1972–73 to 1983–84

First British player to score three penalties in one European game
John Wark (Ipswich Town) v Aris Salonika 17.9.80 UEFA Cup. Wark scored four goals in the game

Players scoring 5 goals in one match
Ray Crawford (Ipswich Town) v Floriana, European Cup 25.9.62; Peter Osgood (Chelsea) v Jeunesse Hautcharage, Cup-Winners' Cup, 29.9.71

Aggregate scores by individuals
11 goals Stan Bowles (Queen's Park Rangers) UEFA Cup, 1976–77; 7 goals in two games (five in first leg) Kevin Hector (Derby County) UEFA Cup, 1976–77; 4 goals on two occasions Trevor Whymark (Ipswich Town) v Lazio UEFA Cup, 24.10.73; v Landskrona Bois, UEFA Cup 28.9.77

Ray Crawford (Ipswich Town). (JB).

LEFT: Peter Lorimer (Leeds United). (ASP). BELOW: John Wark (Ipswich Town). (ASP). CENTRE: Denis Law (Manchester United). (ASP). BOTTOM RIGHT: Peter Osgood (Chelsea). (ASP). BOTTOM LEFT: Kevin Hector (Derby County). (ASP).

Golden Boot Award

for Europe's leading goalscorer

Season	First	Goals	Second	Goals	Third	Goals
1967–68	Eusebio (Benfica)	43	Antal Dunai (Ujpest Dozsa)	36	Bobby Lennox (Celtic)	32
1968–69	Petar Jekov (CSKA Sofia)	36	George Sideris (Olympiakos)	35	Helmut Kogelberger (FK Austria)	31
					Antal Dunai (Ujpest Dozsa)	31
1969–70	Gerd Muller (Bayern Munich)	38	Jan Devillet (Spora Luxembourg)	31		
			Petar Jekov (CSKA Sofia)	31		
1970–71	Josip Skoblar (Marseilles)	44	Salif Keita (St Etienne)	42	George Dedes (Panionios)	28
1971–72	Gerd Muller (Bayern Munich)	40	Antonis Antoniadis (Panathinaikos)	39	Joe Harper (Aberdeen)	33
					Slobodan Santrac (OFK Belgrade)	33
					Francis Lee (Manchester City)	33
1972–73	Eusebio (Benfica)	40	Gerd Muller (Bayern Munich)	36	Petar Jekov (CSKA Sofia)	29
1973–74	Hector Yazalde (Sporting Lisbon)	46	Hans Krankl (Rapid Vienna)	36	Gerd Muller (Bayern Munich)	30
					Jupp Heynckes (Borussia Moenchengladbach)	30
					Carlos Bianchi (Reims)	30
1974–75	Dudu Georgescu (Dinamo Bucharest)	33	Hector Yazalde (Sporting Lisbon)	30		
			Ruud Geels (Ajax)	30		
			Delio Onnis (Monaco)	30		
1975–76	Sotiris Kaiafas (Omonia Nicosia)	39	Carlos Bianchi (Reims)	34	Peter Risi (Zurich)	33
1976–77	Dudu Georgescu (Dinamo Bucharest)	47	Bela Varadi (Vasas Budapest)	36	Ruud Geels (Ajax)	34
					Dieter Muller (FC Cologne)	34
1977–78	Hans Krankl (Rapid Vienna)	41	Carlos Bianchi (Paris St Germain)	37	Ruud Geels (Ajax)	34
1978–79	Kees Kist (AZ 67 Alkmaar)	34	Thomas Mavros (AEK Athens)	31		
			Laszlo Fekete (Ujpest Dozsa)	31		
1979–80	Erwin Van Den Bergh (Lierse)	39	Laszlo Fazekas (Ujpest Dozsa)	36	Walter Schachner (Austria Vienna)	34
1980–81	Georgi Slavkov (Trakia Plovdiv)	31	Tibor Nyilasi (Ferencvaros)	30	Karl-Heinz Rummenigge (Bayern Munich)	29
1981–82	Wim Kieft (Ajax)	32	Kees Kist (AZ 67 Alkmaar)	29	Allan Hansen (Odense BK)	28
			Delio Onnis (Tours)	29		
1982–83	Francisco Gomes (Porto)	36	Peter Houtman (Feyenoord)	30	Nikos Anastopoulous (Olympiakos)	29
					Charlie Nicholas (Celtic)	29
1983–84	Ian Rush (Liverpool)	32	Marco Van Basten (Ajax)	28	Nico Claesen (Seraing)	27
1984–85	Not to hand at press time					

In the days before the Golden Boot Award, Arsenal goalkeeper George Swindin saves from the dubbined foot of a Liverpool attack in the 1950 FA Cup Final. (PA).

Goalkeeping

International

Dino Zoff, Italy unbeaten in 1142 minutes from September 1972 to June 1974

Football League

Steve Death, Reading 1103 minutes from 24 March to 18 August 1979

Most cup-winning medals

FA Cup-winning medals

5 James Forrest (Blackburn Rovers) 1884–86, 1890–91; the Hon Sir Arthur Fitzgerald Kinnaird, Kt (Wanderers) 1873, 1877–78, (Old Etonians) 1879, 1882; and Charles H. R. Wollaston (Wanderers) 1872–73, 1876–78

Scottish Cup-winning medals

8 Charles Campbell (Queen's Park), 1874–76, 1880–82, 1884 and 1886

Most League appearances

Football League

824 Terry Paine (713 Southampton, 111 Hereford United) 1957–77
770 John Trollope (Swindon Town) 1960–80
764 Jimmy Dickinson (Portsmouth) 1946–65
777 Alan Oakes (565 Manchester City, 211 Chester, 1 Port Vale) 1959–84
762 Roy Sproson (Port Vale) 1950–72
757 Pat Jennings (48 Watford, 472 Tottenham Hotspur, 237 Arsenal)
743 Alan Ball (146 Blackpool, 208 Everton, 177 Arsenal, 195 Southampton, 17 Bristol Rovers) 1962–84
743 John Hollins (465 Chelsea, 151 Queen's Park Rangers, 127 Arsenal) 1964–84

Scottish League

626 Bob Ferrier (Motherwell) 1918–37

TOP RIGHT: Lord Kinnaird was a versatile player accomplished in almost every position on the field. On his retirement as President of the FA he was presented with the FA Cup itself. BOTTOM RIGHT: Terry Paine (Southampton) who holds the record for the most appearances in the Football League. (ASP). FACING PAGE, LEFT TO RIGHT: Alan Oakes (Manchester City) and Alan Ball (Arsenal), both with a wealth of League experience. (ASP).

Football League analysis

Most points in a season

Football League (two points system)

Division	Team	Points	Season
1	Liverpool	68	1978–79
2	Tottenham Hotspur	70	1919–20
3	Aston Villa	70	1971–72
3S	Nottingham Forest	70	1950–51
	Bristol City	70	1954–55
3N	Doncaster Rovers	72	1946–47
4	Lincoln City	74	1975–76

Football League (three points system)

1	Everton	90	1984–85
2	Luton Town	88	1981–82
3	Oxford United	95	1983–84
4	York City	101	1983–84

Scottish League

Pr	Aberdeen	59	1984–85
1	Rangers	76	1920–21
2	Morton	69	1966–67

Fewest points (minimum 34 games)

Football League

Division	Team	Points	Season
1	Stoke City	17	1984–85
2	Doncaster Rovers	8	1904–05
	Loughborough Town	8	1899–1900
3	Rochdale	21	1973–74
3S	Merthyr Town	21	1924–25 and 1929–30
	Queen's Park Rangers	21	1925–26
3N	Rochdale	11	1931–32
4	Workington	19	1976–77

Scottish League (minimum 30 games)

Pr	St Johnstone	11	1975–76
1	Stirling Albion	6	1954–55
2	Edinburgh City	7	1936–37

Highest individual goalscorers in League games

Current Football League clubs (in descending order)

Goals	Player	Team	Division	Season
60	Dixie Dean	Everton	1	1927–28
59	George Camsell	Middlesbrough	2	1926–27
55	Joe Payne	Luton Town	3S	1936–37
55	Ted Harston	Mansfield Town	3N	1936–37
52	Terry Bly	Peterborough United	4	1960–61
49	Pongo Waring	Aston Villa	1	1930–31
49	Clarrie Bourton	Coventry City	3S	1931–32
47	Harry Morris	Swindon Town	3S	1926–27
46	Peter Simpson	Crystal Palace	3S	1930–31
46	Derek Dooley	Sheffield Wednesday	2	1951–52
46	Alf Lythgoe	Stockport County	3N	1933–34
45	Jimmy Hampson	Blackpool	2	1929–30
44	Jimmy Cookson	Chesterfield	3N	1925–26
44	Arthur Rowley	Leicester City	2	1956–57
44	Albert Whitehurst	Rochdale	3N	1926–27
44	Tom Bamford	Wrexham	3N	1933–34
43	Ted Harper	Blackburn Rovers	1	1925–26

43	Jimmy McConnell	Carlisle United	3N	1928–29
43	Dave Halliday	Sunderland	1	1928–29
42	Ted Drake	Arsenal	1	1934–35
42	Clarrie Jordan	Doncaster Rovers	3N	1946–47
42	Pat Glover	Grimsby Town	2	1933–34
42	John Charles	Leeds United	2	1953–54
42	Allan Hall	Lincoln City	3N	1931–32
42	Cliff Holton	Watford	4	1959–60
42	Ted MacDougall	Bournemouth	4	1970–71
41	Jimmy Greaves	Chelsea	1	1960–61
41	Frank Newton	Fulham	3S	1931–32
41	Ted Phillips	Ipswich Town	3S	1956–57
41	Roger Hunt	Liverpool	2	1961–62
41	Jimmy Dunne	Sheffield United	1	1930–31
41	Vic Watson	West Ham United	1	1929–30
40	Billy Haines	Portsmouth	2	1926–27
40	Sammy Collins	Torquay United	3S	1955–56
40	Gilbert Alsop	Walsall	3N and	1933–34 1934–35
40	Bobby Hunt	Colchester United	4	1961–62
39	David Brown	Darlington	3N	1924–25
39	Bill McNaughton	Hull City	3N	1932–33
39	Tom Keetley	Notts County	3S	1930–31
39	Ginger Richardson	West Bromwich Albion	1	1935–36
39	Derek Reeves	Southampton	3	1959–60
38	Tommy Johnson	Manchester City	1	1928–29
38	Arthur Rowley	Shrewsbury Town	4	1958–59
38	Wally Ardron	Rotherham United	3N	1946–47
38	Joe Smith	Bolton Wanderers	1	1920–21
38	Ronnie Blackman	Reading	3S	1951–52
38	Jack Holliday	Brentford	3S	1932–33
38	Wilf Kirkham	Port Vale	2	1926–27
37	Jack Bowers	Derby County	1	1930–31
37	Ray Straw	Derby County	3N	1956–57
37	Richard Parker	Millwall	3S	1926–27
37	Ted Harper	Preston North End	2	1932–33
37	George Goddard	Queen's Park Rangers	3S	1929–30
37	Jimmy Greaves	Tottenham Hotspur	1	1962–63
37	Dennis Westcott	Wolverhampton Wanderers	1	1946–47
36	Don Clark	Bristol City	3S	1946–47
36	Dick Yates	Chester	3N	1946–47
36	Cliff Holton	Northampton Town	3	1961–62
36	Wally Ardron	Nottingham Forest	3S	1950–51
36	Hughie Gallacher	Newcastle United	1	1926–27
35	George Beel	Burnley	1	1927–28
35	Craig Madden	Bury	4	1981–82
35	Dixie McNeil	Hereford United	3	1975–76
35	Tom Johnston	Orient	2	1957–58
35	Bunny Bell	Tranmere Rovers	3N	1933–34
35	Sam Taylor	Huddersfield Town	2	1919–20
35	George Brown	Huddersfield Town	1	1925–26
35	Cyril Pearce	Swansea City	2	1931–32
34	David Layne	Bradford City	4	1961–62
34	Terry Harkin	Crewe Alexandra	4	1964–65
34	Fred Whitlow	Exeter City	3S	1932–33
34	Tudor Martin	Newport County	3S	1929–30
34	Albert Valentine	Halifax Town	3N	1934–35
33	Cecil McCormack	Barnsley	2	1950–51
33	Geoff Bradford	Bristol Rovers	3S	1952–53
33	Freddie Steele	Stoke City	1	1936–37
33	Tom Davis	Oldham Athletic	3N	1936–37
32	Peter Ward	Brighton & Hove Albion	3	1976–77
32	Ralph Allen	Charlton Athletic	3S	1934–35
32	Dennis Viollet	Manchester United	1	1959–60
32	Jack Cock	Plymouth Argyle	3S	1925–26
31	Stan Richards	Cardiff City	3S	1946–47
31	Ernie Morgan	Gillingham	3S	1954–55
31	Brian Yeo	Gillingham	4	1973–74
31	Barrie Thomas	Scunthorpe United	2	1961–62
31	Bill Fenton	York City	3N	1951–52
31	Arthur Bottom	York City	3N	1955–56
31	Ralph Hunt	Norwich City	3S	1955–56
31	Jim Shankly	Southend United	3S	1928–29
31	Sammy McCrory	Southend United	3S	1957–58
30	John Aldridge	Oxford United	2	1984–85
29	Joe Bradford	Birmingham City	1	1927–28
29	Alan Cork	Wimbledon	3	1983–84
28	William Robinson	Hartlepool United	3N	1927–28
26	John Dungworth	Aldershot	4	1978–79
21	Alan Biley	Cambridge United	3	1977–78
19	Les Bradd	Wigan Athletic	4	1981–82

BELOW LEFT: Dennis Westcott (Wolverhampton Wanderers). BELOW RIGHT: Alf Bottom (York City). TOP RIGHT: Peter Ward (Brighton and Hove Albion). (ASP). INSET: Ted MacDougall (Norwich City). (ASP).

Bukta

Current Scottish League clubs (in descending order)

Goals	Player	Team	Division	Season
66	Jimmy Smith	Ayr United	2	1927–28
53	Robert Skinner	Dunfermline Athletic	2	1925–26
52	Bill McFadyen	Motherwell	1	1931–32
50	Jimmy McGrory	Celtic	1	1935–36
49	Wee Willie Crilley	Alloa	2	1921–22
45	Harry Yarnall	Airdrieonians	1	1916–17
45	Dave Easson	Arbroath	2	1958–59
45	Davie Kilgour	Forfar Athletic	2	1929–30
45	Dunky Walker	St Mirren	1	1921–22
44	Barney Battles	Heart of Midlothian	1	1930–31
44	Sam English	Rangers	1	1931–32
43	Evelyn Morrison	Falkirk	1	1928–29
42	Jimmy Wood	East Fife	2	1926–27
42	Joe Baker	Hibernian	1	1959–60
41	Jim Renwick	Albion Rovers	2	1932–33
41	John Coyle	Dundee United	2	1955–56
41	Allan McGraw	Morton	2	1963–64
41	Alec Hair	Partick Thistle	1	1926–27
40	Willie Devlin	Cowdenbeath	1	1925–26
38	Benny Yorston	Aberdeen	1	1929–30
38	Ken Bowron	Berwick Rangers	2	1963–64
38	Kenny Wilson	Dumbarton	2	1971–72
38	Dave Halliday	Dundee	1	1923–24
38	Norman Haywood	Raith Rovers	2	1937–38
36	Billy McPhail	Clyde	2	1951–52
36	Malcolm Morrison	East Stirlingshire	2	1938–39
36	Jimmy Benson	St Johnstone	2	1931–32
36	Peerie Cunningham	Kilmarnock	1	1927–28
34	David Wilson	Hamilton Academical	1	1936–37
33	Jimmy Gray	Queen of the South	2	1927–28
30	Willie Martin	Queen's Park	1	1937–38
29	Evelyn Morrison	Stenhousmuir	2	1928–29
29	Bobby Murray	Stenhousemuir	2	1936–37
28	Blair Miller	Clydebank	1	1978–79
28	Brian Third	Montrose	2	1972–73
27	Derek Frye	Stranraer	2	1977–78
26	Mickey Lawson	Stirling Albion	2	1975–76
26	Bill McIntosh	Brechin City	2	1959–60
17	John Jobson	Meadowbank Thistle	2	1979–80

Roger Hunt (Liverpool) pictured above, scored 41 goals in the 1961–62 season. (ASP). RIGHT: Jimmy Greaves (Tottenham Hotspur) who hit the same number in the previous season. (ASP).

Transfers

British players £1 million and over
£1 500 000 Bryan Robson, West Bromwich Albion to Manchester United, October 1981

£1 500 000 Ray Wilkins, Manchester United to AC Milan, June 1984

£1 469 000 Andy Gray, Aston Villa to Wolverhampton Wanderers, September 1979

£1 437 500 Steve Daley, Wolverhampton Wanderers to Manchester City, September 1979

£1 350 000 Kenny Sansom, Crystal Palace to Arsenal, August 1980

£1 250 000 Kevin Reeves, Norwich City to Manchester City, March 1980

£1 250 000 Ian Wallace, Coventry City to Nottingham Forest, July 1980

£1 250 000 Clive Allen, Arsenal to Crystal Palace, August 1980

£1 250 000 Garry Birtles, Nottingham Forest to Manchester United, October 1980

£1 200 000 Clive Allen, Queen's Park Rangers to Arsenal, June 1980

£1 200 000 Trevor Francis, Nottingham Forest to Manchester City, September 1981

£1 180 000 Trevor Francis, Birmingham City to Nottingham Forest, February 1979

£1 100 000 Frank Stapleton, Arsenal to Manchester United, August 1981

£1 000 000 Justin Fashanu, Norwich City to Nottingham Forest, August 1981

£1 000 000 Luther Blissett, Watford to AC Milan, July 1983

Milestones in British transfers
£1000 Alf Common, Sunderland to Middlesbrough, 1905

£10 000 David Jack, Bolton Wanderers to Arsenal, 1928

£100 000 Denis Law, Torino to Manchester United, 1962

£200 000 Martin Peters, West Ham United to Tottenham Hotspur, 1970

£500 000 Kevin Keegan, Liverpool to SV Hamburg, 1977

World records
£6 900 000 Diego Maradona, Barcelona to Napoli, 1984

£4 800 000 Diego Maradona, Argentinos Juniors to Barcelona, 1982

£3 000 000 Karl-Heinz Rummenigge, Bayern Munich to Internazionale, 1984

£2 500 000 Artur Antunes Coimbra (Zico), Flamengo to Udinese, 1983

Kevin Keegan, the first British player to be transferred for half a million, does a spot of hurdling over Belgium's Raymond Mommens in June 1980. (ASP). INSET: Luther Blissett whose move from Watford to AC Milan cost £1 million in July 1983. (ASP).

Scottish League and Cup honours

Championship wins

Rangers 37 (including one shared); Celtic 33; Aberdeen, Heart of Midlothian, Hibernian 4; Dumbarton 2 (including one shared); Dundee, Dundee United, Kilmarnock, Motherwell, Third Lanark 1

Scottish FA Cup

Celtic 27; Rangers 24; Queen's Park 10; Aberdeen, Heart of Midlothian 5; Clyde, Vale of Leven 3; Dunfermline Athletic, Falkirk, Hibernian, Kilmarnock, Renton, St Mirren, Third Lanark 2; Airdrieonians, Dumbarton, Dundee, East Fife, Morton, Motherwell, Partick Thistle, St Bernard's 1

Scottish League Cup

Rangers 12; Celtic 9; Heart of Midlothian 4; Aberdeen, Dundee, East Fife 3; Dundee United 2; Hibernian, Motherwell, Partick Thistle 1

Oldest and youngest players

Youngest players

Football League
Albert Geldard, 15 years 158 days, Bradford Park Avenue v Millwall, Division 2, 16.9.29; and Ken Roberts, 15 years 158 days, Wrexham v Bradford Park Avenue, Division 3N, 1.9.51
Football League scorer
Ronnie Dix, 15 years 180 days, Bristol Rovers v Norwich City, Division 3S, 3.3.28
Division 1
Derek Forster, 15 years 185 days, Sunderland v Leicester City, 22.8.64

Division 1 scorer
Jason Dozzell, 16 years 57 days as substitute Ipswich Town v Coventry City, 4.2.84
FA Cup
Scott Endersby, 15 years 288 days, Kettering v Tilbury, 1st rd, 26.11.77
FA Cup final
Paul Allen, 17 years 256 days, West Ham United v Arsenal, 1980
FA Cup final scorer
Norman Whiteside, 18 years 18 days, Manchester United v Brighton & Hove Albion, 1983
FA Cup final captain
Ron Harris, 22 years, 6 months, 17 days, Chelsea v Tottenham Hotspur, 1967

Internationals

England
Duncan Edwards (Manchester United), 18 years 183 days, v Scotland, 2.4.55

Northern Ireland
Norman Whiteside (Manchester United), 17 years 42 days, v Yugoslavia, 17.6.82
Scotland
Johnny Lambie (Queen's Park), 17 years 92 days, v Ireland, 20.3.1886
Wales
John Charles (Leeds United), 18 years 71 days, v Ireland, 8.3.50
Republic of Ireland
Jimmy Holmes, 17 years 200 days, v Austria, 30.5.71.

Oldest players

Football League
Neil McBain, 52 years 4 months, New Brighton v Hartlepools United, Div 3N, 15.3.47 (McBain was New Brighton's manager and had to play in an emergency)
Division 1
Stanley Matthews, 50 years 5 days, Stoke City v Fulham, 6.2.65
FA Cup final
Walter Hampson, 41 years 8 months, Newcastle United v Aston Villa, 1924
FA Cup
Billy Meredith, 49 years 8 months, Manchester City v Newcastle United, 29.3.24
International debutant
Leslie Compton, 38 years 2 months, England v Wales, 15.11.50
International
Billy Meredith, 45 years 229 days, Wales v England, 15.3.20

Ron Harris (Chelsea) was the youngest FA Cup Final captain in 1967. (ASP).

Duncan Edwards (England) a teenage debutant for his country.

John Charles (Wales) similarly youthful on his bow.

Highest attendances

Record
205 000 (199 854 paid) Brazil v Uruguay 1950 World Cup final series, 16.7.50, Maracana, Rio de Janeiro

International
149 547 Scotland v England, Hampden Park, Glasgow, 17.4.37

European Cup
136 505, Celtic v Leeds United semi-final, Hampden Park, Glasgow 15.4.70

FA Cup final
160 000 (126 047 counted admissions) West Ham United v Bolton Wanderers, Wembley 28.4.23

Scottish Cup final
146 433, Celtic v Aberdeen, Hampden Park, Glasgow, 24.4.37

Football League

Division 1
83 260, Manchester United v Arsenal, Maine Road, 17.1.48

Division 2
68 029, Aston Villa v Coventry City, Villa Park, 30.10.37

Division 3S
51 621, Cardiff City v Bristol City, Ninian Park, 7.4.47

Division 3N
49 655, Hull City v Rotherham United, Boothferry Park, 25.12.48

Division 3
49 309, Sheffield Wednesday v Sheffield United, Hillsborough, 26.12.79

Division 4
37 774, Crystal Palace v Millwall, Selhurst Park, 31.3.61

Scottish League
118 567, Rangers v Celtic, Ibrox Park, 2.1.39

Lowest attendances

International
2315, Wales v Northern Ireland, Racecourse Ground, Wrexham, 27.5.82

Football League (under 500)
484, Gateshead v Accrington Stanley, Div 3N, 26.3.52; 469, Thames v Luton Town, Div 3S, 6.12.30; and 450, Rochdale v Cambridge United, Div 3, 5.2.74

NB Although the Stockport County v Leicester City Division 2 game at Old Trafford on 7.5.21 was reported to have had an official attendance of only 13, contemporary reports estimated the crowd at 2000. Similarly, for the FA Cup third round second replay between Bradford City and Norwich City at Lincoln in 1915 the official attendance was nil, but although it was played behind closed doors so as not to interfere with war work in nearby factories, several hundred spectators gained admittance without paying.

Scottish League
80, Meadowbank Thistle v Stenhousemuir, Div 2, 22.12.79 at Meadowbank

World Cup 1930–82

Winning countries

Year	Winners	P	W	D	L	F	A	Players	Final	Venue	Attendance
1930	Uruguay	4	4	0	0	16	3	15	Uruguay 4 Argentina 2	Montevideo, Uruguay	90 000
1934	Italy	5	4	1	0	12	3	17	Italy 2 Czechoslovakia 1 (aet)	Rome, Italy	50 000
1938	Italy	4	4	0	0	11	5	14	Italy 4 Hungary 2	Paris, France	45 000
1950	Uruguay	4	3	1	0	15	5	14	*Uruguay 2 Brazil 1	Rio de Janeiro, Brazil	199 859
1954	West Germany	6	5	0	1	25	14	18	West Germany 3 Hungary 2	Berne, Switzerland	60 000
1958	Brazil	6	5	1	0	16	4	16	Brazil 5 Sweden 2	Stockholm, Sweden	49 737
1962	Brazil	6	5	1	0	14	5	12	Brazil 3 Czechoslovakia 1	Santiago, Chile	68 679
1966	England	6	5	1	0	11	3	15	England 4 West Germany 2 (aet)	Wembley, England	93 802
1970	Brazil	6	6	0	0	19	7	15	Brazil 4 Italy 1	Mexico City, Mexico	107 412
1974	West Germany	7	6	0	1	13	4	18	West Germany 2 Holland 1	Munich, West Germany	77 833
1978	Argentina	7	5	1	1	15	4	17	Argentina 3 Holland 1 (aet)	Buenos Aires, Argentina	77 000
1982	Italy	7	4	3	0	12	6	15	Italy 3 West Germany 1	Madrid, Spain	90 080

Referee	Aggregate attendances	Average attendance	Matches	Goals	Average	Top scorer	Goals
Langenus, Belgium	434 500	24 139	18	70	3.88	Guillermo Stabile (Argentina)	8
Eklind, Sweden	395 000	23 235	17	70	4.11	Angelo Schiavio (Italy); Oldrich Nejedly (Czechoslovakia); Edmund Cohen (Germany)	4
Capdeville, France	483 000	26 833	18	84	4.66	Leonidas Da Silva (Brazil)	8
Reader, England	1 337 000	60 772	22	88	4.00	Ademir (Brazil)	9
Ling, England	943 000	36 270	26	140	5.38	Sandor Kocsis (Hungary)	11
Guigue, France	868 000	24 800	35	126	3.60	Just Fontaine (France)	13
Latychev, USSR	776 000	24 250	32	89	2.78	Drazen Jerkovic (Yugoslavia)	5
Dienst, Switzerland	614 677	50 458	32	89	2.78	Eusebio (Portugal)	9
Glockner, East Germany	1 673 975	52 312	32	95	2.96	Gerd Muller (West Germany)	10
Taylor, England	1 774 002	46 685	38	97	2.55	Grzegorz Lato (Poland)	7
Gonella, Italy	1 610 215	42 374	38	102	2.68	Mario Kempes (Argentina)	6
Coelho, Brazil	1 766 277	33 967	52	146	2.81	Paolo Rossi (Italy)	6

*Deciding match

Most appearances in finals: Antonio Carbajal (Mexico) 5 — 1950, 1954, 1958, 1962 and 1966

Most appearances in all matches: Uwe Seeler (West Germany) 21 — 1958, 1962, 1966 and 1970

Most appearances in winning teams: Pelé (Brazil) 3 — 1958, 1962 and 1970

Oldest winning medallist: Dino Zoff (Italy) 40 — 1982 (captain)

Youngest finalist: Norman Whiteside (Northern Ireland) 17 — 1982

Highest aggregate goalscorer: Gerd Muller (West Germany) 14 — 1970 (10), 1974 (4). Muller scored 19 goals in the 1970 competition including 9 in qualifying games.

Highest scores (Finals): Hungary 10 El Salvador 1 (1982); Hungary 9 South Korea 0 (1954); Yugoslavia 9 Zaire O (1974)

Highest score (Qualifying Game): New Zealand 13 Fiji 0 (1981)

First World Cup (Finals): Louis Laurent (France v Mexico, 13 July 1930)

Fastest World Cup goal (Finals): Bryan Robson (England v France, 16 June 1982)

Hat-trick scorer (Final): Geoff Hurst (England v West Germany, 1966)

Scorers in every match (Finals): 13 goals: Just Fontaine (France) 1958; 7 goals: Jairzinho (Brazil) 1970

Highest Individual Scorers (Finals): 4 goals: Gustav Wetterstroem (Sweden v Cuba), Leonidas Da Silva (Brazil v Poland), Ernest Willimowski (Poland v Brazil) 1938; Ademir (Brazil v Sweden), Juan Schiaffino (Uruguay v Bolivia) 1950; Sandor Kocsis (Hungary v West Germany), 1954; Just Fontaine (France v West Germany) 1958; Eusebio (Portugal v North Korea) 1966

ABOVE: **Mario Kempes (Argentina) scoring in the 1978 World Cup final in Buenos Aires.** FAR LEFT: **Argentine captain Daniel Passarella is carried shoulder high by fans.** LEFT: **Geoff Hurst (England) the only player to score a hat-trick in a World Cup final. (ASP).**

National records in final series 1930–82

Country	P	W	D	L	F	A
Brazil	57	37	10	10	134	62
West Germany*	54	31	11	12	122	78
Italy	43	24	9	10	74	46
Argentina	34	16	5	13	63	50
England	29	13	8	8	40	29
Uruguay	29	14	5	10	57	39
Hungary	29	14	3	12	85	48
USSR	24	12	5	7	37	25
Poland	21	12	4	5	38	22
Yugoslavia	28	12	4	12	47	36
Sweden	28	11	6	11	48	46
France	27	11	3	13	59	50
Austria	23	11	2	10	38	40
Spain	23	8	5	10	26	30
Czechoslovakia	25	8	5	12	34	40
Holland	16	8	3	5	32	19
Chile	21	7	3	11	26	32
Switzerland	18	5	2	11	28	44
Scotland	14	3	5	6	20	29
Peru	15	4	3	8	19	31
Portugal	6	5	0	1	17	8
Northern Ireland	10	3	4	3	11	17
Mexico	24	3	4	17	21	62
Belgium	14	3	2	9	15	30
East Germany	6	2	2	2	5	5
Paraguay	7	2	2	3	12	19
USA	7	3	0	4	12	21
Wales	5	1	3	1	4	4
Rumania	8	2	1	5	12	17
Algeria	3	2	0	1	5	5
Bulgaria	12	0	4	8	9	29
Tunisia	3	1	1	1	3	2
Cameroon	3	0	3	0	1	1
Cuba	3	1	1	1	5	12
North Korea	4	1	1	2	5	9
Turkey	3	1	0	2	10	11
Honduras	3	0	2	1	2	3
Israel	3	1	0	2	1	3
Kuwait	3	0	1	2	2	6
Morocco	3	0	1	2	2	6
Australia	3	0	1	2	0	5
Colombia	3	0	1	2	5	11
Iran	3	0	1	2	2	8
Norway	1	0	0	1	1	2
Egypt	1	0	0	1	2	4
Dutch East Indies	1	0	0	1	0	6
South Korea	2	0	0	2	0	16
New Zealand	3	0	0	3	2	12
Haiti	3	0	0	3	2	14
Zaire	3	0	0	3	0	14
Bolivia	3	0	0	3	0	16
El Salvador	6	0	0	6	1	22

Brazil have appeared in all World Cup final tournaments.
*Includes matches as Germany 1930–38

European Championship

Year	Winners	Runners-up	Venue	Attendance	Referee	Entries	Top scorer (3 or more goals)
1960	USSR 2	Yugoslavia 1 (aet)	Paris, France	17 966	Ellis, England	17	–
1964	Spain 2	USSR 1	Madrid, Spain	120 000	Holland, England	29	–
1968	Italy 2 (after 1–1 draw)	Yugoslavia 0 (aet)	Rome, Italy	60 000 75 000	Dienst, Switzerland	31	–
1972	West Germany 3	USSR 0	Brussels, Belgium	43 437	Marschall, Austria	32	Gerd Muller (West Germany) 4
1976	Czechoslovakia 2 (Czechs won 5–3 on penalties)	West Germany 2 (aet)	Belgrade, Yugoslavia	45 000	Gonella, Italy	32	Dieter Muller (West Germany) 4
1980	West Germany 2	Belgium 1	Rome, Italy	47 864	Rainea, Rumania	32	Klaus Allofs (West Germany) 3
1984	France 2	Spain 0	Paris, France	80 000	Christov, Czechoslovakia	33	Michel Platini (France) 8

South American Championship

Year	Venue	Teams	Matches	Goals	Champions	Pts
1916	Buenos Aires, Argentina	4	6	18	Uruguay	5
1917	Montevideo, Uruguay	4	6	21	Uruguay	6
1919	Rio de Janeiro, Brazil (1)	4	7	26	Brazil	7
1920	Valparaiso, Chile	4	6	16	Uruguay	5
1921	Buenos Aires, Argentina	4	6	14	Argentina	6
1922	Rio de Janeiro, Brazil (2)	5	11	23	Brazil	7
1923	Uruguay, Montevideo	4	6	18	Uruguay	6
1924	Montevideo, Uruguay	4	6	15	Uruguay	5
1925	Buenos Aires, Argentina (3)	3	6	26	Argentina	7
1926	Santiago de Chile, Chile	5	10	55	Uruguay	8
1927	Lima, Peru	4	6	37	Argentina	6
1929	Buenos Aires, Argentina	4	6	23	Argentina	6
1935	Lima, Peru*	4	6	18	Uruguay	6
1937	Buenos Aires, Argentina (4)	6	16	68	Argentina	10
1939	Lima, Peru	5	10	47	Peru	8
1941	Santiago de Chile, Chile*	5	10	32	Argentina	8
1942	Montevideo, Uruguay (5)	7	21	81	Uruguay	12
1945	Santiago de Chile, Chile*	7	21	89	Argentina	11
1946	Buenos Aires, Argentina*	6	15	61	Argentina	10
1947	Guayaquil, Ecuador	8	28	102	Argentina	13
1949	Rio de Janeiro, Brazil (6)	8	29	130	Brazil	14
1953	Lima, Peru (7)	7	21	67	Paraguay	10
1955	Santiago de Chile, Chile	6	15	73	Argentina	9
1956	Montevideo, Uruguay*	6	15	38	Uruguay	9
1957	Lima, Peru	7	21	101	Argentina	10
1959	Buenos Aires, Argentina	7	21	86	Argentina	11
1959	Guayaquil, Ecuador*	5	20	39	Uruguay	7
1963	La Paz & Cochabamba, Bolivia	7	21	91	Bolivia	11
1967	Montevideo, Uruguay	6	15	49	Uruguay	9
1975	(Reorganized on home and away basis)	10	25	79	Peru	N/A
1979		10	25	63	Paraguay	N/A
1983		10	24	55	Uruguay	N/A

* extraordinary tournaments

(1) play-off; Brazil 1 Uruguay 0
(2) play-off; Brazil 3 Paraguay 1; Uruguay withdrew
(3) two legs were played (home and away)
(4) play-off; Argentina 2 Brazil 0
(5) Chile withdrew
(6) play-off; Brazil 7 Paraguay 0
(7) play-off; Paraguay 3 Brazil 2 (organized by the Paraguayan Football League)

British International Championship 1883–1984

89 tournaments including one not completed (1980–81)

Outright wins

England 34, Scotland 24, Wales 7, Northern Ireland 3

Shared titles

England 20, Scotland 17, Wales and Northern Ireland 5

National record in championships

Goal average or goal difference did not determine the winner until 1978–79. If countries were level on points at the top they shared the title.*

Season ending	Order of finishing* and points total							
1884	Scotland	6	England	4	Wales	2	Ireland	0
1885	Scotland	5	England	4	Wales	3	Ireland	0
1886	Scotland	5	England	5	Wales	2	Ireland	0
1887	Scotland	6	England	4	Ireland	2	Wales	0
1888	England	6	Scotland	4	Wales	2	Ireland	0
1889	Scotland	5	England	4	Wales	3	Ireland	0
1890	Scotland	5	England	5	Wales	2	Ireland	0
1891	England	6	Scotland	4	Ireland	2	Wales	0
1892	England	6	Scotland	4	Ireland	1	Wales	1
1893	England	6	Scotland	4	Ireland	2	Wales	0
1894	Scotland	5	England	4	Wales	2	Ireland	1
1895	England	5	Scotland	3	Wales	2	Ireland	2
1896	Scotland	5	England	4	Wales	2	Ireland	1
1897	Scotland	5	England	4	Ireland	2	Wales	1
1898	England	6	Scotland	4	Ireland	2	Wales	0
1899	England	6	Scotland	4	Ireland	2	Wales	0
1900	Scotland	6	England	3	Wales	3	Ireland	0
1901	England	5	Scotland	4	Wales	3	Ireland	0
1902	Scotland	5	England	4	Ireland	2	Wales	1
1903	Scotland	4	England	4	Ireland	4	Wales	0
1904	England	5	Ireland	3	Scotland	2	Wales	2
1905	England	5	Wales	3	Ireland	2	Scotland	2
1906	England	4	Scotland	4	Wales	3	Ireland	1
1907	Wales	5	England	4	Scotland	3	Ireland	0
1908	England	5	Scotland	5	Ireland	2	Wales	0
1909	England	6	Wales	4	Scotland	2	Ireland	0
1910	Scotland	4	England	3	Ireland	3	Wales	2
1911	England	5	Scotland	4	Wales	3	Ireland	0
1912	England	5	Scotland	5	Ireland	2	Wales	0
1913	England	4	Scotland	3	Wales	3	Ireland	2
1914	Ireland	5	Scotland	4	England	2	Wales	1
1915–19 no competitions								
1920	Wales	4	Scotland	3	England	3	Ireland	2
1921	Scotland	6	Wales	3	England	3	Ireland	0
1922	Scotland	4	Wales	3	England	3	Ireland	2
1923	Scotland	5	England	4	Ireland	2	Wales	1
1924	Wales	6	Scotland	3	Ireland	2	England	1
1925	Scotland	6	England	4	Wales	1	Ireland	1
1926	Scotland	6	Ireland	3	Wales	2	England	1
1927	Scotland	4	England	4	Ireland	2	Wales	2
1928	Wales	5	Ireland	4	Scotland	3	England	0
1929	Scotland	6	England	4	Wales	1	Ireland	1
1930	England	6	Scotland	4	Ireland	2	Wales	0
1931	England	4	Scotland	4	Wales	3	Ireland	1
1932	England	6	Scotland	4	Ireland	2	Wales	0
1933	Wales	5	Scotland	4	England	3	Ireland	0
1934	Wales	5	England	4	Ireland	3	Scotland	0
1935	England	4	Scotland	4	Wales	2	Ireland	2
1936	Scotland	4	England	3	Wales	3	Ireland	2
1937	Wales	6	Scotland	4	England	2	Ireland	0
1938	England	4	Scotland	3	Ireland	3	Wales	2
1939	England	4	Scotland	4	Wales	4	Ireland	0
1940–46 no competitions								
1947	England	5	Ireland	3	Scotland	2	Wales	2
1948	England	5	Wales	4	Ireland	3	Scotland	0
1949	Scotland	6	England	4	Wales	2	Ireland	0
1950	England	6	Scotland	4	Wales	1	Ireland	1
1951	Scotland	6	England	4	Wales	2	Ireland	0
1952	England	5	Wales	5	Scotland	2	Ireland	0
1953	England	4	Scotland	4	Wales	2	Ireland	2
1954	England	6	Scotland	3	Ireland	2	Wales	1
1955	England	6	Scotland	3	Wales	2	Ireland	1
1956	England	3	Scotland	3	Wales	3	Ireland	3
1957	England	5	Scotland	3	Wales	2	Ireland	2
1958	England	4	Ireland	4	Scotland	2	Wales	2
1959	England	4	Ireland	4	Scotland	3	Wales	1
1960	England	4	Scotland	4	Wales	4	Ireland	0
1961	England	6	Wales	4	Scotland	2	Ireland	0
1962	Scotland	6	Wales	3	England	2	Ireland	1
1963	Scotland	6	England	4	Wales	2	Ireland	0
1964	England	4	Scotland	4	Ireland	4	Wales	0
1965	England	5	Wales	4	Scotland	3	Ireland	0
1966	England	5	Ireland	4	Scotland	2	Wales	1
1967	Scotland	5	England	4	Wales	2	Ireland	1
1968	England	5	Scotland	3	Wales	2	Ireland	2
1969	England	6	Scotland	3	Ireland	2	Wales	1
1970	England	4	Scotland	4	Wales	4	Ireland	0
1971	England	5	Scotland	3	Wales	2	Ireland	2
1972	England	4	Scotland	4	Ireland	3	Wales	1
1973	England	6	Ireland	4	Scotland	2	Wales	0
1974	England	4	Scotland	4	Wales	2	Ireland	2
1975	England	4	Scotland	3	Ireland	3	Wales	2
1976	Scotland	6	England	4	Wales	2	Ireland	0
1977	Scotland	5	Wales	4	England	2	Ireland	1
1978	England	6	Wales	3	Scotland	2	Ireland	1
1979	England	5	Wales	4	Scotland	2	Ireland	1
1980	Ireland	5	England	3	Wales	2	Scotland	2
1981 not completed								
1982	England	6	Scotland	3	Wales	2	Ireland	1
1983	England	5	Scotland	3	Ireland	2	Wales	2
1984	Ireland	3	Wales	3	England	3	Scotland	3

The final British Championship match between England and Northern Ireland at Wembley in April 1984. (ASP).

International records

Most capped players in the Home Countries

England
Bobby Moore 108 appearances, 1962–73

Northern Ireland
Pat Jennings, 110 appearances, 1964–85

Scotland
Kenny Dalglish, 97 appearances, 1971–

Wales
Ivor Allchurch, 68 appearances, 1950–68

Most capped players in the world

Hector Chumpitaz (Peru) 150 appearances, 1963–82
Rivelino (Brazil) 120 appearances, 1968–79
Bjorn Nordqvist (Sweden) 115 appearances, 1963–78
Dino Zoff (Italy) 112 appearances, 1968–83
Pelé (Brazil) 111 appearances, 1957–71
(Of the above named players only Nordqvist's and Zoff's totals do not include matches against club sides and other representative selections.)

Highest international goalscorers in the Home Countries

England
Bobby Charlton 49 goals

Northern Ireland
Billy Gillespie, Joe Bambrick and Gerry Armstrong 12 goals

Scotland
Kenny Dalglish and Denis Law 30 goals

Wales
Ivor Allchurch and Trevor Ford 23 goals

ABOVE: Pat Jennings (Northern Ireland) became the most capped British footballer in 1985. (ASP). Right: England's record goalscorer Bobby Charlton. (ASP).

Most capped players

With each Football League club

In descending order of appearances, with number of all international appearances in brackets where figures differ.

Player	Club	Caps	Country
Bobby Moore	West Ham United	108	England
Bobby Charlton	Manchester United	106	England
Billy Wright	Wolverhampton Wanderers	105	England
Tom Finney	Preston North End	76	England
Pat Jennings	Tottenham Hotspur	66 (110)	Northern Ireland
Emlyn Hughes	Liverpool	59 (62)	England
Johnny Haynes	Fulham	56	England
Billy Bremner	Leeds United	54	Scotland
Jimmy McIlroy	Burnley	52 (55)	Northern Ireland
Pat Rice	Arsenal	49	Northern Ireland
Colin Bell	Manchester City	48	England
Jimmy Dickinson	Portsmouth	48	England
Allan Hunter	Ipswich Town	47 (53)	Northern Ireland
Mick Channon	Southampton	45 (46)	England
Jimmy Armfield	Blackpool	43	England
Ivor Allchurch	Swansea	42 (68)	Wales
Bob Crompton	Blackburn Rovers	41	England
Alf McMichael	Newcastle United	40	Northern Ireland
Alf Sherwood	Cardiff City	39 (41)	Wales
Alan Ball	Everton	39 (72)	England
Gordon Banks	Leicester City	37 (73)	England
Gordon Banks	Stoke City	36 (73)	England
Martin O'Neill	Nottingham Forest	36 (64)	Northern Ireland
Ron Springett	Sheffield Wednesday	33	England
Peter McParland	Aston Villa	33 (34)	Northern Ireland
Martin Harvey	Sunderland	34	Northern Ireland
Nat Lofthouse	Bolton Wanderers	33	England
Stuart Williams	West Bromwich Albion	33 (43)	Wales
Jimmy Nicholson	Huddersfield Town	31 (41)	Northern Ireland
Mal Donaghy	Luton Town	36	Northern Ireland
Rod Thomas	Swindon Town	30 (50)	Wales
Roy McFarland	Derby County	28	England
Malcolm Page	Birmingham City	28	Wales
Dai Davies	Wrexham	28 (51)	Wales
Billy Wedlock	Bristol City	26	England
Wilf Mannion	Middlesbrough	26	England
Don Givens	Queen's Park Rangers	26 (56)	Republic of Ireland
Ray Wilkins	Chelsea	24 (72)	England
Billy Gillespie	Sheffield United	25	Northern Ireland
Eamonn Dunphy	Millwall	22 (23)	Republic of Ireland
Dave Clements	Coventry City	21 (48)	Northern Ireland
Gerry Armstrong	Watford	21 (57)	Northern Ireland
Moses Russell	Plymouth Argyle	20 (23)	Wales
John Hewie	Charlton Athletic	19	Scotland
Martin O'Neill	Norwich City	18 (64)	Northern Ireland
Terry Neill	Hull City	15 (59)	Northern Ireland
Mick Kearns	Walsall	15 (17)	Republic of Ireland
Gerry Ryan	Brighton & Hove Albion	15 (16)	Republic of Ireland
Len Graham	Doncaster Rovers	14	Northern Ireland
Paddy Mulligan	Crystal Palace	14 (51)	Republic of Ireland
Peter Nicholas	Crystal Palace	14 (38)	Wales
Ian Walsh	Crystal Palace	14 (18)	Wales
Bill Lewis	Crewe Alexandra	12 (30)	Wales
Lloyd Davies	Northampton Town	12 (16)	Wales

Gordon Banks (England).

Pat Rice (Northern Ireland). (ASP). RIGHT: Mick Channon (England).

RANK
XEROX

Idris Hopkins	Brentford	12	Wales
Bill Gorman	Bury	11 (17)	Republic of Ireland and Northern Ireland
Neil Slatter	Bristol Rovers	10	Wales
George Mackenzie	Southend United	9	Republic of Ireland
Albert Gray	Oldham Athletic	9 (24)	Wales
Eddie McMorran	Barnsley	9 (15)	Northern Ireland
Harry Hampton	Bradford City	9	Northern Ireland
Tony Millington	Peterborough United	8 (21)	Wales
Harry Cursham	Notts County	8	England
Pat McConnell	Reading	8	Northern Ireland
Tony Grealish	Orient	7 (42)	Republic of Ireland
Tom Finney	Cambridge United	7 (14)	Northern Ireland
Pat Glover	Grimsby Town	7	Wales
Bill Lewis	Chester City	7 (30)	Wales
Peter Scott	York City	7 (10)	Northern Ireland
Sammy Morgan	Port Vale	7 (18)	Northern Ireland
John McClelland	Mansfield Town	6 (36)	Northern Ireland
David Roberts	Oxford United	6 (17)	Wales
Harold Millership	Rotherham United	6	Wales
Jimmy McLaughlin	Shrewsbury Town	5 (12)	Northern Ireland
Tommy Godwin	Bournemouth	4 (13)	Republic of Ireland
Walter McMillen	Chesterfield	4 (7)	Northern Ireland
Eric Welsh	Carlisle United	4	Northern Ireland
Nigel Vaughan	Newport County	3 (9)	Wales
David Pugh	Lincoln City	3 (7)	Wales
Con Moulson	Lincoln City	3	Republic of Ireland
Albert Gray	Tranmere Rovers	3 (24)	Wales
Damien Richardson	Gillingham	2 (3)	Republic of Ireland
Terry Cochrane	Gillingham	2 (26)	Northern Ireland
Peter Scott	Aldershot	1 (10)	Northern Ireland
Dermot Curtis	Exeter City	1 (17)	Republic of Ireland
Ambrose Fogarty	Hartlepool United	1 (11)	Republic of Ireland
Brian Evans	Hereford United	1 (7)	Wales
Harry Hardy	Stockport County	1	England

Colchester United, Darlington, Halifax Town, Rochdale, Scunthorpe United, Torquay United, Wigan Athletic and Wimbledon have not had one of their players capped.

ABOVE: Martin O'Neill (Northern Ireland). (ASP). BELOW: Dai Davies (Wales). (ASP). RIGHT: Emlyn Hughes (England). (ASP). INSET: Dave Clements (Northern Ireland). (ASP).

Mick Kearns (Republic of Ireland). (ASP).

British

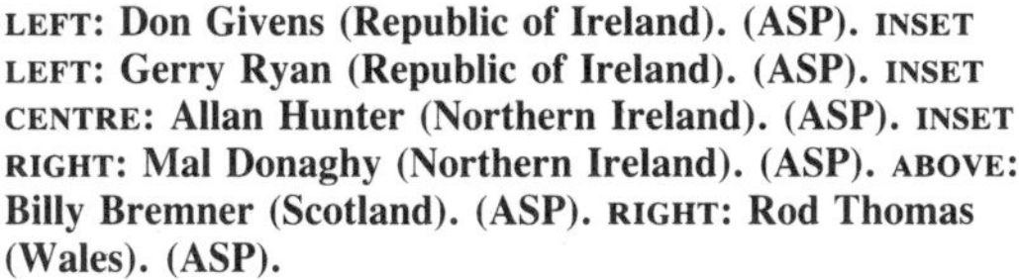

LEFT: Don Givens (Republic of Ireland). (ASP). INSET LEFT: Gerry Ryan (Republic of Ireland). (ASP). INSET CENTRE: Allan Hunter (Northern Ireland). (ASP). INSET RIGHT: Mal Donaghy (Northern Ireland). (ASP). ABOVE: Billy Bremner (Scotland). (ASP). RIGHT: Rod Thomas (Wales). (ASP).

With Scottish League clubs

In descending order of appearances, with number of all international appearances in brackets where figures differ.

Player	Club	Appearances	Country
Danny McGrain	Celtic	62	Scotland
George Young	Rangers	53	Scotland
Alan Rough	Partick Thistle	51	Scotland
Lawrie Reilly	Hibernian	38	Scotland
Willie Miller	Aberdeen	40	Scotland
Tommy Walker	Heart of Midlothian	29	Scotland
Dave Narey	Dundee United	25	Scotland
Jimmy Cowan	Morton	25	Scotland
Alec Hamilton	Dundee	24	Scotland
Watty Arnott	Queen's Park	14	Scotland
Alec Parker	Falkirk	14 (15)	Scotland
Tommy Ring	Clyde	12	Scotland
George Stevenson	Motherwell	12	Scotland
Joe Nibloe	Kilmarnock	11	Scotland
Jimmy Crapnell	Airdrieonians	9	Scotland
John Lindsay	Dumbarton	8	Scotland
James McAulay	Dumbarton	8	Scotland
Iain Munro	St Mirren	7	Scotland
Andy Wilson	Dunfermline Athletic	6 (12)	Scotland
Dave Morris	Raith Rovers	6	Scotland
George Aitken	East Fife	5 (8)	Scotland
Humphrey Jones	East Stirlingshire	5	Wales
Sandy McLaren	St Johnstone	5	Scotland
Jim Nisbet	Ayr United	3	Scotland
Jim Paterson	Cowdenbeath	3	Scotland
Billy Houliston	Queen of the South	3	Scotland
Alexander Keillor	Montrose	2 (6)	Scotland
Ned Doig	Arbroath	2 (5)	Scotland
Jimmy King	Hamilton Academical	2	Scotland
Bobby Howe	Hamilton Academical	2	Scotland
Jock White	Albion Rovers	1 (2)	Scotland
Jock Hepburn	Alloa	1	Scotland

Berwick Rangers, Brechin City, Clydebank, Forfar Athletic, Meadowbank Thistle, Stenhousemuir, Stirling Albion and Stranraer have not had one of their players capped.

Players who played in the winning teams for England v Scotland and in the FA Cup final in the same year

Year	Player	For England at	Date	Cup-winning team	Opponents	Date
1873	A. G. Bonsor	Oval	March 8	Wanderers	Oxford University	March 29
1879	E. Christian	Oval	April 5	Old Etonians	Clapham Rovers	March 29
1888	G. Woodhall	Hampton Park	March 17	West Bromwich Albion	Preston North End	March 24
1892	J. Reynolds	Ibrox Park	April 2	West Bromwich Albion	Aston Villa	March 19
	W. I. Bassett	Ibrox Park	April 2	West Bromwich Albion	Aston Villa	
	G. Kinsey	Richmond	April 1	Wolverhampton Wanderers	Everton	March 25
1895	J. Reynolds	Goodison	April 6	Aston Villa	West Bromwich Albion	April 20
	S. Smith	Goodison	April 6	Aston Villa	West Bromwich Albion	
1899	H. Thickett	Villa Park	April 8	Sheffield United	Derby County	April 15
	E. Needham	Villa Park	April 8	Sheffield United	Derby County	
1904	H. Burgess	Parkhead	April 9	Manchester City	Bolton Wanderers	April 23
1905	H. Spencer	Crystal Palace	April 1	Aston Villa	Newcastle United	April 15
	A. Leake	Crystal Palace	April 1	Aston Villa	Newcastle United	
	J. Bache	Crystal Palace	April 1	Aston Villa	Newcastle United	
1909	G. Wall	Crystal Palace	April 3	Manchester United	Bristol City	April 24
*1913	S. Hardy	Stamford Bridge	April 5	Aston Villa	Sunderland	April 19
	H. Hampson	Stamford Bridge	April 5	Aston Villa	Sunderland	April 19
1920	S. Hardy	Hillsborough	April 10	Aston Villa	Huddersfield Town	April 24
	A. Ducat	Hillsborough	April 10	Aston Villa	Huddersfield Town	April 24
	C. Wallace	Hillsborough	April 10	Aston Villa	Huddersfield Town	April 24
1930	D. B. N. Jack	Wembley	April 5	Arsenal	Huddersfield Town	April 26
1932	S. Weaver	Wembley	April 9	Newcastle United	Arsenal	April 23
1934	E. Brook	Wembley	April 14	Manchester City	Portsmouth	April 28
⋆1948	H. Cockburn	Hampden Park	April 10	Manchester United	Blackpool	April 24
	S. Pearson	Hampden Park	April 10	Manchester United	Blackpool	April 24
1954	R. Allen	Hampden Park	April 3	West Bromwich Albion	Preston North End	May 1
	J. Nicholls	Hampden Park	April 3	West Bromwich Albion	Preston North End	May 1
1958	E. Hopkinson	Hampden Park	April 19	Bolton Wanderers	Manchester United	May 3
+1961	R. Smith	Wembley	April 15	Tottenham Hotspur	Leicester City	May 6
1969	F. Lee	Wembley	May 10	Manchester City	Leicester City	April 26
+1971	P. Storey	Wembley	May 22	Arsenal	Liverpool	May 8
1972	P. Madeley	Hampden Park	May 27	Leeds United	Arsenal	May 6
	N. Hunter	Hampden Park	May 27	Leeds United	Arsenal	May 6
1978	M. Mills	Hampden Park	May 20	Ipswich Town	Arsenal	May 6
	P. Mariner	Hampden Park	May 20	Ipswich Town	Arsenal	May 6
⋆1980	T. Brooking	Hampden Park	May 24	West Ham United	Arsenal	May 10
1983	B. Robson	Wembley	June 1	Manchester United	Brighton	May 21

* Hardy kept goal without conceding a goal in either match.
⋆ Allen and Brooking scored in both matches.
\+ Smith and Storey both played in Cup-League 'double' winning teams. Smith scored in both matches.

Club records in European cup competitions

In ties decided on away goals or penalty kicks, results are as at full-time or after extra time.

Football League

	P	W	D	L	F	A
Arsenal						
European	6	4	0	2	13	4
Cup Winners	9	4	5+	0	13	5
Fairs	24	12	5	7	46	19
UEFA	12	6	1	5	19	15
Aston Villa						
European	15	9	3	3	24	10
UEFA	14	5	4	5	24	16
Super	2	1	0	1	3	1
Birmingham City						
Fairs	25	14	6	5	51	38
Burnley						
European	4	2	0	2	8	8
Fairs	8	4	3	1	16	5
Cardiff City						
Cup Winners	41	15	12	14	58	44
Chelsea						
Cup Winners	14	9	4	1	39	7
Fairs	20	10	5	5	33	24
Coventry City						
Fairs	4	3	0	1	9	8
Derby County						
European	12	6	3	3	18	11
UEFA	10	5	2	3	32	17
Everton						
European	8	2	5	1	12	6
Cup Winners	13	9	3	1	19	5
Fairs	12	7	2	3	22	15
UEFA	8	3	1	4	12	5
Ipswich Town						
European	4	3	0	1	16	5
Cup Winners	6	3	2	1	6	3
UEFA	40	23	10	7	78	43
Leeds United						
European	17	12	1	4	42	11
Cup Winners	9	5	3	1	13	3
*Fairs	53	28	17	8	91	38
UEFA	12	5	3	4	18	13

***Includes match for final possession of trophy**

	P	W	D	L	F	A
Leicester City						
Cup Winners	4	2	1	1	8	5
Liverpool						
European	77	48	13	16	159	64
Cup Winners	17	8	4	5	29	12
Fairs	22	12	4	6	46	15
UEFA	24	16	5	3	44	15
Super	4	2	1	1	10	5
Manchester City						
European	2	0	1	1	1	2
Cup Winners	18	11	2	5	32	13
UEFA	14	4	6	4	21	19
Manchester United						
European	41	26	7	8	100	45
Cup Winners	18	8	5	5	35	27
Fairs	11	6	3	2	29	10
UEFA	16	7	5	4	18	14
Newcastle United						
Fairs	24	13	6	5	37	21
UEFA	4	1	1	2	6	5
Newport County						
Cup Winners	6	2	3	1	12	3
Nottingham Forest						
European	20	12	4	4	32	14
Fairs	6	3	0	3	8	9
UEFA	12	7	3	2	12	7
Super	4	2	1	1	4	3
Queen's Park Rangers						
UEFA	12	8	1	3	39	20
Sheffield Wednesday						
Fairs	10	5	0	5	25	18
Southampton						
Cup Winners	6	4	0	2	16	8
Fairs	6	2	3	1	11	6
UEFA	10	2	5	3	10	12
Stoke City						
UEFA	4	1	2	1	4	6
Sunderland						
Cup Winners	4	3	0	1	5	3
Swansea City						
Cup Winners	14	3	3	8	26	21
Tottenham Hotspur						
European	8	4	1	3	21	13
Cup Winners	25	16	3	6	58	31
UEFA	54	33	12	9	129	41
Watford						
UEFA	6	2	1	3	10	12
West Bromwich Albion						
Cup Winners	6	2	2	2	8	5
Fairs	4	1	1	2	7	9
UEFA	12	5	2	5	15	13

David Jack (Arsenal and England) about to tread on an elusive piece of paper before trapping the ball . . .

West Ham United						
Cup Winners	30	15	6	9	58	42
Wolverhampton Wanderers						
European	8	2	2	4	12	16
Cup Winners	4	1	1	2	6	5
UEFA	20	13	3	4	41	23
Wrexham						
Cup Winners	18	7	4	7	24	27

Scottish League

Aberdeen						
European	6	2	1	3	4	8
Cup Winners	29	17	4	8	62	28
Fairs	4	2	1	1	4	4
UEFA	20	7	6	7	33	32
Super	2	1	1	0	2	0
Celtic						
European	70	39	13	18	134	67
Cup Winners	30	18	3	9	60	22
Fairs	6	1	3	2	9	10
UEFA	8	3	2	3	13	9
Dundee						
European	8	5	0	3	20	14
Cup Winners	2	0	1	1	3	4
Fairs	8	5	1	2	14	7
UEFA	10	4	0	6	17	21
Dundee United						
European	8	5	1	2	14	5
Cup Winners	4	1	1	2	3	3
Fairs	10	5	1	4	11	12
UEFA	38	14	13	11	60	37
Dunfermline Athletic						
Cup Winners	14	7	2	5	34	14
Fairs	28	16	3	9	49	31
Heart of Midlothian						
European	4	1	0	3	4	11
Cup Winners	4	1	0	3	8	11
Fairs	12	4	4	4	20	20
UEFA	2	0	1	1	2	6
Hibernian						
European	6	3	1	2	9	5
Cup Winners	6	3	1	2	19	10
Fairs	36	18	5	13	66	60
UEFA	18	8	5	5	27	23
Kilmarnock						
European	4	1	2	1	4	7
Fairs	20	8	3	9	34	32
Morton						
Fairs	2	0	0	2	3	9
Partick						
Fairs	4	3	0	1	10	7
UEFA	2	0	0	2	0	4
Rangers						
European	43	20	5	18	72	77
Cup Winners	54	27	11	16	100	62
Fairs	18	8	4	6	27	17
UEFA	8	4	1	3	11	13
Super	2	0	0	2	3	6
St Johnstone						
UEFA	6	3	0	3	8	8
St Mirren						
UEFA	6	1	2	3	2	6

Irish League

Ards						
European	2	0	0	2	3	10
Cup Winners	4	0	1	3	2	17
UEFA	2	1	0	1	4	8
Ballymena United						
Cup Winners	6	0	0	6	1	15
UEFA	2	1	0	1	2	4
Carrick Rangers						
Cup Winners	4	1	0	3	7	12
Cliftonville						
Cup Winners	2	0	0	2	0	8

Trevor Brooking (West Ham United and England). (ASP).

Norman Hunter (Leeds United and England). (ASP).

Coleraine						
European	2	0	0	2	1	11
Cup Winners	8	0	1	7	7	34
Fairs	8	2	1	5	15	23
UEFA	2	0	1	1	1	5
Crusaders						
European	4	0	0	4	0	19
Cup Winners	6	0	2	4	5	18
Derby City						
European	3	1	0	2	8	15
Cup Winners	2	0	0	2	0	5
Distillery						
European	2	0	1	1	3	8
Cup Winners	2	0	0	2	1	7
Glenavon						
European	2	0	1	1	0	3
Cup Winners	2	0	0	2	2	7
UEFA	4	0	0	4	2	13
Glentoran						
European	16	3	5	8	17	26
Cup Winners	10	2	3	5	11	20
Fairs	8	1	1	6	7	22
UEFA	12	1	3	8	8	34
Linfield						
European	31	4	8	19	35	69
Cup Winners	4	2	0	2	5	6
Fairs	4	1	0	3	3	11
UEFA	2	0	0	2	0	8
Portadown						
Cup Winners	2	1	0	1	4	7
UEFA	4	1	2	1	3	7

Paul Mariner (in Ipswich Town colours). (ASP).

League of Ireland

Athlone Town						
European	4	0	2	2	7	14
UEFA	4	1	2	1	4	4
Bohemians						
European	6	1	2	3	4	13
Cup Winners	6	2	1	3	6	9
UEFA	8	1	1	6	4	15
Cork Celtic						
European	2	0	0	2	1	7
Cup Winners	2	0	1	1	1	3
Cork Hibs						
European	2	0	0	2	1	7
Cup Winners	6	2	1	3	7	8
Fairs	2	0	0	2	1	6
Drogheda						
UEFA	2	0	0	2	0	14
Drumcondra						
European	6	1	0	5	3	25
Fairs	6	2	0	4	8	19
Dundalk						
European	14	3	3	8	12	30
Cup Winners	6	2	1	3	7	8
Fairs	6	1	1	4	4	25
UEFA	2	0	1	1	0	1
Finn Harps						
Cup Winners	2	0	1	1	2	4
UEFA	6	0	0	6	3	33
Home Farm						
Cup Winners	2	0	1	1	1	7
Limerick						
European	4	0	0	4	4	16
Cup Winners	6	0	1	5	2	11
UEFA	2	0	1	1	1	4
Shamrock Rovers						
European	8	0	3	5	6	19
Cup Winners	16	5	2	9	19	27
Fairs	4	0	2	2	4	6
UEFA	4	2	0	2	7	5
Shelbourne						
European	2	0	0	2	1	7
Cup Winners	2	0	0	2	1	5
Fairs	5	1	2	2	3	4
UEFA	2	0	1	1	1	2
Sligo Rovers						
Cup Winners	2	0	0	2	0	4
St Patrick's Athletic						
Cup Winners	2	0	0	2	1	8
Fairs	2	0	0	2	4	9
University College, Dublin						
Cup Winners	2	0	1	1	0	1
Waterford						
European	14	3	0	11	15	46
Cup Winners	6	1	1	4	5	8

Welsh Non-League clubs

Bangor City						
Cup Winners	3	1	0	2	4	5
Borough United						
Cup Winners	4	1	1	2	2	4

Representative teams

London						
Fairs	8	4	1	3	14	13

Managerial magic

Since the 1946–47 season there have been 19 managers who have won three or more competitions in one or other of the principal tournaments, excluding the Charity Shield and European Super Cup, both of which are one-off games.

Bob Paisley of Liverpool with 13 such achievements between seasons 1975–76 and 1982–83 established a lengthy lead over all others.

Alf Ramsey has been the only one who has managed a club which won the championships of the First, Second and Third Divisions.

	Divisions 1	2	3	4	FA Cup	Milk League Cup	World Cup	European Cup	Cup Winners' Cup	UEFA/ Fairs Cup	Total
Bob Paisley	6					3		3		1	13
Matt Busby	5				2			1			8
Bill Nicholson	1				3	2			1	1	8
Brian Clough	2	1				2		2			7
Joe Mercer	1	2			1	2			1		7
Don Revie	2	1			1	1				2	7
Bill Shankly	3	1			2					1	7
Stan Cullis	3				2						5
Harry Catterick	2	1			1						4
Alf Ramsey	1	1	1				1				4
Ron Saunders	1	1				2					4
Keith Burkinshaw					2					1	3
Tommy Docherty		1			1	1					3
Joe Fagan	1							1			3
John Lyall		1			2	1					3
Lawrie McMenemy				2	1						3
Bertie Mee	1				1					1	3
Alec Stock			2			1					3

ABOVE RIGHT: Brian Clough – hardly clapped out. (ASP).
BELOW: Alf Ramsey in thought. (ASP).

Bill Shankly in playing days.

The FA Cup

Year	Date	Winners		Runners-up		Venue	Attendance	Referee	Entries
1872	16 March	Wanderers	1	Royal Engineers	0	Oval	2 000	A. Stair	15
1873	29 March	Wanderers	2	Oxford University	0	Lillie Bridge	3 000	A. Stair	16
1874	14 March	Oxford University	2	Royal Engineers	0	Oval	2 000	A. Stair	28
1875	13 March	Royal Engineers	1	Old Etonians	1*	Oval	3 000	C. W. Alcock	29
Replay	16 March	Royal Engineers	2	Old Etonians	0	Oval	3 000	C. W. Alcock	
1876	11 March	Wanderers	1	Old Etonians	1	Oval	3 000	W. S. Rawson	32
Replay	18 March	Wanderers	3	Old Etonians	0	Oval	3 500	W. S. Rawson	
1877	24 March	Wanderers	2	Oxford University	1*	Oval	3 000	S. H. Wright	37
1878	23 March	Wanderers	3	Royal Engineers	1	Oval	4 500	S. R. Bastard	43
1879	29 March	Old Etonians	1	Clapham Rovers	0	Oval	5 000	C. W. Alcock	43
1880	10 April	Clapham Rovers	1	Oxford University	0	Oval	6 000	Major Marindin	54
1881	9 April	Old Carthusians	3	Old Etonians	0	Oval	4 500	W. Pierce Dix	63
1882	25 March	Old Etonians	1	Blackburn Rovers	0	Oval	6 500	J. C. Clegg	73
1883	31 March	Blackburn Olympic	2	Old Etonians	1*	Oval	8 000	C. Crump	84
1884	29 March	Blackburn Rovers	2	Queen's Park	1	Oval	4 000	Major Marindin	100
1885	4 April	Blackburn Rovers	2	Queen's Park	0	Oval	12 500	Major Marindin	116
1886	3 April	Blackburn Rovers	0	West Bromwich Albion	0	Oval	15 000	Major Marindin	130
Replay	10 April	Blackburn Rovers	2	West Bromwich Albion	0	Baseball Ground	12 000	Major Marindin	
1887	2 April	Aston Villa	2	West Bromwich Albion	0	Oval	15 500	Major Marindin	126
1888	24 March	West Bromwich Albion	2	Preston North End	1	Oval	19 000	Major Marindin	149
1889	30 March	Preston North End	3	Wolverhampton Wanderers	0	Oval	22 000	Major Marindin	149
1890	29 March	Blackburn Rovers	6	Sheffield Wednesday	1	Oval	20 000	Major Marindin	132
1891	25 March	Blackburn Rovers	3	Notts County	1	Oval	23 000	C. J. Hughes	161
1892	19 March	West Bromwich Albion	3	Aston Villa	0	Oval	25 000	J. C. Clegg	163
1893	26 March	Wolverhampton Wanderers	1	Everton	0	Fallowfield	45 000	C. J. Hughes	183
1894	31 March	Notts County	4	Bolton Wanderers	1	Goodison Park	37 000	C. J. Hughes	155
1895	20 April	Aston Villa	1	West Bromwich Albion	0	Crystal Palace	42 560	J. Lewis	179
1896	18 April	Sheffield Wednesday	2	Wolverhampton Wanderers	1	Crystal Palace	48 836	Capt. W. Simpson	210
1897	10 April	Aston Villa	3	Everton	2	Crystal Palace	65 891	J. Lewis	244
1898	16 April	Nottingham Forest	3	Derby County	1	Crystal Palace	62 017	J. Lewis	213
1899	15 April	Sheffield United	4	Derby County	1	Crystal Palace	73 833	A. Scragg	235
1900	21 April	Bury	4	Southampton	0	Crystal Palace	68 945	A. G. Kingscott	242
1901	20 April	Tottenham Hotspur	2	Sheffield United	2	Crystal Palace	110 820	A. G. Kingscott	220
Replay	27 April	Tottenham Hotspur	3	Sheffield United	1	Burnden Park	20 470	A. G. Kingscott	
1902	19 April	Sheffield United	1	Southampton	1	Crystal Palace	76 914	T. Kirkham	226
Replay	26 April	Sheffield United	2	Southampton	1	Crystal Palace	33 068	T. Kirkham	
1903	18 April	Bury	6	Derby County	0	Crystal Palace	63 102	J. Adams	223
1904	23 April	Manchester City	1	Bolton Wanderers	0	Crystal Palace	61 374	A. J. Barker	252
1905	15 April	Aston Villa	2	Newcastle United	0	Crystal Palace	101 117	P. R. Harrower	274
1906	21 April	Everton	1	Aston Villa	0	Crystal Palace	75 609	T. Kirkham	280
1907	20 April	Sheffield Wednesday	2	Everton	1	Crystal Palace	84 584	N. Whittaker	305

1908	25 April	Wolverhampton Wanderers	3	Newcastle United	1	Crystal Palace	74 967	T. P. Campbell	348
1909	26 April	Manchester United	1	Bristol City	0	Crystal Palace	71 401	J. Mason	361
1910	23 April	Newcastle United	1	Barnsley	1	Crystal Palace	77 747	J. T. Ibbotson	424
Replay	28 April	Newcastle United	2	Barnsley	0	Goodison Park	69 000	J. T. Ibbotson	
1911	22 April	Bradford City	0	Newcastle United	0	Crystal Palace	69 098	J. H. Pearson	403
Replay	26 April	Bradford City	1	Newcastle United	0	Old Trafford	58 000	J. H. Pearson	
1912	20 April	Barnsley	0	West Bromwich Albion	0	Crystal Palace	54 556	J. R. Schumacher	410
Replay	24 April	Barnsley	1	West Bromwich Albion	0*	Bramall Lane	38 555	J. R. Schumacher	
1913	19 April	Aston Villa	1	Sunderland	0	Crystal Palace	120 081	A. Adams	457
1914	25 April	Burnley	1	Liverpool	0	Crystal Palace	72 778	H. S. Bamlett	476
1915	24 April	Sheffield United	3	Chelsea	0	Old Trafford	49 557	H. H. Taylor	454
1920	24 April	Aston Villa	1	Huddersfield Town	0*	Stamford Bridge	50 018	J. T. Howcroft	445
1921	23 April	Tottenham Hotspur	1	Wolverhampton Wanderers	0	Stamford Bridge	72 805	J. Davies	674
1922	29 April	Huddersfield Town	1	Preston North End	0	Stamford Bridge	53 000	J. W. D. Fowler	656
1923	28 April	Bolton Wanderers	2	West Ham United	0	Wembley	126 047	D. H. Asson	548
1924	26 April	Newcastle United	2	Aston Villa	0	Wembley	91 695	W. E. Russell	555
1925	25 April	Sheffield United	1	Cardiff City	0	Wembley	91 763	G. N. Watson	548
1926	24 April	Bolton Wanderers	1	Manchester City	0	Wembley	91 447	I. Baker	570
1927	23 April	Cardiff City	1	Arsenal	0	Wembley	91 206	W. F. Bunnell	552
1928	21 April	Blackburn Rovers	3	Huddersfield Town	1	Wembley	92 041	T. G. Bryan	544
1929	27 April	Bolton Wanderers	2	Portsmouth	0	Wembley	92 576	A. Josephs	520
1930	26 April	Arsenal	2	Huddersfield Town	0	Wembley	92 488	T. Crew	525
1931	25 April	West Bromwich Albion	2	Birmingham	1	Wembley	92 406	A. H. Kingscott	526
1932	23 April	Newcastle United	2	Arsenal	1	Wembley	92 298	W. P. Harper	529
1933	29 April	Everton	3	Manchester City	0	Wembley	92 950	E. Wood	543
1934	28 April	Manchester City	2	Portsmouth	1	Wembley	93 258	S. F. Rous	554
1935	27 April	Sheffield Wednesday	4	West Bromwich Albion	2	Wembley	93 204	A. E. Fogg	573
1936	25 April	Arsenal	1	Sheffield United	0	Wembley	93 384	H. Nattrass	571
1937	1 May	Sunderland	3	Preston North End	1	Wembley	93 495	R. G. Rudd	563
1938	30 April	Preston North End	1	Huddersfield Town	0*	Wembley	93 497	A. J. Jewell	574
1939	29 April	Portsmouth	4	Wolverhampton Wanderers	1	Wembley	99 370	T. Thompson	556
1946	27 April	Derby County	4	Charlton Athletic	1*	Wembley	98 000	E. D. Smith	294
1947	26 April	Charlton Atheltic	1	Burnley	0*	Wembley	99 000	J. M. Wiltshire	438
1948	24 April	Manchester United	4	Blackpool	2	Wembley	99 000	C. J. Barrick	510
1949	30 April	Wolverhampton Wanderers	3	Leicester City	1	Wembley	99 500	R. A. Mortimer	617
1950	29 April	Arsenal	2	Liverpool	0	Wembley	100 000	H. Pearce	617
1951	28 April	Newcastle United	2	Blackpool	0	Wembley	100 000	W. Ling	615
1952	3 May	Newcastle United	1	Arsenal	0	Wembley	100 000	A. Ellis	478
1953	2 May	Blackpool	4	Bolton Wanderers	3	Wembley	100 000	M. Griffiths	477
1954	1 May	West Bromwich Albion	3	Preston North End	2	Wembley	100 000	A. Luty	460
1955	7 May	Newcastle United	3	Manchester City	1	Wembley	100 000	R. Leafe	504
1956	5 May	Manchester City	3	Birmingham City	1	Wembley	100 000	A. Bond	460
1957	4 May	Aston Villa	2	Manchester United	1	Wembley	100 000	F. Coultas	438
1958	3 May	Bolton Wanderers	2	Manchester United	0	Wembley	100 000	J. Sherlock	442
1959	2 May	Nottingham Forest	2	Luton Town	1	Wembley	100 000	J. Clough	447
1960	7 May	Wolverhampton Wanderers	3	Blackburn Rovers	0	Wembley	100 000	K. Howley	462

PLAYER'S CIGARETTES
HOWARTH
HOLMES
Dr MILLS-ROBERTS
DRUMMOND
GRAHAM
RUSSELL
GORDON
DEWHURST (F.)
ROSS
GOODALL
THOMPSON
ASSOCIATION CUP WINNERS
PRESTON NORTH END. 1889

PLAYER'S CIGARETTES
SOUTHWORTH (Jas)
FORBES
HORNE (J. K.)
BARTON
FORREST
DEWAR
LOFTHOUSE
TOWNLEY
CAMPBELL
SOUTHWORTH
WALTON
ASSOCIATION CUP WINNERS
BLACKBURN ROVERS. 1890

PLAYER'S CIGARETTES
BRANDON
FORBES
PENNINGTON
BARTON
FORREST
DEWAR
LOFTHOUSE
TOWNLEY
WALTON
SOUTHWORTH
HALL
ASSOCIATION CUP WINNERS
BLACKBURN ROVERS. 1891

PLAYER'S CIGARETTES
NICHOLSON
McCULLOCH
READER
REYNOLDS
GROVES
PERRY
BASSETT
GEDDES
McLEOD
NICHOLLS
PEARSON
ASSOCIATION CUP WINNERS
WEST BROMWICH ALBION. 1892

PLAYER'S CIGARETTES
BAUGH
SWIFT
ROSE
MALPASS
KINSEY
ALLEN
TOPHAM (R.)
GRIFFIN
WYKES
BUTCHER
WOOD
ASSOCIATION CUP WINNERS
WOLVERHAMPTON WANDERERS. 1893

PLAYER'S CIGARETTES
HARPER
HENDRY
TOONE
BRAMLEY
SHELTON
CALDERHEAD
WATSON
DAFT
DONNELLY
LOGAN
BRUCE
ASSOCIATION CUP WINNERS
NOTTS COUNTY. 1894

PLAYER'S CIGARETTES
SPENCER
WELFORD
WILKES
REYNOLDS
RUSSELL
COWAN (Jas.)
ATHERSMITH
SMITH (S.)
CHATT
DEVEY
HODGETTS
ASSOCIATION CUP WINNERS
ASTON VILLA. 1895

PLAYER'S CIGARETTES
EARP
LANGLEY
MASSEY
BRANDON
PETRIE
CRAWSHAW
BRASH
SPIKESLEY
BRADY
BELL
DAVIS
ASSOCIATION CUP WINNERS
SHEFFIELD WEDNESDAY. 1896

PLAYER'S CIGARETTES
SPENCER
EVANS
WHITEHOUSE
REYNOLDS
CRABTREE
COWAN (Jas.)
ATHERSMITH
COWAN (John)
DEVEY
CAMPBELL
WHELDON
ASSOCIATION CUP WINNERS
ASTON VILLA. 1897

PLAYER'S CIGARETTES
RITCHIE
SCOTT
ALLSOP
FOREMAN (Frank)
WRAGG
McPHERSON
McINNES
CAPES
RICHARDS
BENBOW
SPOUNCER
ASSOCIATION CUP WINNERS
NOTTS FOREST. 1898

PLAYER'S CIGARETTES
THICKETT
BOYLE
FOULKE
JOHNSON
NEEDHAM
MORREN
BENNETT
PRIEST
BEERS
HEDLEY
ALMOND
ASSOCIATION CUP WINNERS
SHEFFIELD UNITED. 1899

PLAYER'S CIGARETTES
DARROCK
DAVIDSON
THOMPSON
PRAY
ROSS
LEEMING
RICHARDS
PLANT
WOODS
McLUCKIE
SAGAR
ASSOCIATION CUP WINNERS
BURY. 1900

PLAYER'S CIGARETTES
THICKETT
FOULKE
BOYLE
JOHNSON
NEEDHAM
MORREN
BENNETT
LIPSHAM
FIELD
HEDLEY
PRIEST
ASSOCIATION CUP WINNERS
SHEFFIELD UTD. DRAWN GAME. 1901

PLAYER'S CIGARETTES
CLAWLEY
TAIT
MORRIS
JONES
HUGHES
SMITH
KIRWAN
CAMERON
BROWN
COPELAND
ASSOCIATION CUP WINNERS
TOTTENHAM HOTSPUR. 1901

PLAYER'S CIGARETTES
C. B. FRY
ROBINSON
MOLYNEAUX
LEE
MESTON
BOWMAN
A. TURNER
J. TURNER
WOOD
BROWN
E. CHADWICK
ASSOCIATION CUP WINNERS
SOUTHAMPTON. DRAWN GAME. 1902

PLAYER'S CIGARETTES
THICKETT
FOULKE
BOYLE
NEEDHAM
JOHNSON
WILKINSON
BARNES
LIPSHAM
COMMON
HEDLEY
PRIEST
ASSOCIATION CUP WINNERS
SHEFFIELD UNITED. 1902

PLAYER'S CIGARETTES
LINDSAY
MONTEITH
McEWEN
JOHNSTON
ROSS
THORPE
RICHARDS
PLANT
WOOD
SAGAR
LEEMING
ASSOCIATION CUP WINNERS
BURY. 1903

PLAYER'S CIGARETTES
BURGESS
HILLMAN
McMAHON
ASHWORTH (S. B.)
FROST
HYNDS
MEREDITH
BOOTH
LIVINGSTONE
GILLESPIE
TURNBULL (A.)
ASSOCIATION CUP WINNERS
MANCHESTER CITY. 1904

PLAYER'S CIGARETTES
SPENCER
GEORGE
MILES
PEARSON
WINDMILL
LEAKE
BRAWN
HALL
GARRATTY
HAMPTON
BACHE
ASSOCIATION CUP WINNERS
ASTON VILLA. 1905

PLAYER'S CIGARETTES
BALMER (W.)
SCOTT
CRELLY
MAKEPEACE
ABBOTT
TAYLOR
SHARP
HARDMAN (H.P.)
BOLTON
YOUNG
SETTLE
ASSOCIATION CUP WINNERS
EVERTON. 1906

PLAYER'S CIGARETTES
LAYTON
LYALL
BURTON
BRITTLETON
BARTLETT
CRAWSHAW
CHAPMAN
SIMPSON
BRADSHAW
WILSON
STEWART
ASSOCIATION CUP WINNERS
SHEFFIELD WEDNESDAY. 1907

PLAYER'S CIGARETTES
JONES
LUNN
COLLINS
HUNT (K.R.G.)
BISHOP
WOOLDRIDGE
HARRISON
PEDLEY
SHELTON
HEDLEY
RADFORD
ASSOCIATION CUP WINNERS
WOLVERHAMPTON WANDERERS. 1908

PLAYER'S CIGARETTES
STACEY
MOGER
HAYES
DUCKWORTH
BELL
ROBERTS
MEREDITH
WALL
HALSE
TURNBULL (J.)
TURNBULL (A.)
ASSOCIATION CUP WINNERS
MANCHESTER UNITED. 1909

PLAYER'S CIGARETTES
McCRACKEN
LAWRENCE
CARR
VEITCH
McWILLIAM
LOW
RUTHERFORD
WILSON
HOWIE
SHEPHERD
HIGGINS
ASSOCIATION CUP WINNERS
NEWCASTLE UNITED. 1910

PLAYER'S CIGARETTES
McCRACKEN
LAWRENCE
WHITSON
VEITCH
WILLIS
LOW
RUTHERFORD
WILSON
STEWART
JOBEY
HIGGINS
ASSOCIATION CUP WINNERS
NEWCASTLE UTD. DRAWN GAME. 1911

PLAYER'S CIGARETTES
CAMPBELL
TAYLOR
MELLORS
ROBINSON
McDONALD
TORRANCE
LOGAN
THOMPSON
O'ROURKE
SPIERS
DEVINE
ASSOCIATION CUP WINNERS
BRADFORD CITY, 1911

PLAYER'S CIGARETTES
PENNINGTON
PEARSON
BADDELEY
McNEAL
BUCK
JEPHCOTT
SHEARMAN
PAILOR
WRIGHT
BOWSER
ASSOCIATION CUP WINNERS
W. BROMWICH A. DRAWN GAME. 1912

PLAYER'S CIGARETTES
DOWNS
TAYLOR
COOPER
GLENDINNING
UTLEY
BRATLEY
BARTROP
MOORE
LILLYCROP
TUFNELL
TRAVERS
ASSOCIATION CUP WINNERS
BARNSLEY. 1912

PLAYER'S CIGARETTES
LYONS
WESTON
HARDY
BARBER
LEACH
HARROP
WALLACE
BACHE
HAMPTON
HALSE
STEPHENSON
ASSOCIATION CUP WINNERS
ASTON VILLA. 1913

PLAYER'S CIGARETTES
BAMFORD
TAYLOR
SEWELL
HALLEY
WATSON
BOYLE
NESBIT
FREEMAN
LINDLEY
HODGSON
ASSOCIATION CUP WINNERS
BURNLEY. 1914

PLAYER'S CIGARETTES
COOK
ENGLISH
GOUGH
STURGESS
UTLEY
BRELSFORD
SIMMONS
EVANS
KITCHEN
FAZACKERLEY
MASTERMAN
ASSOCIATION CUP WINNERS
SHEFFIELD UNITED. 1915

PLAYER'S CIGARETTES
SMART
WESTON
HARDY
DUCAT
MOSS
BARSON
WALLACE
DORRELL
WALKER
KIRTON
STEPHENSON
ASSOCIATION CUP WINNERS
ASTON VILLA. 1920

PLAYER'S CIGARETTES
CLAY
McDONALD
HUNTER
SMITH
GRIMSDELL
WALTERS
BANKS
DIMMOCK
CANTRELL
SEED
BLISS
ASSOCIATION CUP WINNERS
TOTTENHAM HOTSPUR. 1921

PLAYER'S CIGARETTES
WOOD
WADSWORTH
MUTCH
SLADE
WATSON
WILSON
RICHARDSON
SMITH
ISLIP
MANN
STEPHENSON
ASSOCIATION CUP WINNERS
HUDDERSFIELD TOWN. 1922

PLAYER'S CIGARETTES
HAWORTH
FINNEY
PYM
NUTTALL
JENNINGS
SEDDON
BUTLER
VIZARD
SMITH (J. R.)
JACK
SMITH (J.)
ASSOCIATION CUP WINNERS
BOLTON WANDERERS. 1923

PLAYER'S CIGARETTES
HAMPSON
HUDSPETH
BRADLEY
MOONEY
GIBSON
SPENCER
LOW
SEYMOUR
HARRIS
COWAN
McDONALD
ASSOCIATION CUP WINNERS
NEWCASTLE UNITED. 1924

1961	6 May	Tottenham Hotspur	2	Leicester City	0	Wembley	100 000	J. Kelly	433
1962	5 May	Tottenham Hotspur	3	Burnley	1	Wembley	100 000	J. Finney	414
1963	25 May	Manchester United	3	Leicester City	1	Wembley	100 000	K. Aston	411
1964	2 May	West Ham United	3	Preston Northend	2	Wembley	100 000	A. Holland	400
1965	1 May	Liverpool	2	Leeds United	1*	Wembley	100 000	W. Clements	395
1966	14 May	Everton	3	Sheffield Wednesday	2	Wembley	100 000	J. K. Taylor	403
1967	20 May	Tottenham Hotspur	2	Chelsea	1	Wembley	100 000	K. Dagnall	406
1968	18 May	West Bromwich Albion	1	Everton	0*	Wembley	100 000	L. Callaghan	429
1969	26 April	Manchester City	1	Leicester City	0	Wembley	100 000	G. McCabe	438
1970	11 April	Chelsea	2	Leeds United	2*	Wembley	100 000	E. Jennings	451
Replay	29 April	Chelsea	2	Leeds United	1*	Old Trafford	62 078	E. Jennings	
1971	8 May	Arsenal	2	Liverpool	1	Wembley	100 000	N. Burtenshaw	464
1972	6 May	Leeds United	1	Arsenal	0	Wembley	100 000	D. W. Smith	471
1973	5 May	Sunderland	1	Leeds United	0	Wembley	100 000	K. Burns	471
1974	4 May	Liverpool	3	Newcastle United	0	Wembley	100 000	G. C. Kew	468
1975	3 May	West Ham United	2	Fulham	0	Wembley	100 000	P. Partridge	453
1976	1 May	Southampton	1	Manchester United	0	Wembley	100 000	C. Thomas	441
1977	21 May	Manchester United	2	Liverpool	1	Wembley	100 000	R. Matthewson	454
1978	6 May	Ipswich Town	1	Arsenal	0	Wembley	100 000	D. R. G. Nippard	469
1979	12 May	Arsenal	3	Manchester United	2	Wembley	100 000	R. Challis	466
1980	10 May	West Ham United	1	Arsenal	0	Wembley	100 000	G. Courtney	475
1981	9 May	Tottenham Hotspur	1	Manchester City	1*	Wembley	100 000	K. Hackett	480
Replay	14 May	Tottenham Hotspur	3	Manchester City	2	Wembley	100 000	K. Hackett	
1982	22 May	Tottenham Hotspur	1	Queen's Park Rangers	1*	Wembley	100 000	C. White	486
Replay	27 May	Tottenham Hotspur	1	Queen's Park Rangers	0	Wembley	100 000	C. White	

1983	21 May	Manchester United	2	Brighton & H.A.	2*	Wembley	100 000	A. Grey	479
Replay	26 May	Manchester United	4	Brighton & H.A.	0	Wembley	100 000	A. Grey	
1984	19 May	Everton	2	Watford	0	Wembley	100 000	J. Hunting	487
1985	18 May	Manchester United	1	Everton	0*	Wembley	100 000	P. Willis	494

* after extra time

The Giant-Killers

Since the re-organization of the FA Cup in 1925 the following non-League clubs have reached the 3rd round

1925–26
Chilton Colliery, lost 0–3 South Shields (A); Clapton, lost 2–3 Swindon Town (H); *Corinthians, lost 0–4 Manchester City (A) after 3–3 (H); Boston, lost 1–8 Sunderland (A).

1926–27
Rhyl Athletic, lost 1–2 Darlington (A); Carlisle United, lost 0–2 Wolverhampton Wanderers (H); Poole, lost 1–3 Everton (A); *Corinthians, beat Walsall 4–0 (A), 4th round, lost 1–3 Newcastle United (H).

1927–28
*Corinthians, lost 1–2 New Brighton (A); Peterborough United, lost 3–4 Birmingham City (A); London Caledonians, lost 2–3 Crewe Alexandra (H).

1928–29
*Corinthians, beat Norwich City 5–0 (A); 4th round, lost 0–3 West Ham United (A); Mansfield Town, beat Wolverhampton Wanderers 1–0 (A), 4th round, lost 0–2 Arsenal (A).

1929–30
*Corinthians, lost 1–5 Millwall (at Chelsea) after 2–2 (H), 1–1 (A) aet.

1930–31
*Corinthians, lost 1–3 Port Vale (H); Scarborough, lost 1–2 Grimsby Town (H); Aldershot Town, lost 0–1 Bradford City (H).
*Corinthians exempted to 3rd round.

1931–32
Darwen, lost 1–11 Arsenal (A); *Corinthians, lost 1–2 Sheffield United (A); Bath City, lost 0–2 Brentford (A); Burton Town, lost 0–4 Blackburn Rovers (H); Crook Town, lost 0–7 Leicester City (A).

1932–33
*Corinthians, lost 0–2 West Ham United (H); Folkestone, lost 0–2 Huddersfield Town (A).

1933–34
Workington Town, beat Gateshead 4–1 (H), 4th round, lost 1–2 Preston North End (H); Cheltenham Town, lost 1–3 Blackpool (H).

1934–35
Bath City, lost 0–2 Norwich City (A); Wigan Athletic, lost 1–4 Millwall (H); Yeovil and Petters, lost 2–6 Liverpool (H).

1935–36
Southall, lost 1–4 Watford (H); Margate, lost 1–3 Blackpool (A); Dartford, lost 2–3 Derby County (A).

1936–37
Spennymoor United, lost 1–7 West Bromwich Albion (A); Dartford, lost 0–1 Darlington (H).

1937–38
Yeovil and Petters, lost 0–3 Manchester United (A); Scarborough, lost 1–5 Luton Town (A), after 1–1 (H).

1938–39
Runcorn, lost 2–4 Preston North End (H); Chelmsford City, beat Southampton 4–1 (H), 4th round, lost 0–6 Birmingham (A); Yeovil and Petters, lost 1–2 Sheffield Wednesday (H), after 1–1 (A).

1945–46
Lovell's Athletic, lost on aggregate Wolverhampton Wanderers 2–4 (H), 1–8 (A).

1946–47
Gillingham, lost 1–4 Swansea Town (A).

1947–48
Colchester United, beat Huddersfield Town 1–0 (H), 4th round, beat Bradford 3–2 (H), 5th round, lost 0–5 Blackpool (A); Gillingham, lost 1–3 Queen's Park Rangers (A) after 1–1 aet (H).

1948–49
Yeovil Town, beat Bury 3–1 (H), 4th round, beat Sunderland 2–1 (H) aet, 5th round, lost 0–8 Manchester United (A).

1949–50
Yeovil Town, lost 1–3 Chesterfield (A); Weymouth, lost 0–4 Manchester United (A); Nuneaton Borough, lost 0–3 Exeter City (A).

1950–51
None.

1951–52
Stockton, lost 0–4 Notts County (A); Buxton, lost 0–2 Doncaster Rovers (A).

1952–53
Finchley, lost 0–2 Shrewsbury Town (A); Walthamstow Avenue, beat Stockport County 2–1 (H), 4th round, lost 2–5 Manchester United (H) after 1–1 (A).

1953–54
Wigan Athletic, lost 2–3 Newcastle United (H) after 2–2 (A); Peterborough United, lost 1–3 Cardiff City (A); Hastings

United, lost 0–3 Norwich City (A) after 3–3 (H); Headington United, beat Stockport County 1–0 (H) after 0–0 (A), 4th round, lost 2–4 Bolton Wanderers (H).

1954–55
Bishop Auckland, beat Ipswich Town 3–0 (H) after 2–2 (A), 4th round, lost 1–3 York City (H); Hastings United, lost 1–2 Sheffield Wednesday (A).

1955–56
Bedford Town, lost 1–2 Arsenal (H) after 2–2 (A); Burton Albion, lost 0–7 Charlton Athletic (A); Worksop Town, lost 0–1 Swindon Town (A); Boston United, lost 0–4 Tottenham Hotspur (A).

1956–57
Rhyl, beat Notts County 3–1 (A), 4th round, lost 0–3 Bristol City (A); New Brighton, beat Torquay United 2–1 (H), 4th round, lost 0–9 Burnley (A); Peterborough United, beat Lincoln City 5–4 (A) after 2–2 (H), 4th round, lost 1–3 Huddersfield Town (A); Goole Town, lost 0–6 Nottingham Forest (A).

1957–58
Hereford United, lost 0–3 Sheffield Wednesday (H); Yeovil Town, lost 0–4 Fulham (A).

1958–59
Worcester City, beat Liverpool 2–1 (H), 4th round, lost 0–2 Sheffield United (H); Peterborough United, lost 0–1 Fulham (H) after 0–0 (A); Tooting and Mitcham United, lost 0–3 Nottingham Forest (A) after 2–2 (H).

1959–60
Peterborough United, beat Ipswich Town 3–2 (A), 4th round, lost 0–2 Sheffield Wednesday (A); Bath City, lost 0–1 Brighton & Hove Albion (H).

1960–61
Oxford United, lost 1–3 Leicester City (A).

1961–62
King's Lynn, lost 0–4 Everton (A); Morecambe, lost 0–1 Weymouth (H); Weymouth, beat Morecambe 1–0 (A), 4th round, lost 0–2 Preston North End (A).

1962–63
Gravesend and Northfleet, beat Carlisle United 1–0 (A), 4th round, lost 2–5 Sunderland (A) after 1–1 (H).

1963–64
Yeovil Town, lost 0–2 Bury (H); Bedford Town, beat Newcastle United 2–1 (A), 4th round, lost 0–3 Carlisle United (H); Bath City, lost 0–3 Bolton Wanderers (A) after 1–1 (H).

1964-65
Barnet, lost 2–3 Preston North End (H).

1965–66
Bedford Town, beat Hereford United 2–1 (H), 4th round, lost 0–3 Everton (H); Folkestone Town, lost 1–5 Crewe Alexandra (H); Altrincham, lost 0–5 Wolverhampton Wanderers (A); Corby Town, lost 0–6 Plymouth Argyle (A).

1966–67
Bedford Town, lost 2–6 Peterborough United (H); Nuneaton Borough, lost 0–1 Rotherham United (A) after 1–1 (H).

1967–68
Macclesfield, lost 2–4 Fulham (A).

1968–69
Kettering Town, lost 1–2 Bristol Rovers (H) after 1–1 (A).

1969–70
South Shields, lost 1–4 Queen's Park Rangers (A); Brentwood Town, lost 0–1 Northampton Town (H); Hillingdon Borough, lost 1–4 Sutton United (A) after 0–0 (H). Sutton United, beat Hillingdon Borough 4–1 (H) after 0–0 (A), 4th round, lost 0–6 Leeds United (H).

1970–71
Yeovil Town, lost 0–3 Arsenal (H); Wigan Athletic, lost 0–1 Manchester City (A); Barnet, lost 0–1 Colchester United (H); Rhyl, lost 1–6 Swansea City (A).

1971–72
Boston United, lost 0–1 Portsmouth (H); Hereford United, beat Newcastle United 2–1 (H) after 2–2 (A), 4th round, lost 1–3 West Ham United (A) after 0–0 (H); Blyth Spartans, lost 1–6 Reading (A) after 2–2 (H).

1972–73
Chelmsford, lost 1–3 Ipswich Town (H); Margate, lost 0–6 Tottenham Hotspur (H); Barnet, lost 0–3 Queen's Park Rangers (H) after 0–0 (A).

1973–74
Boston United, lost 1–6 Derby County (H) after 0–0 (A); Alvechurch, lost 2–4 Bradford City (A); Grantham, lost 0–2 Middlesbrough (H); Hendon, lost 0–4 Newcastle United (H) after 1–1 (A).

Stan Cullis (Wolves) on the left shakes hands with Jimmy Guthrie (Portsmouth) while referee Tommy Thompson officiates in the 1939 FA Cup Final.

Ken Dagnall.

Bill Clements.

George McCabe.

Jim Finney.

1974–75
Leatherhead, beat Brighton 1–0 (A), 4th round, lost 2–3 Leicester City (A); Wimbledon, beat Burnley 1–0 (A), 4th round, lost 0–1 Leeds United (H) after 0–0 (A); Stafford Rangers, beat Rotherham United 2–0 (A) after 0–0 (H), 4th round, lost 1–2 Peterborough United (H); Wycombe Wanderers, lost 0–1 Middlesbrough (A) after 0–0 (H); Altrincham, lost 0–2 Everton (H) after 1–1 (A).

1975–76
Tooting and Mitcham United, beat Swindon Town 2–1 (H) after 2–2 (A), 4th round, lost 1–3 Bradford City (A); Scarborough, lost 1–2 Crystal Palace (H).

1976–77
Kettering Town, lost 2–3 Colchester United (H); Wimbledon, lost 0–1 Middlesbrough (A) after 0–0 (H); Northwich Victoria, beat Watford 3–2 (H), 4th round, lost 1–3 Oldham Athletic (H); Matlock Town, lost 1–5 Carlisle United (A).

1977–78
Scarborough, lost 0–3 Brighton (A); Wigan Athletic, lost 0–4 Birmingham City (A); Wealdstone, lost 0–4 Queen's Park Rangers (A); Tilbury, lost 0–4 Stoke City (A); Blyth Spartans, beat Enfield 1–0 (H), 4th round, beat Stoke City 3–2 (A), 5th round, lost Wrexham 1–2 (H) after 1–1 (A).

1978–79
Maidstone United, lost 1–2 Charlton Athletic (H) after 1–1 (A); Altrincham, lost 0–3 Tottenham Hotspur (H) after 1–1 (A).

1979–80
Yeovil Town, lost 0–3 Norwich City (H); Harlow Town, beat Leicester City 1–0 (H) after 1–1 (A), 4th round, lost 3–4 Watford (A); Chesham United, lost 0–2 Cambridge United (H); Altrincham, lost 1–2 Orient (A) after 1–1 (H).

1980–81
Altrincham, lost 1–4 Liverpool (A); Maidstone United, lost 2–4 Exeter City (H); Enfield, beat Port Vale 3–0 (H) after 1–1 (A), 4th round, lost 0–3 Barnsley (H) after 1–1 (A).

1981–82
Altrincham, lost 1–6 Burnley (A); Barnet, lost 1–3 Brighton (A) after 0–0 (H)

1982–83
Bishop's Stortford, lost 1–2 Middlesbrough (H) after 2–2 (A); Weymouth, lost 0–1 Cambridge United (A); Worcester City, lost 1–3 Coventry City (A).

1983–84
Maidstone United, lost 1–4 Darlington (A); Telford United, beat Rochdale 4–1 (A); 4th round, lost 2–3 Derby County (A).

1984–85
Burton Albion, lost 1–6 Leicester City (H); Dagenham, lost 0–1 Carlisle United (A); Telford United, beat Bradford City 2–1 (H), 4th round, beat Darlington 3–0 (H) after 1–1 draw (A); 5th round, lost 0–3 Everton (A).

Jack Taylor.

Kevin Howley.

FA Cup attendances from 1966–67 to 1983–84

Season	1st Rd	2nd Rd	3rd Rd	4th Rd	5th Rd	6th Rd	S F+F	Total	Matches	Average
1966–67	390 292	295 112	1 288 341	921 303	602 111	252 672	217 378	3 967 209	169	23 475
1967–68	322 121	236 195	1 229 519	771 284	563 779	240 095	223 831	3 586 824	160	22 418
1968–69	331 858	252 710	1 094 043	883 675	464 915	188 121	216 232	3 431 554	157	21 857
1969–70	345 229	195 102	925 930	651 374	319 893	198 537	390 700	3 026 765	170	17 805
1970–71	329 687	230 942	956 683	757 852	360 687	304 937	279 644	3 220 432	162	19 879
1971–72	277 726	236 127	986 094	711 399	468 378	230 292	248 546	3 158 562	160	19 741
1972–73	259 432	169 114	938 741	735 825	357 386	241 934	226 543	2 928 975	160	18 306
1973–74	214 236	125 295	840 142	747 909	346 012	233 307	273 051	2 779 952	167	16 646
1974–75	283 956	170 466	914 994	646 434	393 323	268 361	291 369	2 968 903	172	17 261
1975–76	255 533	178 099	867 880	573 843	471 925	206 851	205 810	2 759 941	161	17 142
1976–77	379 230	192 159	942 523	631 265	373 330	205 379	258 216	2 982 102	174	17 139
1977–78	258 248	178 930	881 406	540 164	400 751	137 059	198 020	2 594 578	160	16 216
1978–79	243 773	185 343	880 345	537 748	243 683	263 213	249 897	2 604 002	166	15 687
1979–80	267 121	204 759	804 701	507 725	364 039	157 530	355 541	2 661 416	163	16 328
1980–81	246 824	194 502	832 578	534 402	320 530	288 714	339 250	2 756 800	169	16 312
1981–82	236 220	127 300	513 185	356 987	203 334	124 308	279 621	1 840 955	160	11 506
1982–83	191 312	150 046	670 503	452 688	260 069	193 845	291 162	2 209 625	159	13 897
1983–84	192 276	151 647	625 965	417 298	181 832	185 382	187 000	1 941 400	166	11 695
1984–85	(Official figures not available at press time)							1 903 874	158	

Scottish Cup finals

Year	Date	Winners		Runners-up		Venue	Attendance
1874	21 March	Queen's Park	2	Clydesdale	0	First Hampden	3 500
1875	10 April	Queen's Park	3	Renton	0	First Hampden	7 000
1876	11 March	Queen's Park	1	3rd Lanark Rifles	1	Hamilton Crescent	10 000
Replay	18 March	Queen's Park	2	3rd Lanark Rifles	0	Hamilton Crescent	6 000
1877	17 March	Vale of Leven	1	Rangers	1	Hamilton Crescent	10 000
Replay	7 April	Vale of Leven	1	Rangers	1	Hamilton Crescent	15 000
2nd Replay	13 April	Vale of Leven	3	Rangers	2	First Hampden	12 000
1878	30 March	Vale of Leven	1	3rd Lanark Rifles	0	First Hampden	5 000
(1) 1879	19 April	Vale of Leven	1	Rangers	1	First Hampden	9 000
1880	21 February	Queen's Park	3	Thornliebank	0	First Cathkin	4 000
1881	26 March	Queen's Park	2	Dumbarton	1	Kinning Park	15 000
(2) Replay	9 April	Queen's Park	3	Dunbarton	1	Kinning Park	7 000
1882	18 March	Queen's Park	2	Dunbarton	2	First Cathkin	12 500
Replay	1 April	Queen's Park	4	Dumbarton	1	First Cathkin	14 000
1883	31 March	Dumbarton	2	Vale of Leven	2	First Hampden	9 000
Replay	7 April	Dumbarton	2	Vale of Leven	1	First Hampden	12 000
(3) 1884		Queen's Park	W.O.	Vale of Leven Scr.			
1885	21 February	Renton	0	Vale of Leven	0	Second Hampden	2 500
Replay	28 February	Renton	3	Vale of Leven	1	Second Hampden	3 500
1886	13 February	Queen's Park	3	Renton	1	First Cathkin	7 000
1887	12 February	Hibernian	2	Dumbarton	1	Second Hampden	12 000
1888	4 February	Renton	6	Cambuslang	1	Second Hampden	11 000
1889	2 February	Third Lanark	3	Celtic	0	Second Hampden	18 000
(4) Replay	9 February	Third Lanark	2	Celtic	1	Second Hampden	13 000
1890	15 February	Queen's Park	1	Vale of Leven	1	Ibrox	11 000
Replay	22 February	Queen's Park	2	Vale of Leven	1	Ibrox	14 000
1891	7 February	Heart of Midlothian	1	Dumbarton	0	Second Hampden	10 836
1892	12 March	Celtic	1	Queen's Park	0	Ibrox	40 000
(5) Replay	9 April	Celtic	5	Queen's Park	1	Ibrox	26 000
1893	25 February	Queen's Park	0	Celtic	1	Ibrox*	18 771
Replay	11 March	Queen's Park	2	Celtic	1	Ibrox	13 239
1894	17 February	Rangers	3	Celtic	1	Second Hampden	17 000
1895	20 April	St Bernard's	2	Renton	1	Ibrox	15 000
1896	14 March	Heart of Midlothian	3	Hibernian	1	Logie Green	17 034
1897	20 March	Rangers	5	Dumbarton	1	Second Hampden	14 000
1898	26 March	Rangers	2	Kilmarnock	0	Second Hampden	13 000
1899	22 April	Celtic	2	Rangers	0	Second Hampden	25 000
1900	14 April	Celtic	4	Queen's Park	3	Ibrox	15 000
1901	6 April	Heart of Midlothian	4	Celtic	3	Ibrox	12 000
1902	26 April	Hibernian	1	Celtic	0	Celtic Park	16 000
1903	11 April	Rangers	1	Heart of Midlothian	1	Celtic Park	40 000
Replay	18 April	Rangers	0	Heart of Midlothian	0	Celtic Park	35 000
2nd Replay	25 April	Rangers	2	Heart of Midlothian	0	Celtic Park	32 000
1904	16 April	Celtic	3	Rangers	2	Hampden Park	65 000
1905	8 April	Third Lanark	0	Rangers	0	Hampden Park	54 000
Replay	15 April	Third Lanark	3	Rangers	1	Hampden Park	55 000
1906	28 April	Heart of Midlothian	1	Third Lanark	0	Ibrox	25 000
1907	20 April	Celtic	3	Heart of Midlothian	0	Hampden Park	50 000
1908	18 April	Celtic	5	St Mirren	1	Hampden Park	55 000
(6) 1909	10 April	Celtic	2	Rangers	2	Hampden Park	70 000
Replay	17 April	Celtic	1	Rangers	1	Hampden Park	61 000
1910	9 April	Dundee	2	Clyde	2	Ibrox	62 300
Replay	16 April	Dundee	0	Clyde	0		24 500
2nd Replay	20 April	Dundee	2	Clyde	1		25 400
1911	8 April	Celtic	0	Hamilton Acad.	0	Ibrox	45 000
Replay	15 April	Celtic	2	Hamilton Acad.	0	Ibrox	24 700
1912	6 April	Celtic	2	Clyde	0	Ibrox	46 000
1913	12 April	Falkirk	2	Raith Rovers	0	Celtic Park	45 000
1914	11 April	Celtic	0	Hibernian	0	Ibrox	56 000
Replay	16 April	Celtic	4	Hibernian	1	Ibrox	40 000
1920	17 April	Kilmarnock	3	Albion Rovers	2	Hampden Park	95 000
1921	16 April	Partick Thistle	1	Rangers	0	Celtic Park	28 300
1922	15 April	Morton	1	Rangers	0	Hampden Park	75 000
1923	31 March	Celtic	1	Hibernian	0	Hampden Park	80 100
1924	19 April	Airdrieonians	2	Hibernian	0	Ibrox	59 218
1925	11 April	Celtic	2	Dundee	1	Hampden Park	75 137
1926	10 April	St Mirren	2	Celtic	0	Hampden Park	98 620
1927	16 April	Celtic	3	East Fife	1	Hampden Park	80 070
1928	14 April	Rangers	4	Celtic	0	Hampden Park	118 115
1929	6 April	Kilmarnock	2	Rangers	0	Hampden Park	114 708
1930	12 April	Rangers	0	Partick Thistle	0	Hampden Park	107 475
Replay	16 April	Rangers	2	Partick Thistle	1	Hampden Park	103 686
1931	11 April	Celtic	2	Motherwell	2	Hampden Park	105 000

Replay	15 April	Celtic	4	Motherwell	2	Hampden Park	98 579
1932	16 April	Rangers	1	Kilmarnock	1	Hampden Park	111 982
Replay	2 April	Rangers	3	Kilmarnock	0	Hampden Park	104 965
1933	15 April	Celtic	1	Motherwell	0	Hampden Park	102 339
1934	21 April	Rangers	5	St Mirren	0	Hampden Park	113 403
1935	20 April	Rangers	2	Hamilton Acad.	1	Hampden Park	87 286
1936	18 April	Rangers	1	Third Lanark	0	Hampden Park	88 859
1937	24 April	Celtic	2	Aberdeen	1	Hampden Park	147 365
1938	23 April	East Fife	1	Kilmarnock	1	Hampden Park	80 091
Replay	27 April	East Fife	4	Kilmarnock	2	Hampden Park	92 716
1939	22 April	Clyde	4	Motherwell	0	Hampden Park	94 799
1947	19 April	Aberdeen	2	Hibernian	1	Hampden Park	82 140
1948	17 April	Rangers	1	Morton	1	Hampden Park	129 176
Replay	21 April	Rangers	1	Morton	0	Hampden Park	133 570
1949	23 April	Rangers	4	Clyde	1	Hampden Park	108 435
1950	22 April	Rangers	3	East Fife	0	Hampden Park	118 262
1951	21 April	Celtic	1	Motherwell	0	Hampden Park	131 943
1952	19 April	Motherwell	4	Dundee	0	Hampden Park	136 274
1953	25 April	Rangers	1	Aberdeen	1	Hampden Park	129 681
Replay	29 April	Rangers	1	Aberdeen	0	Hampden Park	112 619
1954	24 April	Celtic	2	Aberdeen	1	Hampden Park	129 926
1955	23 April	Clyde	1	Celtic	1	Hampden Park	106 111
Replay	27 April	Clyde	1	Celtic	0	Hampden Park	68 735
1956	21 April	Heart of Midlothian	3	Celtic	1	Hampden Park	133 339
1957	20 April	Falkirk	1	Kilmarnock	1	Hampden Park	83 000
Replay	24 April	Falkirk	2	Kilmarnock	1	Hampden Park	79 785
1958	26 April	Clyde	1	Hibernian	0	Hampden Park	95 124
1959	25 April	St Mirren	3	Aberdeen	1	Hampden Park	108 591
1960	23 April	Rangers	2	Kilmarnock	0	Hampden Park	108 017
1961	22 April	Dunfermline Athletic	0	Celtic	0	Hampden Park	113 618
Replay	26 April	Dunfermline Athletic	2	Celtic	0	Hampden Park	87 866
1962	21 April	Rangers	2	St Mirren	0	Hampden Park	126 930
1963	4 May	Rangers	1	Celtic	1	Hampden Park	129 527
Replay	15 May	Rangers	3	Celtic	0	Hampden Park	120 263
1964	25 April	Rangers	3	Dundee	1	Hampden Park	120 982
1965	24 April	Celtic	3	Dunfermline Athletic	2	Hampden Park	108 800
1966	23 April	Rangers	0	Celtic	0	Hampden Park	126 552
Replay	27 April	Rangers	1	Celtic	0	Hampden Park	98 202
1967	29 April	Celtic	2	Aberdeen	0	Hampden Park	127 117
1968	27 April	Dunfermline Athletic	3	Heart of Midlothian	1	Hampden Park	56 366
1969	26 April	Celtic	4	Rangers	0	Hampden Park	132 874
1970	11 April	Aberdeen	3	Celtic	1	Hampden Park	108 434
1971	9 May	Celtic	1	Rangers	1	Hampden Park	120 092
Replay	12 May	Celtic	2	Rangers	1	Hampden Park	103 332
1972	6 May	Celtic	6	Hibernian	1	Hampden Park	106 102
1973	5 May	Rangers	3	Celtic	2	Hampden Park	122 714
1974	4 May	Celtic	3	Dundee United	0	Hampden Park	75 959
1975	3 May	Celtic	3	Airdrieonians	1	Hampden Park	75 457
1976	1 May	Rangers	3	Heart of Midlothian	1	Hampden Park	85 354
1977	7 May	Celtic	1	Rangers	0	Hampden Park	54 252
1978	6 May	Rangers	2	Aberdeen	1	Hampden Park	61 563
1979	12 May	Rangers	0	Hibernian	0	Hampden Park	50 610
Replay	16 May	Rangers	0	Hibernian	0	Hampden Park	33 506
2nd Replay	28 May	Rangers	3	Hibernian	2	Hampden Park	30 602
1980	10 May	Celtic	1	Rangers	0	Hampden Park	70 303
1981	9 May	Rangers	0	Dundee United	0	Hampden Park	55 000
Replay	12 May	Rangers	4	Dundee United	1	Hampden Park	43 009
1982	22 May	Aberdeen	4	Rangers	1	Hampden Park	53 788
1983	21 May	Aberdeen	1	Rangers	0	Hampden Park	62 979
1984	19 May	Aberdeen	2	Celtic	1	Hampden Park	58 900
1985	18 May	Celtic	2	Dundee United	1	Hampden Park	60 346

(1) Vale of Leven awarded cup; Rangers failed to appear for replay after 1–1 draw
(2) After Dumbarton protested the first game, which Queen's Park won 2–1
(3) Queen's Park awarded cup, Vale of Leven failing to appear
(4) Replay by order of Scottish FA because of playing conditions in first match, won 3–0 by Third Lanark
(5) After mutually protested first game which Celtic won 1–0
(6) Owing to riot, the cup was withheld after two drawn games
*Declared a friendly due to fog and frost

Record individual scoring feats – for and against – of all clubs in Football League matches

This table shows the best individual goalscoring performance for each Football League club in one game and also the highest number of goals scored by an opponent against that same team. Only Football League matches are included and feats of four or more goals shown.

	For				Against			
	Player	Gls	Against		Player	Club	Gls	
Aldershot	C. Mortimore	5	Orient	25.2.50	P. Simpson	Palace	4	18.11.33
					T. Cheetham	Q.P.R.	4	14.9.35
	D. Banton	5	Halifax	7.5.83	T. Cheetham	Q.P.R.	4	12.11.38
					M. Tadman	Plymouth	4	14.10.50
					R. Smith	Peterborough	4	4.3.61
Arsenal	E. J. Drake	7	Villa	14.12.35	S. Bloomer	Middlesbro	4	5.1.07
					A. Turnbull	Man. U.	4	23.11.07
					W. Walker	Villa	4	28.8.20
					F. Morris	West Brom.	4	14.10.22
					N. Harris	Notts C.	4	26.12.25
					H. Johnson	Sheff. U.	4	7.1.28
Aston Villa	H. Hampton	5	Sheff. W.	5.10.12	E. J. Drake	Arsenal	7	14.12.35
	H. J. Halse	5	Derby C.	19.10.12				
	L. Capewell	5	Burnley	29.8.25				
	G. Brown	5	Leicester	2.1.32				
	G. Hitchens	5	Charlton	14.11.59				
Barnsley	F. Eaton	5	Sth Shields	9.4.27	A. Chandler	Leicester	5	26.2.25
	P. Cunningham	5	Darlington	4.2.33	T. Phillipson	Wolves	5	26.4.26
	B. Asquith	5	Darlington	12.12.38	B. R. Mills	Notts C.	5	19.12.27
	C. McCormack	5	Luton	9.9.50	J. Hallows	Bradford C.	5	2.1.32
					W. R. Scott	Brentford	5	15.12.34
					K. Hector	Bradford PA	5	20.11.65
Birmingham	W. Abbott	5	Darwen	26.11.98	L. A. Page	Burnley	6	10.4.26
	J. McMillan	5	Blackpool	2.3.01				
	J. Windridge	5	Glossop	23.1.15				
Blackburn	T. Briggs	7	Bristol R.	5.2.55	G. Henson	Bradford PA	6	29.1.38
Blackpool	J. Hampson	5	Reading	10.11.28	J. Cookson	West Brom	6	17.9.27
	J. McIntosh	5	Preston	1.5.48				
Bolton W.	T. Caldwell	5	Walsall	10.9.83	R. Gurney	Sunderland	5	7.12.35
Bournemouth	J. Russell	4	Orient	7.1.33	C. Bourton	Coventry	5	17.10.31
	J. Russell	4	Bristol C.	28.1.33				
	H. Mardon	4	Southend	1.1.38				
	J. McDonald	4	Torquay	8.11.47				
Bradford C.	A. Whitehurst	7	Tranmere	6.3.29	T. Phillipson	Wolves	5	25.12.26
Brentford	W. R. Scott	5	Barnsley	15.12.34	G. Whitworth	Northampton	4	2.4.21
	P. McKennan	5	Bury	19.2.49	L. Thompson	Swansea	4	8.11.24
					W. Arblaster	Merthyr	4	17.4.26
					F. White	Birmingham	4	10.12.38
					S. Cooper	Newport	4	26.1.85
Brighton	J. Doran	5	Northampton	5.11.21	J. Riley	Bristol C.	5	7.2.34
	A. Thorne	5	Watford	30.4.58	R. Blackman	Reading	5	11.11.50
					B. Clough	Middlesbro.	5	23.8.58
Bristol C.	T. Walsh	6	Gillingham	15.1.27	K. McDonald	Hull C.	5	17.11.26
Bristol R.	R. A. Leigh	4	Exeter	2.5.21	J. Payne	Luton	10	13.4.36
	J. Wilcox	4	Bournemouth	26.12.25				
	W. Culley	4	Q.P.R.	5.3.27				
Burnley	L. A. Page	6	Birmingham	10.4.26	R. Jardine	Notts C.	5	27.10.88
					L. Capewell	Villa	5	29.8.25
					T. Browell	Manchester C.	5	24.10.25
					H. Ferguson	Cardiff	5	5.9.28
Bury	E. Quigley	5	Millwall	15.2.47	P. McKennan	Brentford	5	19.2.49
	R. Pointer	5	Rotherham U.	2.10.65				
Cambridge	B. Greenhalgh	4	Darlington	18.9.71	J. Howarth	Aldershot	4	13.4.74

Club	Player	Goals	Opponent	Date	Player	Opponent	Goals	Date
Cardiff	H. Ferguson W. Robbins W. Henderson	5 5 5	Burnley Thames Northampton	5.9.28 6.2.32 22.4.33	A. G. Dawes	Palace	5	1.9.34
Carlisle	H. Mills J. Whitehouse	5 5	Halifax Scunthorpe	11.9.37 25.12.52	T. Bamford G. Alsop	Wrexham Walsall	5 5	17.3.34 2.2.35
Charlton	W. Lennox E. Firmani J. Summers J. Summers	5 5 5 5	Exeter Villa Huddersfield T. Portsmouth	2.2.29 5.2.55 21.12.57 1.10.60	J. Fowler W. Carter G. Hitchens	Swansea Plymouth Villa	5 5 5	27.9.24 27.12.60 14.11.59
Chelsea	G. Hilsdon J. Greaves J. Greaves J. Greaves R. Tambling	5 5 5 5 5	Glossop Wolves Preston West Brom Villa	1.9.06 30.8.58 19.12.59 3.12.60 17.9.66	W. R. Dean A. Lochhead	Everton Burnley	5 5	14.12.31 24. 4.65
Chester	T. Jennings B. Jepson	5 5	Walsall York	30.1.32 8.2.58	E. Gemmell	Oldham	7	19.1.52
Chesterfield	J. Cookson J. Cookson J. Cookson T. Lyon	4 4 4 4	Accrington Ashington Wigan Southampton	16.1.26 1.5.26 4.9.26 3.12.38	S. Littlewood	Port Vale	6	24.9.32
Colchester	R. R. Hunt M. King R. R. Hunt	4 4 4	Bradford C. Bradford C. Doncaster	30.12.61 30.12.61 30.4.62	D. Pacey R. Poole I. Towers	Orient Chesterfield Oldham	4 4 4	30.4.53 3.3.61 4.2.67
Coventry	C. Bourton A. Bacon	5 5	Bournemouth Gillingham	17.10.31 30.12.33	T. Hunt	Norwich	5	15.3.30
Crewe A.	W. Caulfield A. Rice	4 4	Stalybe York	28.1.22 27.12.38	A. Graver	Lincoln	6	29.9.51
Crystal P.	P. P. Simpson	6	Exeter	4.10.30	J. Moore R. V. Hoten	Derby Northampton	5 5	25.12.22 27.10.28
Darlington	T. Ruddy M. Wellock	5 5	Sth Shields Rotherham	23.4.27 15.2.30	P. Cunningham B. Asquith	Barnsley Barnsley	5 5	4.2.33 12.11.38
Derby C.	S. Bloomer	6	Sheffield W.	21.1.99	H. J. Halse D. Mangnall F. Steele S. Garner	Villa Hudds. T. Stoke Blackburn	5 5 5 5	19.10.12 21.11.31 11.9.37 10.9.83
Doncaster	T. Keetley	6	Ashington	16.2.29	T. Eglington J. Hill	Everton Fulham	5 5	27.9.52 15.3.58
Everton	J. Southworth	6	W.B.A.	30.12.93	T. Johnson D. Kevan	Man. C. West Brom	5 5	15.9.28 19.3.60
Exeter C.	H. Kirk F. Dent F. Whitlow	4 4 4	Portsmouth Bristol R. Watford	3.3.23 5.11.27 29.10.32	P. Simpson	Palace	6	4.10.30
Fulham	F. Harrison B. Jezzard J. Hill S. Earle	5 5 5 5	Stockport Hull Doncaster Halifax	5.9.08 8.10.55 15.3.58 16.9.69	H. Leonard G. Camsell W. Kirkham T. Keetley	Derby Middlesbro Port Vale Notts C.	4 4 4 4	4.11.11 20.11.26 2.4.27 6.9.30
Gillingham	F. Cheesemuir	6	Merthyr	26.4.30	T. Walsh	Bristol C.	6	15.1.27
Grimsby	T. McCairns	6	Leicester	11.4.96	J. W. Glover	Southport	6	22.10.21
Halifax	W. Chambers A. Valentine	6 5	Hartlepools New Btn	7.4.34 9.3.35	F. Keetley	Lincoln	6	16.1.32
Hartlepools	H. Simmons D. Folland	5 5	Wigan B. Oldham	1.1.31 15.4.61	E. Harston	Mansfield	7	23.1.37
Hereford	R. McNeil	4	Chester	10.3.76	M. Sanford	Aldershot	4	26.12.80
Hudds T.	D. Mangnall A. Lythgoe	5 5	Derby C. Blackburn	21.11.31 13.4.35	J. Summers	Charlton	5	21.12.57
Hull City	K. McDonald S. Raleigh	5 5	Bristol C. Halifax	17.11.28 26.12.30	W. McLeod B. Jezzard	Leeds City Fulham	5 5	16.1.15 8.10.55
Ipswich	A. Brazil	5	Southampton	16.2.81	T. Lawton	Notts C.	4	9.9.48

Leeds United	G. Hodgson	5	Leicester	1.10.38	V. Watson	West Ham	6	9.2.29
Leicester	J. Duncan	6	Port Vale	25.12.24	T. McCairns	Grimsby	6	11.4.96
	A. Chandler	6	Portsmouth	20.10.28				
Lincoln C.	F. Keetley	6	Halifax	16.1.32	N. Coleman	Stoke	7	23.2.57
	A. Graver	6	Crewe	29.9.51				
Liverpool	A. McGuigan	5	Stoke	4.1.02	C. M. Buchan	Sunderland	5	7.12.12
	J. Evans	5	Bristol R.	15.9.54				
	I. Rush	5	Luton	29.10.83				
Luton Town	J. Payne	10	Bristol R.	13.4.36	C. McCormack	Barnsley	5	9.9.50
					B. Thomas	Scunthorpe	5	24.4.65
					R. Davies	Derby C.	5	29.3.75
					I. Rush	Liverpool	5	29.10.83
Manchester C.	F. Williams	5	Darwen	18.2.99	G. Camsell	Middlesbro	5	25.12.26
	T. Browell	5	Burnley	24.10.25				
	T. Johnson	5	Everton	15.9.28				
	G. Smith	5	Newport	14.6.47				
Manchester U.	A. Turnbull	4	Arsenal	23.11.07				
	J. Spence	4	West Ham	1.2.30				
	J. Rowley	4	Charlton	30.8.47				
	C. Mitten	4	Villa	8.3.50				
Mansfield	E. Harston	7	Hartlepools	23.1.37	W. Evans	Walsall	5	5.10.35
					W. McNaughton	Stockport	5	14.12.35
					K. East	Swindon	5	20.11.65
Middlesbrough	A. Wilson	5	Forest	6.10.23	J. Cantrell	Spurs	4	13.2.15
	G. Camsell	5	Man C.	25.12.26	E. J. Drake	Arsenal	4	19.4.35
	B. Clough	5	Brighton	23.8.58	W. Richardson	West B.	4	26.12.35
					T. Lawton	Everton	4	11.3.39
					E. J. Dodds	Blackpool	4	15.4.39
Millwall	R. Parker	5	Norwich	28.8.26	E. Quigley	Bury	5	15.2.47
Newcastle	L. Shackleton	6	Newport	6.10.46	E. C. Harper	Blackburn	5	9.9.25
Newport C.	T. J. Martin	5	Merthyr	10.4.30	L. Shackleton	Newcastle	6	5.10.46
Northampton	R. V. Hoten	5	Palace	7.10.28	J. Doran	Brighton	5	5.11.21
Norwich	T. Hunt	5	Coventry	15.3.30	D. A. Hunt	Sheffield W.	6	19.11.38
	R. Hollis		Walsall	29.12.51	W. Henderson	Cardiff	5	22.4.33
Nottingham F.	T. Peacock	4	Port Vale	23.12.33	A. Wilson	Middlesbro	5	6.10.23
	T. Peacock	4	Barnsley	9.11.35	J. Robson	Burnley	5	21.11.59
	T. Peacock	4	Port Vale	23.11.35				
	T. Peacock	4	Doncaster	26.12.35				
	T. Capel		Gillingham	18.11.50				
Notts C.	R. Jardine	5	Burnley	27.10.88	F. Morris	West Brom.	5	25.10.19
	D. Bruce	5	Port Vale	26.2.95	W. Hartill	Wolves	5	12.10.29
	B. R. Mills	5	Barnsley	19.11.27	D. Dooley	Sheffield W.	5	3.11.51
Oldham	E. Gemmell	7	Chester	19.1.52	R. C. Bell	Tranmere	9	26.12.35
Orient	W. Leigh	4	Bradford C	13.4.06	W. Boyd	Luton	5	28.12.35
	A. A. Pape	4	Oldham	1.9.24	C. Mortimore	Aldershot	5	25.2.50
	P. Kitchen	4	Millwall	21.4.84				
Oxford	A. Jones	4	Newport	22.9.62	R. Jenkins	Watford	4	23.9.78
Peterbro.	T. Bly	4	Darlington	24.12.61	W. Best	Southend	4	28.3.70
	T. Bly	4	Chester	13.3.61				
	R. Smith	4	Aldershot	4.3.61				
	J. Hall	4	Oldham	26.11.69				
Plymouth	W. Carter	5	Charlton	27.12.60	W. R. Dean	Everton	4	27.12.30
					J. Stein	Everton	4	27.12.30
					B. Clough	Middlesbro	4	5.9.59
Portsmouth	A. H. Strange	5	Gillingham	27.1.22	A. Chandler	Leicester	6	20.10.28
	P. Harris	5	Villa	3.9.58				
Port Vale	S. Littlewood	6	Chesterfield	24.9.32	J. Duncan	Leicester	6	25.12.24
Preston	+J. Ross	7	Stoke	6.10.88	J. McIntosh	Blackpool	5	1.5.48
					J. Greaves	Chelsea	5	19.12.59

Q.P.R.	G. Goddard	4	Merthyr	9.3.29	D. H. Morris	Swindon	5	18.12.26
	G. Goddard	4	Swindon	12.4.30				
	G. Goddard	4	Exeter	20.12.30				
	G. Goddard	4	Watford	19.9.31				
	T. Cheetham	4	Aldershot	14.9.35				
	T. Cheetham	4	Aldershot	12.11.38				
Reading	A. Bacon	6	Stoke	3.4.31	J. Hampson	Blackpool	5	10.11.28
					E. C. Harper	Tottenham	5	30.8.30
Rochdale	T. Tippett	6	Hartlepools	21.4.30	F. Watts	Tranmere	5	25.12.31
					E. Harston	Mansfield	5	9.9.36
					J. Campbell	Lincoln	5	21.11.36
Rotherham	R. Bastow	4	York	9.11.35	M. Wellock	Darlington	5	15.2.30
	R. Bastow	4	Rochdale	7.3.36	F. Watkin	Port Vale	5	22.2.30
	W. Ardron	4	Crewe	5.10.46	H. Gallacher	Gateshead	5	17.9.38
	W. Ardron	4	Carlisle	13.9.47	A. Patrick	York	5	20.11.48
	W. Ardron	4	Hartlpls	13.10.48	R. Pointer	Bury	5	2.10.65
Scunthorpe	B. Thomas	5	Luton	24.4.65	J. Whitehouse	Carlisle	5	25.12.52
Sheffield U.	H. Hammond	5	Bootle	26.12.92	J. Lambert	Arsenal	5	24.12.32
	H. Johnson	5	West Ham	26.12.27				
Sheffield W.	D. A. Hunt	6	Norwich	19.11.38	S. Bloomer	Derby C.	6	21.1.99
Shrewsbury	A. Wood	5	Blackburn	2.10.71	J. Gilfillan	Southend	4	4.4.64
					J. Atyeo	Bristol C.	4	19.4.65
					G. Yardley	Tranmere	4	8.9.67
Southampton	C. Wayman	5	Leicester	23.10.48	A. Brazil	Ipswich	5	16.2.82
Southend	J. Shankly	5	Merthyr	1.3.30	R. Blackman	Reading	5	14.8.51
Stockport	J. Smith	5	Southport	7.1.28	F. Harrison	Fulham	5	5.9.08
	J. Smith	5	Lincoln	15.9.28	J. Trotter	Sheffield W.	5	21.9.25
	F. Newton	5	Nelson	19.9.29				
	A. Lythgoe	5	Southport	25.8.34				
	W. McNaughton	5	Mansfield	14.12.35				
	J. Connor	5	Workington	8.11.52				
	J. Connor	5	Southport	7.4.56				
Stoke	N. Coleman	7	Lincoln	23.2.57	+J. Ross	Preston	7	6.10.88
Sunderland	C. M. Buchan	5	Liverpool	7.12.12	G. Hurst	West Ham	6	19.10.68
	R. Gurney	5	Bolton	7.12.35				
	D. Sharkey	5	Norwich	20.3.63				
Swansea	J. Fowler	5	Charlton	17.9. 24	G. Camsell	Middlesbrough	4	18.12.26
					T. Glidden	West Brom	4	26.10.29
Swindon	D. H. Morris	5	Q.P.R.	18.12.26	T. Tait	Luton	5	16.4.32
	D. H. Morris	5	Norwich	26.4.30				
	K. East	5	Mansfield	20.11.65				
Torquay	R. Stubbs	5	Newport C.	19.10.63	J. Devlin	Walsall	5	1.9.49
Tottenham	E. C. Harper	5	Reading	30.8.30	F. Pagnum	Liverpool	4	31.10.14
	A. Stokes	5	Birmingham	18.9.57	J. H. Carter	West Brom	4	8.12.23
	R. Smith	5	Aston Villa	29.3.58	J. W. Bowers	Derby C.	4	7.4.34
					E. J. Drake	Arsenal	4	20.10.34
Tranmere	R. C. Bell	9	Oldham	26.12.35	A. Whitehurst	Bradford	7	6.3.29
Walsall	G. Alsop	5	Carlisle	2.2.35	Adrian Capes	Burton W.	5	12.1.95
	W. Evans	5	Mansfield	5.10.35	T. Jennings	Chester	5	30.1.32
	J. Devlin	5	Torquay	1.9.49	R. Hollis	Norwich	5	29.12.51
Watford	A. Mummery	5	Newport	5.1.24	J. C. Martin	Aberdare	5	2.1.26
					A. Thorne	Brighton	5	30.4.58
West B.A.	J. Cookson	6	Blackpool	17.9.27	J. Southworth	Everton	6	30.12.93
West Ham	W. Watson	6	Leeds	9.2.29	H. Johnson	Sheffield U.	5	26.12.27
	G. Hurst	6	Sunderland	19.10.68				
Wigan A.	Never more than three goals				Never more than three goals			
Wimbledon	A. Cork	4	Torquay	28.2.79	Never more than three goals			

+There is a great deal of doubt about J. Ross scoring 7 goals in a game

Wolves	J. H. Butcher	5	Accrington	19.11.92	J. McMillan	Derby C.	5	10.1.91
	T. Phillipson	5	Barnsley	26.4.26	J. Greaves	Chelsea	5	30.8.58
	T. Phillipson	5	Bradford C.	25.12.26				
	W. Hartill	5	Notts C.	12.10.29				
	W. Hartill	5	Villa	3.9.34				
Wrexham	T. H. Lewis	5	Crewe	20.9.30	B. Twell	Southport	5	18.4.30
	T. Bamford	5	Carlisle	17.3.34				
York City	A. Patrick	5	Rotherham	20.11.48	B. Jepson	Chester	5	15.2.58

RIGHT: Before the advent of the League Cup, the FA Cup had the glamour to itself. Here Stan Mortensen scores Blackpool's second goal against Bolton Wanderers at Wembley in the 1953 FA Cup Final. (PA).

Milk Cup (League Cup)

Year	Winners	Runners-up	Venue	Attendance	Referee	Aggregate attendances
1961	Aston Villa 3	+ Rotherham United 2	home/away	12 226 31 202	K. A. Collinge C. W. Kingston	1 204 580
1962	Norwich City 4	+ Rochdale 0	home/away	11 123 19 708	A. Holland R. H. Mann	1 030 534
1963	+Birmingham City 3	Aston Villa 1	home/away	31 850 37 920	E. Crawford A. W. Starling	1 029 893
1964	Leicester City 4	+ Stoke City 3	home/away	22 309 25 372	W. Clements A. Jobling	945 265
1965	+Chelsea 3	Leicester City 2	home/away	20 690 26 958	J. Finney K. Howley	962 802
1966	West Bromwich Albion 5	+ West Ham United 3	home/away	28 341 31 925	D. W. Smith J. Mitchell	1 205 876
1967	Queen's Park Rangers 3	West Bromwich Albion 2	Wembley	97 952	W. Crossley	1 394 553
1968	Leeds United 1	Arsenal 0*	Wembley	97 887	L. Hamer	1 671 326
1969	Swindon Town 3	Arsenal 1*	Wembley	98 189	W. Handley	2 064 647
1970	Manchester City 2	West Bromwich Albion 1	Wembley	97 963	J. James	2 299 819
1971	Tottenham Hotspur 2	Aston Villa 0	Wembley	100 000	J. Finney	2 038 809
1972	Stoke City 2	Chelsea 1	Wembley	100 000	N. C. Burtenshaw	2 397 154
1973	Tottenham Hotspur 1	Norwich City 0	Wembley	100 000	D. W. Smith	1 935 474
1974	Wolverhampton Wanderers 2	Manchester City 1	Wembley	100 000	E. D. Wallace	1 722 629
1975	Aston Villa 1	Norwich City 0	Wembley	100 000	G. W. Hill	1 901 094
1976	Manchester City 2	Newcastle United 1	Wembley	100 000	J. K. Taylor	1 841 735
1977	Aston Villa 3	Everton 2*	Old Trafford	54 749	G. C. Kew	2 236 636
	(After first replay 1–1*)		Hillsborough	55 000	G. C. Kew	
	(After 0–0)		Wembley	100 000	G. C. Kew	
1978	Nottingham Forest 1	Liverpool 0	Old Trafford	54 375	P. Partridge	2 038 295
	(after 0–0*)		Wembley	100 000	P. Partridge	
1979	Nottingham Forest 3	Southampton 2	Wembley	100 000	P. G. Reeves	1 827 464
1980	Wolverhampton Wanderers 1	Nottingham Forest 0	Wembley	100 000	D. Richardson	2 322 866
1981	Liverpool 2	West Ham United 1	Villa Park	36 693	C. Thomas	2 051 576
	(after 1–1*)		Wembley	100 000	C. Thomas	
1982	Liverpool 3	Tottenham Hotspur 1*	Wembley	100 000	P. M. Willis	1 880 682
1983	Liverpool 2	Manchester United 1	Wembley	100 000	G. Courtney	1 679 756
1984	Liverpool 1	Everton 0	Maine Road	52 089	A. Robinson	1 900 491
	(after 0–0*)				A. Robinson	
1985	Norwich City 1	Sunderland 0	Wembley	[1]100 000	N. Midgeley	1 865 517

* after extra time + home team in first leg

[1]unofficial figures

Games	Average attendance	Entries	Top Scorer	
112	10 755	87	Gerry Hitchens (Aston Villa)	11
104	9 909	82	Ray Charnley (Blackpool)	6
102	10 097	80	Ken Leek (Birmingham City)	8
104	9 089	82	John Ritchie (Stoke City)	10
98	9 825	82	Tony Hateley (Aston Villa)	10
106	11 376	83	Tony Brown (West Bromwich Albion) Geoff Hurst (West Ham United)	11
118	11 818	90	Rodney Marsh (Queen's Park Rangers)	11
110	15 194	90	John O'Hare (Derby County) Jim Fryatt (Torquay United)	6
118	17 497	91	Don Rogers (Swindon Town)	7
122	18 851	92	Jeff Astle (West Bromwich Albion) John Byrom (Bolton Wanderers) Francis Lee (Manchester City) Rodney Marsh (Queen's Park Rangers)	5
117	17 425	91	Martin Chivers (Tottenham Hotspur)	7
123	19 489	92	Martin Chivers (Tottenham Hotspur)	7
120	16 129	92	Kevin Keegan (Liverpool) Graham Paddon (Norwich City) Martin Peters (Tottenham Hotspur)	5
132	13 050	92	Francis Lee (Manchester City)	8
127	14 969	92	Lou Macari (Manchester United)	7
140	13 155	92	Dennis Tueart (Manchester City)	8
147	15 215	92	Brian Little (Aston Villa)	10
148	13 772	92	Kenny Dalglish (Liverpool) Ian Bowyer (Nottingham Forest)	6
139	13 148	92	Garry Birtles (Nottingham Forest) Bob Latchford (Everton)	6
169	13 745	92	Alan Mayes (Swindon Town)	6
161	12 743	92	Kenny Dalglish (Liverpool)	7
161	11 681	92	Ian Rush (Liverpool)	8
160	10 498	92	Steve Coppell (Manchester United)	6
168	11 312	92	Ian Rush (Liverpool)	8
167	11 170	92	Kerry Dixon (Chelsea)	8

Tony Brown (West Bromwich Albion), a League Cup marksman in the 1960s. (ASP).

Francis Lee (Manchester City), who twice made a similar mark in the cup. (ASP).

European Champion Clubs Cup

Season	Winners		Runners-up		Venue	Attendance at final
1955–56	Real Madrid	4	Stade de Reims	3	Paris, France	38 000
1956–57	Real Madrid	2	Florentina	0	Madrid, Spain	124 000
1957–58	Real Madrid	3	AC Milan	2	Brussels, Belgium	67 000
1958–59	Real Madrid	2	Stade de Reims	0	Stuttgart, West Germany	80 000
1959–60	Real Madrid	7	Eintracht Frankfurt	3	Glasgow, Scotland	135 000
1960–61	Benfica	3	Barcelona	2	Berne, Switzerland	28 000
1961–62	Benfica	5	Real Madrid	3	Amsterdam, Holland	65 000
1962–63	AC Milan	2	Benfica	1	Wembley, England	45 000
1963–64	Internazionale	3	Real Madrid	1	Vienna, Austria	74 000
1964–65	Internazionale	1	Benfica	0	Milan, Italy	80 000
1965–66	Real Madrid	2	Partizan Belgrade	1	Brussels, Belgium	55 000
1966–67	Celtic	2	Internazionale	1	Lisbon, Portugal	56 000
1967–68	Manchester United	4	Benfica	1	Wembley, England	100 000
1968–69	AC Milan	4	Ajax	1	Madrid, Spain	50 000
1969–70	Feyenoord	2	Celtic	1	Milan, Italy	50 000
1970–71	Ajax	2	Panathinaikos	0	Wembley, England	90 000
1971–72	Ajax	2	Internazionale	0	Rotterdam, Holland	67 000
1972–73	Ajax	1	Juventus	0	Belgrade, Yugoslavia	93 500
1973–74	Bayern Munich	1	Atletico Madrid	1	Brussels, Belgium	65 000
Replay	Bayern Munich	4	Atletico Madrid	0	Brussels, Belgium	65 000
1974–75	Bayern Munich	2	Leeds United	0	Paris, France	50 000
1975–76	Bayern Munich	1	St Etienne	0	Glasgow, Scotland	54 864
1976–77	Liverpool	3	Borussia Moenchengladbach	1	Rome, Italy	57 000
1977–78	Liverpool	1	FC Bruges	0	Wembley, England	92 000
1978–79	Nottingham Forest	1	Malmo	0	Munich, West Germany	57 500
1979–80	Nottingham Forest	1	Hamburg	0	Madrid, Spain	50 000
1980–81	Liverpool	1	Real Madrid	0	Paris, France	48 360
1981–82	Aston Villa	1	Bayern Munich	0	Rotterdam, Holland	46 000
1982–83	Hamburg	1	Juventus	0	Athens, Greece	75 000
1983–84	Liverpool (aet; Liverpool won 4–2 on Penalties)	1	Roma	1	Rome, Italy	69 693
1984–85	Juventus	1	Liverpool	0	Brussels, Belgium	58 000

Referee	Total games played	Total goals scored	Attendances Overall	Attendances Average	Top scorer	Goals
Ellis (England)	29	127	912 000	31 450	Milutinovic (Partizan Belgrade)	7
Horn (Holland)	44	170	1 786 000	40 590	Viollet (Manchester United)	9
Alsteen (Belgium)	48	189	1 790 000	37 290	Di Stefano (Real Madrid)	10
Dutsch (West Germany)	55	199	2 010 000	36 545	Fontaine (Stade de Reims)	10
Mowat (Scotland)	52	218	2 780 000	50 545	Puskas (Real Madrid)	12
Dienst (Switzerland)	51	166	1 850 000	36 274	Aguas (Benfica)	10
Horn (Holland)	55	221	2 135 000	45 727	Di Stefano, Puskas and Tejada (Real Madrid)	7
Holland (England)	59	214	2 158 000	36 593	Altafini (AC Milan)	14
Stoll (Austria)	61	212	2 180 000	35 737	Mazzola (Internazionale)	7
Dienst (Switzerland)	62	215	2 577 000	41 564	Eusebio and Torres (Benfica)	9
Kreitlein (West Germany)	58	234	2 112 000	36 431	Albert (Ferencvaros) and Eusebio (Benfica)	7
Tschenscher (West Germany)	65	211	2 248 000	34 584	Van Himst (Anderlecht)	6
Lo Bello (Italy)	60	162	2 544 000	42 500	Eusebio (Benfica)	6
Ortiz De Mendibil (Spain)	52	176	2 056 000	39 540	Law (Manchester United)	9
Lo Bello (Italy)	63	202	2 345 000	37 222	Jones (Leeds United)	8
Taylor (England)	63	210	2 124 000	33 714	Antoniadis (Panathinaikos)	10
Helies (France)	64	175	2 066 976	32 280	Cruyff (Ajax) Macari (Celtic), Takac (Standard)	5
Guglovic (Yugoslavia)	58	160	1 712 277	30 000	Muller (Bayern Munich)	11
Loraux (Belgium)	60	180	1 586 852	26 448	Muller (Bayern Munich)	9
Delcourt (Belgium)						
Kitabdjian (France)	55	174	1 380 254	25 096	Almquist (Atvidaberg), Kreuz (Feyenoord), Markarov (Ararat) Muller (Bayern Munich), Zungul (Hajduk)	5
Palotai (Hungary)	61	202	1 736 087	28 460	Heynckes (Moenchengladback) Santillana (Real Madrid)	6
Wurtz (France)	61	155	2 010 000	34 325	Cucinotta (Zurich) (Muller (Bayern Munich)	5
Corver (Holland)	59	172	1 509 471	25 584	Simonsen (Moenchengladbach)	5
Linemayr (Austria)	63	185	1 511 291	23 988	Sulser (Grasshoppers)	11
Garrido (Portugal)	63	185	1 729 415	27 451	Lerby (Ajax)	10
Palotai (Hungary)	63	166	1 166 593	26 374	Rummenigge (Bayern Munich), McDermott and Souness (Liverpool)	6
Konrath (France)	63	170	1 530 082	24 287	Hoeness (Bayern Munich), Geurts (Anderlecht)	7
Rainea (Rumania)	61	180	1 718 075	28 165	Rossi (Juventus)	6
Fredriksson (Sweden)	59	165	1 601 065	27 137	Sokol (Dynamo Minsk)	6
Daina (Switzerland)	61	186	N/A	N/A	Platini (Juventus) and Nilsson (Gothenburg)	7

European Cup Winners' Cup

Season	Winners		Runners-up		Venue	Attendance
1960–61	Fiorentina (First Leg)	2	Rangers	0	Glasgow, Scotland	80 000
	Fiorentina (Second Leg)	2	Rangers	1	Florence, Italy	50 000
1961–62	Atletico Madrid	1	Fiorentina	1	Glasgow, Scotland	27 389
Replay	Atletico Madrid	3	Fiorentina	0	Stuttgart, West Germany	45 000
1962–63	Tottenham Hotspur	5	Atletico Madrid	1	Rotterdam, Holland	25 000
1963–64	Sporting Lisbon	3	MTK Budapest	3	Brussels, Belgium	9 000
Replay	Sporting Lisbon	1	MTK Budapest	0	Antwerp, Belgium	18 000
1964–65	West Ham United	2	Munich 1860	0	Wembley, England	100 000
1965–66	Borussia Dortmund (aet)	2	Liverpool	1	Glasgow, Scotland	41 657
1966–67	Bayern Munich (aet)	1	Rangers	0	Nuremberg, West Germany	69 480
1967–68	AC Milan	2	Hamburg	0	Rotterdam, Holland	60 000
1968–69	Slovan Bratislava	3	Barcelona	2	Basle, Switzerland	40 000
1969–70	Manchester City	2	Gornik Zabrze	1	Vienna, Austria	10 000
1970–71	Chelsea	1	Real Madrid	1	Athens, Greece	42 000
Replay	Chelsea	2	Real Madrid	1	Athens, Greece	24 000
1971–72	Rangers	3	Moscow Dynamo	2	Barcelona, Spain	35 000
1972–73	AC Milan	1	Leeds United	0	Salonika, Greece	45 000
1973–74	Magdeburg	2	AC Milan	0	Rotterdam, Holland	5 000
1974–75	Dynamo Kiev	3	Ferencvaros	0	Basle, Switzerland	13 000
1975–76	Anderlecht	4	West Ham United	2	Brussels, Belgium	58 000
1976–77	Hamburg	2	Anderlecht	0	Amsterdam, Holland	65 000
1977–78	Anderlecht	4	Austria/WAC	0	Amsterdam, Holland	48 679
1978–79	Barcelona (aet)	4	Fortuna Dusseldorf	3	Basle, Switzerland	58 000
1979–80	Valencia	0	Arsenal	0	Brussels, Belgium	40 000
	(aet: Valencia won 5–4 on penalties)					
1980–81	Dynamo Tbilisi	2	Carl Zeiss Jena	1	Dusseldorf, West Germany	9 000
1981–82	Barcelona	2	Standard Liege	1	Barcelona, Spain	100 000
1982–83	Aberdeen (aet)	2	Real Madrid	1	Gothenburg, Sweden	17 804
1983–84	Juventus	2	Porto	1	Basle, Switzerland	60 000
1984–85	Everton	3	Rapid Vienna	1	Rotterdam, Holland	30 000

Referee	Total games played	Total goals scored	Attendances		Top scorer	Goals
			Overall	Average		
	18	60	290 000	16 111		
	44	174	650 000	14 733		
Van Leuwen	48	169	1 100 000	22 916		
Van Nuffel	62	202	1 300 000	20 967		
Versyp						
Szolt	61	163	1 100 000	18 032		
Schwinte	59	188	1 546 000	26 203	Emmerich (Dortmund)	14
Lo Bello (Italy)	61	170	1 556 000	25 508	Muller (Bayern Munich)	9
Ortiz de Mendibil (Spain)	64	200	1 683 000	26 269	Seeler (Hamburg)	6
Van Ravens	51	157	957 000	18 765	Ruhl (Cologne)	6
Schiller	64	179	1 675 000	25 890	Lubanski (Gornik)	8
Scheurer	67	203	1 570 000	23 582	Lubanski (Gornik)	8
Bucheni						
Ortiz de Mendibil (Spain)	65	186	1 145 211	17 615	Osgood (Chelsea)	8
Mihas	61	174	908 564	15 000	Chiarugi (AC Milan)	7
Van Gemert	61	169	1 105 494	18 123	Heynckes (Moenchengladbach)	10
Davidson	59	177	1 298 850	22 014	Onishenko (Dynamo Kiev)	7
Wurtz (France)	61	189	1 128 962	18 508	Rensenbrink (Anderlecht)	8
Partridge (England)	63	198	1 537 000	24 400	Milanov (Levski)	13
Adlinger (West Germany)	63	179	1 161 383	18 434	Gritter (Twente)	7
Palotai (Hungary)	59	160	1 041 135	17 646	Altobelli (Internazionale)	7
Christov (Czechoslovakia)	63	176	1 193 682	18 947	Kempes (Valencia)	9
Lattanzi (Italy)	65	176	1 239 795	19 074	Cross (West Ham United)	6
Eschweiler (West Germany)	63	176	1 504 023	23 873	Shengelia (Tbilisi) and Voordeckers (Standard)	6
Menegali (Italy)	65	198	1 424 104	21 909	Santillana (Real Madrid)	8
Prokop (East Germany)	63	198	1 451 136	23 034	McGhee (Aberdeen)	5
Casarin (Italy)	61	156	N/A	N/A	Gazayev (Dynamo Moscow) Panenka (Rapid) and Gray (Everton)	5

UEFA Cup (The Fairs Cup until 1971)

Season	Winners		Runners-up		Venue	Attendance
1955–58	Barcelona (First Leg)	2	London	2	Stamford Bridge, England	45 466
	Barcelona (Second Leg)	6	London	0	Barcelona, Spain	62 000
1958–60	Barcelona (First Leg)	0	Birmingham City	0	Birmingham, England	40 500
	Barcelona (Second Leg)	4	Birmingham City	1	Barcelona, Spain	70 000
1960–61	Roma (First Leg)	2	Birmingham City	2	Birmingham, England	21 005
	Roma (Second Leg)	2	Birmingham City	0	Rome, Italy	60 000
1961–62	Valencia (First Leg)	6	Barcelona	2	Valencia, Spain	65 000
	Valencia (Second Leg)	1	Barcelona	1	Barcelona, Spain	60 000
1962–63	Valencia (First Leg)	2	Dynamo Zagreb	1	Zagreb, Yugoslavia	40 000
	Valencia (Second Leg)	2	Dynamo Zagreb	0	Valencia, Spain	55 000
1963–64	Zaragoza	2	Valencia	1	Barcelona, Spain	50 000
1964–65	Ferencvaros	1	Juventus	0	Turin, Italy	25 000
1965–66	Barcelona (First Leg)	0	Zaragoza	1	Barcelona, Spain	70 000
	Barcelona (Second Leg)	4	Zaragoza	2	Zaragoza, Spain	70 000
1966–67	Dynamo Zagreb (First Leg)	2	Leeds United	0	Zagreb, Yugoslavia	40 000
	Dynamo Zagreb (Second Leg)	0	Leeds United	0	Leeds, England	35 604
1967–68	Leeds United (First Leg)	1	Ferencvaros	0	Leeds, England	25 368
	Leeds United (Second Leg)	0	Ferencvaros	0	Budapest, Hungary	70 000
1968–69	Newcastle United (First Leg)	3	Ujpest Dozsa	0	Newcastle, England	60 000
	Newcastle United (Second Leg)	3	Ujpest Dozsa	2	Budapest, Hungary	37 000
1969–70	Arsenal (First Leg)	1	Anderlecht	3	Brussels, Belgium	37 000
	Arsenal (Second Leg)	3	Anderlecht	0	Highbury, England	51 612
1970–71	Leeds United (Abandoned 51 minutes)	0	Juventus	0	Turin, Italy	65 000
	Leeds United (First Leg)	2	Juventus	2	Turin, Italy	65 000
	Leeds United (Second Leg)	1 (Leeds won on away goals)	Juventus	1	Leeds, England	42 483
1971–72	Tottenham Hotspur (First Leg)	2	Wolverhampton Wanderers	1	Wolverhampton, England	45 000
	Tottenham Hotspur (Second Leg)	1	Wolverhampton Wanderers	1	White Hart Lane, England	48 000
1972–73	Liverpool (First Leg)	3	Moenchengladbach	0	Anfield, England	41 169
	Liverpool (Second Leg)	2	Moenchengladbach	0	Moenchengladbach, West Germany	35 000
1973–74	Feyenoord (First Leg)	2	Tottenham Hotspur	2	White Hart Lane, England	46 281
	Feyenoord (Second Leg)	2	Tottenham Hotspur	0	Rotterdam, Holland	68 000
1974–75	Moenchengladbach (First Leg)	0	Twente	0	Dusseldorf, West Germany	45 000
	Moenchengladbach (Second Leg)	5	Twente	1	Enschede, Holland	24 500
1975–76	Liverpool (First Leg)	3	FC Bruges	2	Anfield, England	56 000
	Liverpool (Second Leg)	1	FC Bruges	1	Bruges, Belgium	32 000
1976–77	Juventus (First Leg)	1	Athletic Bilbao	0	Turin, Italy	75 000
	Juventus (Second Leg)	1	Athletic Bilbao	2	Bilbao, Spain	43 000

1977–78	PSV Eindhoven (First Leg)	0	Bastia	0	Bastia, Corsica	15 000
	PSV Eindhoven (Second Leg)	3	Bastia	0	Eindhoven, Holland	27 000
1978–79	Moenchengladbach (First Leg)	1	Red Star Belgrade	1	Belgrade, Yugoslavia	87 500
	Moenchengladbach (Second Leg)	1	Red Star Belgrade	0	Dusseldorf, West Germany	45 000
1979–80	Eintracht Frankfurt (First Leg)	2	Moenchengladbach	3	Moenchengladbach, West Germany	25 000
	Eintracht Frankfurt (Second Leg)	1	Moenchengladbach (Eintracht won on away goals)	0	Frankfurt, West Germany	60 000
1980–81	Ipswich Town (First Leg)	3	AZ '67	0	Ipswich, England	27 532
	Ipswich Town (Second Leg)	2	AZ '67	4	Amsterdam, Holland	28 500
1981–82	Gothenburg (First Leg)	1	Hamburg	0	Gothenburg, Sweden	42 548
	Gothenburg (Second Leg)	3	Hamburg	0	Hamburg, West Germany	60 000
1982–83	Anderlecht (First Leg)	1	Benfica	0	Brussels, Belgium	45 000
	Anderlecht (Second Leg)	1	Benfica	1	Lisbon, Portugal	80 000
1983–84	Tottenham Hotspur (First Leg)	1	Anderlecht	1	Brussels, Belgium	40 000
	Tottenham Hotspur (Second Leg)	1	Anderlecht (Tottenham won 4-3 on penalties)	1	White Hart Lane, England	46 258
1984–85	Videoton (First Leg)	0	Real Madrid	3	Szekesfehervar	30 000
	Real Madrid (Second Leg)	0	Videoton	1	Madrid, Spain	98 300

European Super Cup

Year	Winners	Runners-up	Scores
1973	Ajax	Rangers	3–1, 3–2
1974	Ajax	AC Milan	0–1, 6–0
1975	Dynamo Kiev	Bayern Munich	1–0, 2–0
1976	Anderlecht	Bayern Munich	4–1, 1–2
1977	Liverpool	Hamburg	1–1, 6–0
1978	Anderlecht	Liverpool	3–1, 1–2
1979	Nottingham Forest	Barcelona	1–0, 1–1
1980	Valencia	Nottingham Forest	1–2, 1–0 (on away goals)
1981	Not Contested		
1982	Aston Villa	Barcelona	0–1, 3–0
1983	Aberdeen	Hamburg	0–0, 2–0
1984	Juventus	Liverpool	2–0 (in Turin)

South American Cup (Copa Libertadores)

Year	Winner	Entries	Matches	Goals
1960	Penarol	8	13	39
1961	Penarol	9	16	52
1962	Santos	10	25	101
1963	Santos	9	19	63
1964	Independiente	10	25	89
1965	Independiente	10	27	72
1966	Penarol	17	94	218
1967	Racing	19	114	355
1968	Estudiantes	21	93	232
1969	Estudiantes	17	74	211
1970	Estudiantes	19	88	253
1971	Nacional	21	73	196
1972	Independiente	20	69	176
1973	Independiente	19	66	190
1974	Independiente	21	76	178
1975	Independiente	21	76	208
1976	Cruzeiro	21	77	211
1977	Boca Juniors	21	75	152
1978	Boca Juniors	21	75	181
1979	Olimpia	21	74	211
1980	Nacional	21	75	160
1981	Flamengo	21	77	220
1982	Penarol	21	73	163
1983	Gremio	21	74	179
1984	Independiente	21	75	206

World Club Championship

Year	Winners	Runners-up	Scores	Venue	First Leg Attendance
1960	Real Madrid	Penarol	0–0, 5–1	Montevideo	75 000
1961	Penarol	Benfica	0–1, 5–0, 2–1	Lisbon	55 000
1962	Santos	Benfica	3–2, 5–2	Rio de Janeiro	90 000
1963	Santos	AC Milan	2–4, 4–2, 1–0	Milan	80 000
1964	Internazionale	Independiente	0–1, 2–0, 1–0	Buenos Aires	70 000
1965	Internazionale	Independiente	3–0, 0–0	Milan	70 000
1966	Penarol	Real Madrid	2–0, 2–0	Montevideo	70 000
1967	Racing Club	Celtic	0–1, 2–1, 1–0	Hampden Park	103 000
1968	Estudiantes	Manchester United	1–0, 1–1	Buenos Aires	65 000
1969	AC Milan	Estudiantes	3–0, 1–2	Milan	80 000
1970	Feyenoord	Estudiantes	2–2, 1–0	Buenos Aires	65 000
1971	Nacional	Panathinaikos	1–1, 2–1	Athens	60 000
1972	Ajax	Independiente	1–1, 3–0	Buenos Aires	65 000
1973	Independiente	Juventus	1–0	Rome	35 000
1974	Atletico Madrid	Independiente	0–1, 2–0	Buenos Aires	60 000
1975	Independiente and Bayern Munich could not agree on dates to play				
1976	Bayern Munich	Cruzeiro	2–0, 0–0	Munich	22 000
1977	Boca Juniors	Borussia Moenchengladbach	2–2, 3–0	Buenos Aires	50 000
1978	Not contested; Liverpool declined to play				
1979	Olimpia	Malmo	1–0, 2–1	Malmo	4 811
1980	Nacional	Nottingham Forest	1–0	Tokyo	62 000
1981	Flamengo	Liverpool	3–0	Tokyo	62 000
1982	Penarol	Aston Villa	2–0	Tokyo	62 000
1983	Gremio	Hamburg	2–1	Tokyo	62 000
1984	Independiente	Liverpool	1–0	Tokyo	62 000

Football League title wins

Division 1

Liverpool 15; Arsenal, Everton 8; Manchester United, Aston Villa 7; Sunderland 6; Newcastle United, Sheffield Wednesday 4; Huddersfield Town. Wolverhampton Wanderers 3; Blackburn Rovers, Portsmouth, Preston North End, Burnley, Manchester City, Tottenham Hotspur, Leeds United, Derby County 2; Chelsea, Sheffield United, West Bromwich Albion, Ipswich Town, Nottingham Forest 1.

Division 2

Leicester City, Manchester City 6; Sheffield Wednesday 5; Birmingham City, Liverpool 4; Notts County, Preston North End, Derby County, Middlesbrough 3; Grimsby Town, Nottingham Forest, Tottenham Hotspur, West Bromwich Albion, Aston Villa, Stoke City, Leeds United, Ipswich Town, Burnley, Manchester United, West Ham United, Wolverhampton Wanderers, Bolton Wanderers 2; Huddersfield Town, Bristol City, Brentford, Bury, Bradford City, Everton, Fulham, Sheffield United, Newcastle United, Coventry City, Blackpool, Blackburn Rovers, Norwich City, Sunderland, Crystal Palace, Luton Town, Queen's Park Rangers, Chelsea, Oxford United 1.

Division 3

Portsmouth, Oxford United 2; Plymouth Argyle, Southampton, Bury, Northampton Town, Coventry City, Carlisle United, Hull City, Queen's Park Rangers, Watford, Leyton Orient, Preston North End, Aston Villa, Bolton Wanderers, Oldham Athletic, Blackburn Rovers, Hereford United, Mansfield Town, Wrexham, Shrewsbury Town, Grimsby Town, Rotherham United, Burnley, Bradford City 1.

Division 4

Doncaster Rovers, Peterborough United, Chesterfield 2; Port Vale, Walsall, Millwall, Brentford, Gillingham, Brighton & Hove Albion, Stockport County, Luton Town, Notts County,Grimsby Town, Southport, Mansfield Town, Lincoln City, Cambridge United, Watford, Reading, Huddersfield Town, Southend United, Sheffield United, Wimblebon, York City 1.

Division 3 Southern

Bristol City 3; Charlton Athletic, Ipswich Town, Millwall, Notts County, Plymouth Argyle, Swansea Town 2; Brentford, Bristol Rovers, Cardiff City, Crystal Palace, Coventry City, Fulham, Leyton Orient, Luton Town, Newport County, Nottingham Forest, Norwich City, Portsmouth, Queen's Park Rangers, Reading, Southampton, Brighton and Hove Albion 1.

Division 3 Northern

Barnsley, Doncaster Rovers, Lincoln City 3; Chesterfield, Grimsby Town, Hull City, Port Vale, Stockport County 2; Bradford Park Avenue, Bradford City, Darlington, Derby County, Nelson, Oldham Athletic, Rotherham United, Stoke City, Tranmere Rovers, Wolverhampton Wanderers, Scunthorpe United 1.

First Leg Referee	Second Leg Venue	Attendance	Referee	Play-off Venue	Attendance	Referee
Praddaude (Argentina)	Madrid	125 000	Aston (England)			
Ebert (Switzerland)	Montevideo	56 358	Nay Foino (Argentina)	Montevideo	62 300	Praddaude (Argentina)
Ramirez (Paraguay)	Lisbon	75 000	Schwinte (France)			
Harbseliner (Austria)	Rio de Janeiro	150 000	Brozzi (Argentina)	Rio de Janeiro	121 000	Brozzi (Argentina)
Armando Marques (Brazil)	Milan	70 000	Geroe (Hungary)	Madrid	45 000	De Mendibil (Spain)
Kreitlein (West Germany)	Buenos Aires	70 000	Yamasaki (Peru)			
Vicuna (Chile)	Madrid	70 000	Lo Bello (Italy)			
Gardeazabal (Spain)	Buenos Aires	80 000	Esteban Marino (Spain)	Montevideo	65 172	Osorio (Paraguay)
Miranda (Paraguay)	Old Trafford	60 000				
Machin (France)	Buenos Aires	65 000	Massaro (Chile)			
Glockner (East Germany)	Rotterdam	70 000	Tejada (Peru)			
	Montevideo	70 000				
Bakhramov (USSR)	Amsterdam	65,000	Romey (Paraguay)			
Belcourt (Belgium)						
Corver (Holland)	Madrid	45 000	Robles (Chile)			
Pestarino (Argentina)	Belo Horizonte	114 000	Partridge (England)			
Doudine (Bulgaria)	Karlsruhe	21 500	Cerullo (Uraguay)			
Partridge (England)	Ascuncion	35 000	Cardellino (Uruguay)			
Klein (Israel)						
Vasquez (Mexico)						
Siles (Costa Rica)						
Vautrot (France)						
Filho (Brazil)						

Football League champions

Season ending	Champions	Matches	Points	Home W	Home D	Home L	Home F	Home A	Home Pts	Away W	Away D	Away L	Away F	Away A	Away Pts	Goal av.	No. of players	Ever present	Winning margin (pts)
1889	Preston North End	22	40	10	1	0	39	7	21	8	3	0	35	8	19	3.36	18	2	11
1890	Preston North End	22	33	8	1	2	41	12	17	7	2	2	30	18	16	3.23	19	3	2
1891	Everton	22	29	9	0	2	39	12	18	5	1	5	24	17	11	2.86	21	3	2
1892	Sunderland	26	42	13	0	0	55	11	26	8	0	5	38	25	16	3.57	15	2	5
1893	Sunderland	30	48	13	2	0	58	17	28	9	2	4	42	19	20	3.33	15	3	11
1894	Aston Villa	30	44	12	2	1	49	13	26	7	4	4	35	29	18	2.80	24	1	6
1895	Sunderland	30	47	13	2	0	51	14	28	8	3	4	29	23	19	2.66	16	2	5
1896	Aston Villa	30	45	14	1	0	47	17	29	6	4	5	31	28	16	2.60	17	2	4
1897	Aston Villa	30	47	10	3	2	36	16	23	11	2	2	37	22	24	2.43	17	4	11
1898	Sheffield United	30	42	9	4	2	27	14	22	8	4	3	29	17	20	1.86	23	1	5
1899	Aston Villa	34	45	15	2	0	58	13	32	4	5	8	18	27	13	2.23	24	1	2
1900	Aston Villa	34	50	12	4	1	45	18	28	10	2	5	32	17	22	2.26	21	2	2
1901	Liverpool	34	45	12	2	3	36	13	26	7	5	5	23	22	19	1.73	18	3	2
1902	Sunderland	34	44	12	3	2	32	14	27	7	3	7	18	21	17	1.47	19	1	3
1903	Sheffield Wednesday	34	42	12	3	2	31	7	27	7	1	9	23	29	15	1.58	23	3	1
1904	Sheffield Wednesday	34	47	14	3	0	34	10	31	6	4	7	14	18	16	1.41	22	2	3
1905	Newcastle United	34	48	14	1	2	41	12	29	9	1	7	31	21	19	2.11	21	0	1
1906	Liverpool	38	51	14	3	2	49	15	31	9	2	8	30	31	20	2.07	21	1	4
1907	Newcastle United	38	51	18	1	0	51	12	37	4	6	9	23	34	14	1.94	27	0	3
1908	Manchester United	38	52	15	1	3	43	19	31	8	5	6	38	29	21	2.13	25	0	9
1909	Newcastle United	38	53	14	1	4	32	20	29	10	4	5	33	21	24	1.71	25	1	7
1910	Aston Villa	38	53	17	2	0	62	19	36	6	5	8	22	23	17	2.21	18	0	5
1911	Manchester United	38	52	14	4	1	47	18	32	8	4	7	25	22	20	1.89	26	0	1
1912	Blackburn Rovers	38	49	13	6	0	35	10	32	7	3	9	25	33	17	1.57	21	0	3
1913	Sunderland	38	54	14	2	3	47	17	30	11	2	6	39	26	24	2.26	22	1	4
1914	Blackburn Rovers	38	51	14	4	1	51	15	32	6	7	6	27	27	19	2.05	21	1	7
1915	Everton	38	46	8	5	6	44	29	21	11	3	5	32	18	25	2.00	24	0	1
No national competition 1916, 1917, 1918 or 1919 when regional leagues in operation																			
1920	West Bromwich Albion	42	60	17	1	3	65	21	35	11	3	7	39	26	25	2.47	18	1	9

Season ending	Champions	Matches	Points	Home W	D	L	F	A	Pts	Away W	D	L	F	A	Pts	Goal av.	No. of players	Ever present	Winning margin (pts)
1921	Burnley	42	59	17	3	1	56	16	37	6	10	5	23	20	22	1.88	23	1	5
1922	Liverpool	42	57	15	4	2	43	15	34	7	9	5	20	21	23	1.50	22	2	6
1923	Liverpool	42	60	17	3	1	50	13	37	9	5	7	20	18	23	1.66	19	3	6
1924	Huddersfield Town	42	57	15	5	1	35	9	35	8	6	7	25	24	22	1.42	22	1	gl av.
1925	Huddersfield Town	42	58	10	8	3	31	10	28	11	8	2	38	18	30	1.64	22	0	2
1926	Huddersfield Town	42	57	14	6	1	50	17	34	9	5	7	42	43	23	2.19	24	0	5
1927	Newcastle United	42	56	19	1	1	64	20	39	6	5	10	32	38	17	2.28	21	3	5
1928	Everton	42	53	11	8	2	60	28	30	9	5	7	42	38	23	2.42	24	2	2
1929	Sheffield Wednesday	42	52	18	3	0	55	16	39	3	7	11	31	46	13	2.04	22	4	1
1930	Sheffield Wednesday	42	60	15	4	2	56	20	34	11	4	6	49	37	26	2.50	22	1	10
1931	Arsenal	42	66	14	5	2	67	27	33	14	5	2	60	32	33	3.02	22	1	7
1932	Everton	42	56	18	0	3	84	30	36	8	4	9	32	34	20	2.76	20	0	2
1933	Arsenal	42	58	14	3	4	70	27	31	11	5	5	48	34	27	2.80	23	1	4
1934	Arsenal	42	59	15	4	2	45	19	34	10	5	6	30	28	25	1.78	23	1	3
1935	Arsenal	42	58	15	4	2	74	17	34	8	8	5	41	29	24	2.73	25	0	4
1936	Sunderland	42	56	17	2	2	71	33	36	8	4	9	38	41	20	2.59	23	2	8
1937	Manchester City	42	57	15	5	1	56	22	35	7	8	6	51	39	22	2.54	22	4	3
1938	Arsenal	42	52	15	4	2	52	16	34	6	6	9	25	28	18	1.83	29	0	1
1939	Everton	42	59	17	3	1	60	18	37	10	2	9	28	34	22	2.09	22	1	4
No national competition 1940, 1941, 1942, 1943, 1944, 1945 or 1946 when regional leagues were in operation																			
1947	Liverpool	42	57	13	3	5	42	24	29	12	4	5	42	28	28	2.00	26	0	1
1948	Arsenal	42	52	15	3	3	56	15	33	8	10	3	25	17	26	1.92	19	2	7
1949	Portsmouth	42	58	18	3	0	52	12	39	7	5	9	32	30	19	2.00	18	2	5
1950	Portsmouth	42	56	12	7	2	44	15	31	10	2	9	30	23	22	1.76	25	2	gl av.
1951	Tottenham Hotspur	42	60	17	2	2	54	21	36	8	8	5	28	23	24	1.95	19	2	4
1952	Manchester United	42	57	15	3	3	55	21	33	8	8	5	40	31	24	2.26	24	1	4
1953	Arsenal	42	54	15	3	3	60	30	33	6	9	6	37	34	21	2.30	21	0	gl av.
1954	Wolverhampton Wanderers	42	57	16	1	4	61	25	33	9	6	6	35	31	24	2.28	22	1	4
1955	Chelsea	42	52	11	5	5	43	29	27	9	7	5	38	28	25	1.92	20	2	4
1956	Manchester United	42	60	18	3	0	51	20	39	7	7	7	32	31	21	1.97	24	1	11
1957	Manchester United	42	64	14	4	3	55	25	32	14	4	3	48	29	22	2.45	24	0	8
1958	Wolverhampton Wanderers	42	64	17	3	1	60	21	37	11	5	5	43	26	27	2.45	21	0	5
1959	Wolverhampton Wanderers	42	61	15	3	3	68	19	33	13	2	6	42	30	28	2.61	22	0	6
1960	Burnley	42	55	15	2	4	52	28	32	9	5	7	33	33	23	2.02	18	3	1
1961	Tottenham Hotspur	42	66	15	3	3	65	28	33	16	1	4	50	27	33	2.73	17	4	8
1962	Ipswich Town	42	56	17	2	2	58	28	36	7	6	8	35	39	20	2.21	16	3	3
1963	Everton	42	61	14	7	0	48	17	35	11	4	6	36	25	26	2.00	20	2	6
1964	Liverpool	42	57	16	0	5	60	18	32	10	5	6	32	27	25	2.19	17	3	4
1965	Manchester United	42	61	16	4	1	52	13	36	10	5	6	37	26	25	2.11	18	4	gl av.
1966	Liverpool	42	61	17	2	2	52	15	36	9	7	5	27	19	25	1.88	14	5	6
1967	Manchester United	42	60	17	4	0	51	13	38	7	8	6	33	32	22	2.00	20	2	4
1968	Manchester City	42	58	17	2	2	52	16	36	9	4	8	34	27	22	2.04	21	1	2
1969	Leeds United	42	67	18	3	0	41	9	39	9	10	2	25	17	28	1.57	17	4	6
1970	Everton	42	66	17	3	1	46	19	37	12	5	4	26	15	29	1.71	17	4	9
1971	Arsenal	42	65	18	3	0	41	6	39	11	4	6	30	23	26	1.69	16	3	1
1972	Derby County	42	58	16	4	1	43	10	36	8	6	7	26	23	22	1.64	16	2	1
1973	Liverpool	42	60	17	3	1	45	19	37	8	7	6	27	23	23	1.17	16	3	3
1974	Leeds United	42	62	12	8	1	38	18	32	12	6	3	28	13	30	1.57	20	2	5
1975	Derby County	42	53	14	4	3	41	18	32	7	7	7	26	31	21	1.59	16	2	2
1976	Liverpool	42	60	14	5	2	41	21	33	9	9	3	25	10	27	1.57	19	2	1
1977	Liverpool	42	57	18	3	0	47	11	39	5	8	8	15	22	18	1.47	17	3	1
1978	Nottingham Forest	42	64	15	6	0	37	8	36	10	8	3	32	16	28	1.64	16	1	7
1979	Liverpool	42	68	19	2	0	51	4	40	11	6	4	34	12	28	2.02	15	4	8
1980	Liverpool	42	60	15	6	0	46	8	36	8	10	4	35	22	24	1.92	17	3	2
1981	Aston Villa	42	60	16	3	2	40	13	35	10	5	6	32	27	25	1.71	14	7	4
1982	Liverpool	42	87	14	3	4	39	14	45	12	6	3	41	18	42	1.90	16	3	4
1983	Liverpool	42	82	16	4	1	55	16	52	8	6	7	32	21	30	2.07	16	4	11
1984	Liverpool	42	80	14	5	2	50	12	47	8	9	4	23	20	33	1.73	15	5	3
1985	Everton	42	90	16	3	2	58	17	51	12	3	6	30	26	42	2.09	25	1	13

Teams with the longest unbeaten runs in Football League matches from the start of a season

Tommy Lawton seen in Notts County colours. This club has twice figured in unbeaten starts to a season. (PA).

Season	Team	Division	Unbeaten in first
1888–89	Preston North End	1	all 22
1889–90	Accrington Stanley	1	3
1889–90	Aston Villa	1	3
1890–91	Everton	1	7
1891–92	Aston Villa	1	4
1891–92	Bolton Wanderers	1	4
1892–93	Sunderland	1	8
1893–94	Liverpool	2	all 28*
1894–95	Everton	1	8
1895–96	Liverpool	2	5
1895–96	Newton Heath	2	5
1896–97	Sheffield United	1	8
1897–98	Sheffield United	1	14
1898–99	Sheffield United	1	11
1899–90	Sheffield United	1	22
1900–01	Small Heath	2	14
1901–02	Lincoln City	2	7
1902–03	Blackpool	2	6
1903–04	Preston North End	2	13
1904–05	Liverpool	2	13
1905–06	Sheffield Wednesday	1	7
1905–06	Manchester United	2	7
1906–07	Bolton Wanderers	1	7
1906–07	Hull City	2	7
1907–08	Everton	1	6
1908–09	Birmingham City	2	8
1909–10	Sheffield United	1	9
1910–11	Sunderland	1	14
1911–12	Clapton Orient	2	7
1912–13	Hull City	2	8
1913–14	Blackburn Rovers	1	10
1914–15	Manchester City	1	11
1919–20	Tottenham Hotspur	2	12
1920–21	South Shields	2	7
1921–22	Portsmouth	3S	10
1922–23	Portsmouth	3S	8
1923–24	Cardiff City	1	11
1924–25	Huddersfield Town	1	10
1925–26	Chelsea	2	14
1926–27	Stoke City	3N	9
1927–28	Charlton Athletic	3S	12
1928–29	Luton Town	3S	10
1928–29	Wrexham	3N	10
1929–30	Plymouth Argyle	3S	18
1930–31	Notts County	3S	18
1931–32	Southend United	3S	15
1932–33	Brentford	3S	14
1933–34	Aldershot	3S	8
1934–35	Tranmere Rovers	3N	8
1935–36	Huddersfield Town	1	9
1935–36	Chesterfield	3N	9
1935–36	Tranmere Rovers	3N	9
1936–37	Chester	3N	9
1936–37	Hull City	3N	9
1937–38	Coventry City	2	15
1938–39	Southport	3N	9
1946–47	Barnsley	2	10
1947–48	Arsenal	1	17
1948–49	Derby County	1	16
1949–50	Liverpool	1	19
1950–51	Newcastle United	1	11
1951–52	Oldham Athletic	3N	9
1952–53	Oldham Athletic	3N	13
1953–54	Norwich City	3S	12
1954–55	Bristol City	3S	13
1955–56	Blackpool	1	8
1956–57	Manchester United	1	12
1957–58	Scunthorpe United	3N	8
1958–59	Fulham	2	12
1959–60	Millwall	4	19
1960–61	Tottenham Hotspur	1	16
1961–62	Bournemouth	3	14
1962–63	Huddersfield Town	2	13
1963–64	Gillingham	4	13
1964–65	Bradford Park Avenue	4	12
1965–66	Bristol City	2	7
1966–67	Chelsea	1	10
1967–68	Torquay United	3	10
1968–69	Darlington	4	14
1969–70	Port Vale	4	18
1970–71	Notts County	4	9
1971–72	Norwich City	2	13
1972–73	Burnley	2	16
1973–74	Leeds United	1	29
1974–75	Manchester United	2	9
1975–76	Bury	3	10
1976–77	Leicester City	1	6
1976–77	Manchester City	1	6
1976–77	Wolverhampton Wanderers	2	6
1976–77	Stockport County	4	6
1977–78	Manchester City	1	8
1977–78	Brighton & Hove Albion	2	8
1977–78	Tottenham Hotspur	2	8
1977–78	Southend United	4	8
1978–79	Everton	1	19
1979–80	Walsall	4	13
1980–81	Ipswich Town	1	14
1981–82	Oldham Athletic	2	9
1982–83	Wimbledon	4	11
1983–84	Sheffield Wednesday	2	15
1984–85	Portsmouth	2	10

* Liverpool also won one test match and then began the next season with two games undefeated.

Record wins

Football League clubs (in descending order of scoring)

Team	Score	Opponents	Competition	Date
Preston North End	26–0	Hyde	FA Cup 1st rd	15.10.1887
Notts County	15–0	Thornhill United	FA Cup 1st rd	24.10.1885
Bristol Rovers	15–1	Weymouth	FA Cup Pr rd	17.11.1900
Wimbledon	15–2	Polytechnic	FA Cup Pr rd	7.2.29
Nottingham Forest	14–0	Clapton	FA Cup 1st rd	17.1.1891
Southampton	14–0	Newbury	FA Cup 1st rd	10.9.1894
Wolverhampton Wanderers	14–0	Crosswell's Brewery	FA Cup 2nd rd	13.11.1886
Aston Villa	13–0	Wednesday Old Alliance	FA Cup 1st rd	30.10.1886
Bolton Wanderers	13–0	Sheffield United	FA Cup 2nd rd	1.2.1890
Chelsea	13–0	Jeunesse Hautcharage	Cup Winners' Cup 1st rd	29.9.71
Newcastle United	13–0	Newport County	Division 2	5.10.46
Stockport County	13–0	Halifax Town	Division 3N	6.1.34
Arsenal	12–0	Loughborough Town	Division 2	12.3.1900
Birmingham City	12–0	Walsall Town Swifts	Division 2	17.12.1892
Birmingham City	12–0	Doncaster Rovers	Division 2	11.4.03
Chester	12–0	York City	Division 3N	1.2.36
Derby County	12–0	Finn Harps	UEFA Cup 3rd rd	15.9.76
Luton Town	12–0	Bristol Rovers	Division 3S	13.4.36
Sheffield Wednesday	12–0	Halliwell	FA Cup 1st rd	10.9.1894
West Bromwich Albion	12–0	Darwen	Division 1	4.4.1892
Bury	12–1	Stockton	FA Cup 1st rd replay	2.2.1897
Tottenham Hotspur	13–2	Crewe Alexandra	FA Cup 4th rd replay	3.2.60
Blackburn Rovers	11–0	Rossendale United	FA Cup 1st rd	25.10.84
Bournemouth	11–0	Margate	FA Cup 1st rd	20.11.71
Bristol City	11–0	Chichester	FA Cup 1st rd	5.11.60
Hereford United	11–0	Thynnes	FA Cup qual rd	13.9.47
Liverpool	11–0	Stromsgodset Drammen	Cup Winners' Cup 1st rd	17.9.74
Oldham Athletic	11–0	Southport	Division 4	26.12.62
Bradford City	11–1	Rotherham United	Division 3N	25.8.28
Hull City	11–1	Carlisle United	Division 3N	14.1.39
Lincoln City	11–1	Crewe Alexandra	Division 3N	29.9.51
Northampton Town	11–1	Southend United	Southern League	30.12.09
Sunderland	11–1	Fairfield	FA Cup 1st rd	2.2.1895
Blackpool	10–0	Lanerossi Vicenza	Anglo-Italian Cup	10.6.72
Chesterfield	10–0	Glossop North End	Division 2	17.1.03
Doncaster Rovers	10–0	Darlington	Division 4	25.1.64
Ipswich Town	10–0	Floriana	Eur. Cup 1st rd	25.9.62
Leeds United	10–0	Lyn Oslo	Eur. Cup 1st rd	17.9.69
Leicester City	10–0	Portsmouth	Division 1	20.10.28
Manchester United	10–0	Anderlecht	Eur. Cup Pr rd	26.9.56
Newport County	10–0	Merthyr Town	Division 3S	10.4.30
Walsall	10–0	Darwen	Division 2	4.3.1899
West Ham United	10–0	Bury	Milk Cup 2nd rd 2nd leg	25.10.83
Tranmere Rovers	13–4	Oldham Athletic	Division 3N	26.12.35
Everton	11–2	Derby County	FA Cup 1st rd	18.1.1890
Sheffield United	11–2	Cardiff City	Division 1	1.1.26
Brighton & Hove Albion	10–1	Wisbech	FA Cup 1st rd	13.11.65
Fulham	10–1	Ipswich Town	Division 1	26.12.63
Gillingham	10–1	Gorleston	FA Cup 1st rd	16.11.57
Hartlepool United	10–1	Barrow	Division 4	4.4.59
Huddersfield Town	10–1	Blackpool	Division 1	13.12.30
Southend United	10–1	Golders Green	FA Cup 1st rd	24.11.34
Southend United	10–1	Brentwood	FA Cup 2nd rd	7.12.68
Swindon Town	10–1	Farnham United Breweries	FA Cup 1st rd	28.11.25
Watford	10–1	Lowestoft Town	FA Cup 1st rd	27.11.26
Wrexham	10–1	Hartlepool United	Division 4	3.3.62
Barnsley	9–0	Loughborough Town	Division 2	29.1.1899
Barnsley	9–0	Accrington Stanley	Division 3N	3.2.34
Brentford	9–0	Wrexham	Division 3	15.10.63
Burnley	9–0	Darwen	Division 1	9.1.1892
Burnley	9–0	Crystal Palace	FA Cup 2nd rd replay	27.1.09
Burnley	9–0	New Brighton	FA Cup 4th rd	26.1.57
Burnley	9–0	Penrith	FA Cup 1st rd	17.11.84
Coventry City	9–0	Bristol City	Division 3S	28.4.34
Crystal Palace	9–0	Barrow	Division 4	10.10.59
Scunthorpe United	9–0	Boston United	FA Cup 1st rd	21.11.53
Torquay United	9–0	Swindon Town	Division 3S	8.3.52
Manchester City	11–3	Lincoln City	Division 2	23.3.1895
Norwich City	10–2	Coventry City	Division 3S	15.3.30
Reading	10–2	Crystal Palace	Division 3S	4.9.46
Colchester United	9–1	Bradford City	Division 4	30.12.61
Millwall	9–1	Torquay United	Division 3S	29.8.27
Millwall	9–1	Coventry City	Division 3S	19.11.27
Portsmouth	9–1	Notts County	Division 2	9.4.27
Port Vale	9–1	Chesterfield	Division 2	24.9.32

York City	9–1	Southport	Division 3N	2.2.57
Carlisle United	8–0	Hartlepool United	Division 3N	1.9.28
Carlisle United	8–0	Scunthorpe United	Division 3N	25.12.52
Crewe Alexandra	8–0	Rotherham United	Division 3N	1.10.32
Rotherham United	8–0	Oldham Athletic	Division 3N	26.5.47
Swansea City	8–0	Hartlepool United	Division 4	1.4.78
Middlesbrough	10–3	Sheffield United	Division 1	18.11.33
Stoke City	10–3	West Bromwich Albion	Division 1	4.2.37
Cardiff City	9–2	Thames	Division 3S	6.2.32
Darlington	9–2	Lincoln City	Division 3N	7.1.28
Grimsby Town	9–2	Darwen	Division 2	15.4.1899
Mansfield Town	9–2	Rotherham United	Division 3N	27.12.32
Mansfield Town	9–2	Hounslow Town	FA Cup 1st rd replay	5.11.62
Orient	9–2	Aldershot	Division 3S	10.2.34
Orient	9–2	Chester	League Cup 3rd rd	17.10.62
Queen's Park Rangers	9–2	Tranmere Rovers	Division 3	3.12.60
Aldershot	8–1	Gateshead	Division 4	13.9.58
Charlton Athletic	8–1	Middlesbrough	Division 1	12.9.53
Exeter City	8–1	Coventry City	Division 3S	4.12.26
Exeter City	8–1	Aldershot	Division 3S	4.5.35
Peterborough United	8–1	Oldham Athletic	Division 4	26.11.69
Plymouth Argyle	8–1	Millwall	Division 2	16.1.32
Rochdale	8–1	Chesterfield	Division 3N	18.12.26
Halifax Town	7–0	Bishop Auckland	FA Cup 2nd rd replay	10.1.67
Oxford United	7–0	Barrow	Division 4	19.12.64
Shrewsbury Town	7–0	Swindon Town	Division 3S	6.5.55
Cambridge United	6–0	Darlington	Division 4	18.9.71
Wigan Athletic	7–2	Scunthorpe United	Division 4	12.3.82

Scottish League clubs (in descending order)

Team	Score	Opponents	Competition	Date
Arbroath	36–0	Bon Accord	Scottish Cup 1st rd	12.9.1885
Stirling Albion	20–0	Selkirk	Scottish Cup 1st rd	9.12.84
Partick Thistle	16–0	Royal Albert	Scottish Cup 1st rd	17.1.31
Queen's Park	16–0	St Peter's	Scottish Cup 1st rd	12.9.1885
Heart of Midlothian	15–0	King's Park	Scottish Cup 2nd rd	13.3.37
St Mirren	15–0	Glasgow University	Scottish Cup 1st rd	10.1.60
Airdrieonians	15–1	Dundee Wanderers	Division 2	1.11.1894
Hibernian	15–1	Peebles Rovers	Scottish Cup 2nd rd	11.2.61
Dundee United	14–0	Nithsdale Wanderers	Scottish Cup 1st rd	17.1.31
Forfar Athletic	14–1	Lindertis	Scottish Cup 1st rd	1.9.1888
Aberdeen	13–0	Peterhead	Scottish Cup 3rd rd	10.2.23
Dumbarton	13–1	Kirkintilloch Central	Scottish Cup 1st rd	1.9.1888
Albion Rovers	12–0	Airdriehill	Scottish Cup 1st rd	3.9.1887
Cowdenbeath	12–0	Johnstone	Scottish Cup 1st rd	21.1.28
Montrose	12–0	Vale of Leithen	Scottish Cup 2nd rd	4.1.75
Rangers	14–2	Whitehill	Scottish Cup 2nd rd	22.9.83
Rangers	14–2	Blairgowrie	Scottish Cup 1st rd	20.1.34
Brechin City	12–1	Thornhill	Scottish Cup 1st rd	28.1.26
Falkirk	12–1	Laurieston	Scottish Cup 2nd rd	1.9.1888
Motherwell	12–1	Dundee United	Division 2	23.1.54
East Fife	13–2	Edinburgh City	Division 2	11.12.37
Celtic	11–0	Dundee	Division 1	26.10.1895
Morton	11–0	Carfin Shamrock	Scottish Cup 1st rd	13.11.1886
Ayr United	11–1	Dumbarton	League Cup	13.8.52
Clyde	11–1	Cowdenbeath	Division 2	6.10.51
Queen of the South	11–1	Stranraer	Scottish Cup 1st rd	16.1.32
Dundee	10–0	Alloa	Division 2	8.3.47
Dundee	10–0	Dunfermline Athletic	Division 2	22.3.47
Dunfermline Athletic	11–2	Stenhousemuir	Division 2	27.9.30
Kilmarnock	13–2	Saltcoats Victoria	Scottish Cup 2nd rd	12.9.1896
East Stirlingshire	10–1	Stenhousemuir	Scottish Cup 1st rd	1.9.1888
Raith Rovers	10–1	Coldstream	Scottish Cup 2nd rd	13.3.54
Hamilton Academical	10–2	Cowdenbeath	Division 1	15.10.32
Alloa	9–2	Forfar Athletic	Division 2	18.3.33
Berwick Rangers	8–1	Forfar Athletic	Division 2	25.12.65
Berwick Rangers	8–1	Vale of Leithen	Scottish Cup 1st rd	30.9.67
Clydebank	8–1	Arbroath	Division 1	3.1.77
St Johnstone	8–1	Partick Thistle	League Cup	16.8.69
Stenhousemuir	9–2	Dundee United	Division 2	17.4.37
Stranraer	7–0	Brechin City	Division 2	6.2.65
Meadowbank Thistle	6–1	Stenhousemuir	Division 2	6.2.82

Heaviest defeats

Football League clubs (in descending order)

Team	Score	Opponents	Competition	Date
Reading	0–18	Preston North End	FA Cup 1st rd	27.1.1894
Halifax Town	0–13	Stockport County	Division 3N	6.1.34
Newport County	0–13	Newcastle United	Division 2	5.10.46
Sheffield United	0–13	Bolton Wanderers	FA Cup 2nd rd	1.2.1890
Bristol Rovers	0–12	Luton Town	Division 3S	13.4.36
Doncaster Rovers	0–12	Small Heath	Division 2	11.4.03
Leicester City	0–12	Nottingham Forest	Division 1	21.4.09
Walsall	0–12	Small Heath	Division 2	17.12.1892
Walsall	0–12	Darwen	Division 2	26.12.1896
York City	0–12	Chester	Division 3N	1.2.36
Crewe Alexandra	2–13	Tottenham Hotspur	FA Cup 4th rd replay	3.2.60
Carlisle United	1–11	Hull City	Division 3N	14.1.39
Charlton Athletic	1–11	Aston Villa	Division 2	14.11.59
Rotherham United	1–11	Bradford City	Division 3N	25.8.28
Burnley	0–10	Aston Villa	Division 1	29.8.25
Burnley	0–10	Sheffield United	Division 1	19.1.29
Bury	0–10	Blackburn Rovers	FA Cup Pr rd	1.10.1887
Bury	0–10	West Ham United	Milk Cup 2nd rd 2nd leg	25.10.83
Darlington	0–10	Doncaster Rovers	Division 4	25.1.64
Northampton Town	0–10	Bournemouth	Division 3S	2.9.39
Portsmouth	0–10	Leicester City	Division 1	20.10.28
Port Vale	0–10	Sheffield United	Division 2	10.12.1892
Port Vale	0–10	Notts County	Division 2	26.2.1895
Sheffield Wednesday	0–10	Aston Villa	Division 1	5.10.12
Stoke City	0–10	Preston North End	Division 1	14.9.1889
Watford	0–10	Wolverhampton Wanderers	FA Cup 1st rd replay	13.1.12
Oldham Athletic	4–13	Tranmere Rovers	Division 3N	26.12.35
Derby County	2–11	Everton	FA Cup 1st rd	18.1.1890
Chester City	2–11	Oldham Athletic	Division 3N	19.1.52
Cardiff City	2–11	Sheffield United	Division 1	1.1.26
Blackpool	1–10	Small Heath	Division 2	2.3.01
Blackpool	1–10	Huddersfield Town	Division 1	13.12.30
Hartlepool United	1–10	Wrexham	Division 4	3.3.62
Ipswich Town	1–10	Fulham	Division 1	26.12.63
Swindon Town	1–10	Manchester City	FA Cup 4th rd replay	25.1.30
Wolverhampton Wanderers	1–10	Newton Heath	Division 1	15.10.1892
Aldershot	0–9	Bristol City	Division 3S	28.12.46
Barnsley	0–9	Notts County	Division 2	19.11.27
Bournemouth	0–9	Lincoln City	Division 3	18.12.82
Brighton & Hove Albion	0–9	Middlesbrough	Division 2	23.8.58
Bristol City	0–9	Coventry City	Division 3S	28.4.34
Exeter City	0–9	Notts County	Division 3S	16.10.48
Exeter City	0–9	Northampton Town	Division 3S	12.4.58
Fulham	0–9	Wolverhampton Wanderers	Division 1	16.9.59
Middlesbrough	0–9	Blackburn Rovers	Division 2	6.11.54
Newcastle United	0–9	Burton Wanderers	Division 2	15.4.1895
Plymouth Argyle	0–9	Stoke City	Division 2	17.12.60
Wrexham	0–9	Brentford	Division 3	15.10.63
Lincoln City	3–11	Manchester City	Division 2	23.3.1895
Coventry City	2–10	Norwich City	Division 3S	15.3.30
Norwich City	2–10	Swindon Town	Southern League	5.9.08
Torquay United	2–10	Fulham	Division 3S	7.9.31
Torquay United	2–10	Luton Town	Division 3S	2.9.33
Birmingham City	1–9	Sheffield Wednesday	Division 1	13.12.30
Birmingham City	1–9	Blackburn Rovers	Division 1	5.1.95
Bradford City	1–9	Colchester United	Division 4	30.12.61
Chesterfield	1–9	Port Vale	Division 2	24.9.32
Grimsby Town	1–9	Arsenal	Division 1	28.1.31
Liverpool	1–9	Birmingham City	Division 2	11.12.54
Luton Town	1–9	Small Heath	Division 2	12.11.1898
Manchester City	1–9	Everton	Division 1	3.9.06
Millwall	1–9	Aston Villa	FA Cup 4th rd	28.1.46
Nottingham Forest	1–9	Blackburn Rovers	Division 2	10.4.37
Notts County	1–9	Blackburn Rovers	Division 1	16.11.1889
Notts County	1–9	Aston Villa	Division 1	29.9.1888
Notts County	1–9	Portsmouth	Division 2	9.4.27
Rochdale	1–9	Tranmere Rovers	Division 3N	25.12.31
Southend United	1–9	Brighton & Hove Albion	Division 3	27.11.65
Tranmere Rovers	1–9	Tottenham Hotspur	FA Cup 3rd rd replay	14.1.53
Arsenal	0–8	Loughborough Town	Division 2	12.12.1896
Blackburn Rovers	0–8	Arsenal	Division 1	25.2.33
Huddersfield Town	0–8	Middlesbrough	Division 1	30.9.50
Hull City	0–8	Wolverhampton Wanderers	Division 2	4.11.11
Orient	0–8	Aston Villa	FA Cup 4th rd	30.1.29
Scunthorpe United	0–8	Carlisle United	Division 3N	25.12.52

Southampton	0–8	Tottenham Hotspur	Division 2	28.3.36
Southampton	0–8	Everton	Division 1	20.11.71
Sunderland	0–8	West Ham United	Division 1	19.10.68
Sunderland	0–8	Watford	Division 1	25.9.82
Wimbledon	0–8	Everton	League Cup 2nd rd	29.8.78
West Bromwich Albion	3–10	Stoke City	Division 1	4.2.57
Gillingham	2–9	Nottingham Forest	Division 3S	18.11.50
Aston Villa	1–8	Blackburn Rovers	FA Cup 3rd rd	16.2.1889
Chelsea	1–8	Wolverhampton Wanderers	Division 1	26.9.53
Leeds United	1–8	Stoke City	Division 1	27.8.34
Mansfield Town	1–8	Walsall	Division 3N	19.1.33
Peterborough United	1–8	Northampton Town	FA Cup 2nd rd 2nd replay	18.12.46
Queen's Park Rangers	1–8	Mansfield Town	Division 3	15.3.65
Queen's Park Rangers	1–8	Manchester United	Division 1	19.3.69
Shrewsbury Town	1–8	Norwich City	Division 3S	13.9.52
Shrewsbury Town	1–8	Coventry City	Division 3	22.10.63
Stockport County	1–8	Chesterfield	Division 2	19.4.02
Swansea City	1–8	Fulham	Division 2	22.1.38
Crystal Palace	4–11	Manchester City	FA Cup 5th rd	20.2.26
Bolton Wanderers	0–7	Manchester City	Division 1	21.3.36
Brentford	0–7	Swansea Town	Division 3S	8.11.24
Brentford	0–7	Walsall	Division 3S	19.1.57
Colchester United	0–7	Leyton Orient	Division 3S	5.1.52
Colchester United	0–7	Reading	Division 3S	18.9.57
Manchester United	0–7	Blackburn Rovers	Division 1	10.4.26
Manchester United	0–7	Aston Villa	Division 1	27.12.30
Manchester United	0–7	Wolverhampton Wanderers	Division 2	26.12.31
Preston North End	0–7	Blackpool	Division 1	1.5.48
Tottenham Hotspur	0–7	Liverpool	Division 1	2.9.78
Everton	4–10	Tottenham Hotspur	Division 1	11.10.58
West Ham United	2–8	Blackburn Rovers	Division 1	26.12.63
Cambridge United	0–6	Aldershot	Division 3	13.4.74
Cambridge United	0–6	Darlington	Division 4	28.9.74
Hereford United	2–7	Arsenal	FA Cup 3rd rd replay	22.1.85
Oxford United	0–5	Cardiff City	Division 2	8.2.69
Oxford United	0–5	Cardiff City	Division 2	12.9.73
Wigan Athletic	0–5	Bristol Rovers	Division 3	26.2.83
Wigan Athletic	0–5	Chelsea	FA Cup 3rd rd replay	26.1.85

Scottish League clubs (in descending order)

Montrose	0–13	Aberdeen Reserves	Division C	17.3.51
Dundee United	1–12	Motherwell	Division 2	23.1.54
East Stirlingshire	1–12	Dundee United	Division 2	13.4.36
Clyde	0–11	Dumbarton	Scottish Cup 4th rd	22.11.79
Clyde	0–11	Rangers	Scottish Cup 4th rd	13.11.80
Dundee	0–11	Celtic	Division 1	26.10.1895
Forfar Athletic	2–12	King's Park	Division 2	2.1.30
Airdrieonians	1–11	Hibernian	Division 1	24.10.59
Cowdenbeath	1–11	Clyde	Division 2	6.10.51
Dumbarton	1–11	Albion Rovers	Division 2	30.1.26
Dumbarton	1–11	Ayr United	League Cup qual rd	13.8.52
Falkirk	1–11	Airdrieonians	Division 1	28.4.51
Hamilton Academical	1–11	Hibernian	Division 1	6.11.65
Stranraer	1–11	Queen of the South	Scottish Cup 1st rd	16.1.32
Dunfermline Athletic	0–10	Dundee	Division 2	22.3.47
Hibernian	0–10	Rangers	Division 1	24.12.1898
Partick Thistle	0–10	Queen's Park	Scottish Cup 5th rd	3.12.81
Brechin City	1–10	Dunfermline Athletic	Division 2	14.12.29
Morton	1–10	Port Glasgow Athletic	Division 2	5.5.1894
St Johnstone	1–10	Third Lanark	Scottish Cup 1st rd	24.1.03
Alloa	2–11	Hibernian	League Cup qual rd	26.9.65
Stenhousemuir	2–11	Dunfermline Athletic	Division 2	27.9.30
Raith Rovers	2–11	Morton	Division 2	18.3.36
Ayr United	0–9	Rangers	Division 1	16.11.29
Ayr United	0–9	Heart of Midlothian	Division 1	28.2.31
East Fife	0–9	Heart of Midlothian	Division 1	5.10.57
Stirling Albion	0–9	Dundee United	Division 1	30.12.67
Albion Rovers	1–9	Motherwell	Division 1	2.1.37
Clydebank	1–9	Gala Fairydean	Scottish Cup qual rd	15.9.65
Aberdeen	0–8	Celtic	Division 1	30.1.65
Arbroath	0–8	Kilmarnock	Division 2	3.1.49
Berwick Rangers	0–8	Morton	Division 2	21.12.57
Celtic	0–8	Motherwell	Division 1	30.4.37
Kilmarnock	0–8	Hibernian	Division 1	22.8.37
Kilmarnock	0–8	Rangers	Division 1	27.2.37
Meadowbank Thistle	0–8	Hamilton Academical	Division 2	14.12.74
Motherwell	0–8	Aberdeen	Division 1	26.3.79
Queen of the South	2–10	Dundee	Division 1	1.12.62
Queen's Park	3–10	Heart of Midlothian	Division 1	24.8.12
St Mirren	2–9	Dundee	Division 1	24.8.12
Heart of Midlothian	0–7	Hibernian	Division 1	1.1.73
Rangers	1–7	Celtic	League Cup final	19.10.57

Highest number of goals scored by each Football League club in one season (in descending order)

Goals	Team	Division	Season
134	Peterborough United	4	1960–61
128	Aston Villa	1	1930–31
128	Bradford City	3N	1928–29
127	Arsenal	1	1930–31
127	Millwall	3S	1927–28
123	Doncaster Rovers	3N	1946–47
122	Middlesbrough	2	1926–27
121	Everton	2	1930–31
121	Lincoln City	3N	1951–52
119	Chester	4	1964–65
118	Barnsley	3N	1933–34
115	Stockport County	3N	1933–34
115	Tottenham Hotspur	1	1960–61
115	Wolverhampton Wanderers	2	1931–32
114	Rotherham United	3N	1946–47
114	Blackburn Rovers	2	1954–55
113	Carlisle United	4	1963–64
112	Brighton & Hove Albion	3S	1955–56
112	Reading	3S	1951–52
112	Southampton	3S	1957–58
111	Derby County	3N	1956–57
111	Fulham	3S	1931–32
111	Queen's Park Rangers	3	1961–62
111	Tranmere Rovers	3N	1930–31
110	Crystal Palace	4	1960–61
110	Nottingham Forest	3S	1950–51
110	Port Vale	4	1958–59
109	Hull City	3	1965–66
109	Leicester City	2	1956–57
109	Northampton Town	3 and 3S	1962–63 and 1952–53
109	Sunderland	1	1935–36
108	Bury	3	1960–61
108	Coventry City	3S	1931–32
108	Darlington	3N	1929–30
108	Manchester City	2	1926–27
108	Mansfield Town	4	1962–63
107	Charlton Athletic	2	1957–58
107	Notts County	4	1959–60
107	Plymouth Argyle	3S	1925–26 and 1951–52
106	Ipswich Town	3S	1955–56
106	Liverpool	2	1895–96
106	Orient	3S	1955–56
106	Sheffield Wednesday	2	1958–59
106	Wrexham	3N	1932–33
105	Rochdale	3N	1926–27
105	West Bromwich Albion	2	1929–30
104	Bristol City	3S	1926–27
104	Colchester United	4	1961–62
103	Birmingham City	2	1893–94
103	Grimsby Town	2	1933–34
103	Luton Town	3S	1936–37
103	Manchester United	1	1956–57 and 1958–59
102	Burnley	1	1960–61
102	Chesterfield	3N	1930–31
102	Sheffield United	1	1925–26
102	Walsall	4	1959–60
101	Huddersfield Town	4	1979–80
101	Shrewsbury Town	4	1958–59
101	West Ham United	2	1957–58
100	Preston North End	2 and 1	1927–28 and 1957–58
100	Swindon Town	3S	1926–27
99	Norwich City	3S	1952–53
98	Blackpool	2	1929–30
98	Brentford	4	1962–63
98	Chelsea	1	1960–61
98	Leeds United	2	1927–28
98	Newcastle United	1	1951–52
97	Wimbledon	3	1983–84
96	Bolton Wanderers	2	1934–35
96	York City	4	1983–84
95	Crewe Alexandra	3N	1931–32
95	Oldham Athletic	4	1962–63
93	Cardiff City	3S	1946–47
92	Bristol Rovers	3S	1952–53
92	Southend United	3S	1950–51
92	Stoke City	3N	1926–27
92	Watford	4	1959–60
91	Oxford United	3	1983–84
91	Portsmouth	4	1979–80
90	Gillingham	3N	1956–57
90	Hartlepool United	3N	1956–57
90	Swansea City	2	1956–57
89	Torquay United	3S	1956–57
88	Bournemouth	3S	1956–57
88	Exeter City	3S	1932–33
88	Scunthorpe United	3N	1957–58
87	Cambridge United	4	1976–77
86	Hereford United	3	1975–76
85	Newport County	4	1964–65
83	Aldershot	4	1963–64
83	Halifax Town	3N	1957–58
80	Wigan Athletic	4	1981–82

Scottish League clubs

Goals	Team	Division	Season
142	Raith Rovers	2	1937–38
135	Morton	2	1963–64
132	Heart of Midlothian	1	1957–58
132	Falkirk	2	1935–36
122	Clyde	2	1956–57
120	Cowdenbeath	2	1938–39
120	Dunfermline Athletic	2	1957–58
119	Motherwell	1	1931–32
118	Rangers	1	1931–32 and 1933–34
117	Ayr United	2	1927–28
115	Celtic	1	1935–36
114	East Fife	2	1929–30
114	St Mirren	2	1935–36
112	Dundee	2	1946–47
111	East Stirling	2	1931–32
108	Dundee United	2	1935–36
107	Airdrieonians	2	1965–66
106	Hibernian	1	1959–60
105	Stirling Albion	2	1959–60
102	St Johnstone	2	1931–32
101	Albion Rovers	2	1929–30
101	Dumbarton	2	1956–57
100	Queen's Park	1	1928–29
99	Stenhousemuir	2	1960–61
96	Aberdeen	1	1935–36
94	Queen of the South	2	1959–60
92	Alloa	2	1961–62
92	Hamilton Academical	1	1932–33
92	Kilmarnock	1	1962–63
91	Partick Thistle	1	1928–29
90	Forfar Athletic	2	1931–32
87	Arbroath	2	1967–68
83	Berwick Rangers	2	1961–62
83	Stranraer	2	1961–62
80	Brechin City	2	1957–58
78	Clydebank	1	1978–79
78	Montrose	2	1970–71
64	Meadowbank Thistle	2	1982–83

Goal bonanzas

There have been only two matches in Football League history in which each side scored as many as six goals — 6–6 draws between Leicester City and Arsenal in 1930 and Charlton Athletic and Middlesbrough in 1960. Below are the details of the matches in which each team scored five times or more:

Match and score				Division		Date
Blackburn Rovers	5	Accrington Stanley	5	F.Lge		9.9.1888
Derby County	8	Blackburn Rovers	5	1		6.9.1890
Crewe Alexandra	5	Walsall Town S.	6	2		5.11.1892
Burton Swifts	8	Walsall Town S.	5	2		24.2.1894
Manchester United	5	Lincoln City	5	2		16.11.1895
Derby County	5	Everton	5	1		15.10.1898
Sheffield Wed.	5	Everton	5	1		12.11.04
Sunderland	5	Liverpool	5	1		19.1.07
Liverpool	6	Newcastle United	5	1		4.12.09
Middlesbrough	7	Tottenham Hotspur	5	1		13.2.15
Tottenham Hotspur	5	Huddersfield Town	5	1		19.9.25
Wrexham	5	Accrington Stanley	6	3N		24.10.25
Crystal Palace	5	Plymouth Argyle	5	3S		28.11.25
Bury	6	Manchester City	5	1		25.12.25
Aberdare Athletic	5	Plymouth Argyle	6	3S		2.1.27
Newcastle United	7	Aston Villa	5	1		10.3.27
Northampton Town	6	Luton Town	5	3S		26.12.27
Swansea Town	5	Blackpool	5	2		27.8.28
Blackburn Rovers	7	Birmingham City	5	1		28.9.29
Sheffield United	5	Blackburn Rovers	7	1		3.3.30
Leicester City	6	Arsenal	6	1		21.4.30
Millwall	5	Preston North End	7	2		4.10.30
Sunderland	6	Liverpool	5	1		6.12.30
West Ham United	5	Aston Villa	5	1		3.1.31
Coventry City	5	Fulham	5	3S		2.1.32
Walsall	5	Accrington Stanley	5	3N		2.4.32
W.B.A.	5	Grimsby Town	6	1		30.4.32
Grimsby Town	5	Port Vale	5	2		15.10.32
Blackburn Rovers	6	Blackpool	5	1		2.1.33
Grimsby Town	5	Charlton Athletic	5	2		7.1.33
Luton Town	5	Brentford	5	3S		1.2.33
Stockport County	8	Chester	5	3N		6.5.33
W.B.A.	6	Sunderland	5	1		24.3.34
Bristol Rovers	5	Exeter City	5	3S		10.11.34
York City	7	Mansfield Town	5	3N		16.11.35
Crewe Alexandra	5	Chesterfield	6	3N		1.2.36
Middlesbrough	5	Sunderland	5	1		17.10.36
Darlington	5	Hartlepool United	5	3N		21.11.36
Bolton Wanderers	5	Chelsea	5	1		30.10.37
Walsall	5	Millwall	6	3S		13.11.48
Derby County	6	Sunderland	5	1		16.12.50
Leicester City	5	Sheffield United	5	2		3.11.51
Chelsea	5	Manchester United	6	1		16.10.54
Charlton Athletic	7	Huddersfield Town	6	2		21.12.57
Chelsea	6	Newcastle United	5	1		10.9.58
Charlton Athletic	6	Middlesbrough	6	2		22.10.60
Newcastle United	5	West Ham United	5	1		10.12.60
Blackburn Rovers	5	Arsenal	5	1		3.11.62
Birmingham City	5	Blackburn Rovers	5	1		24.4.65
Tottenham Hotspur	5	Aston Villa	5	1		19.3.66
Birmingham City	5	Derby County	5	2		
Chelsea	5	West Ham United	5	1		17.12.66
Bristol Rovers	5	Charlton Athletic	5	2		18.11.78
Southampton	5	Coventry City	5	1		4.5.82
Doncaster Rovers	7	Reading	5	3		25.9.82
Q.P.R.	5	Newcastle United	5	1		22.9.84

The great derby showdowns

The League's greatest rivalry — Everton v Liverpool

Everton were founded in 1878 as St Domingo Church Sunday School team, becoming Everton the following year. Liverpool came into being in 1892 following a split which led to the Everton club moving from Anfield to Goodison Park.

Of the 132 matches played between the sides in the League Everton have won 46, Liverpool 46 and 40 have been drawn.

League results at Goodison Park (Everton's score first)

Season	Score	Season	Score
1894–95	3–0	1934–35	1–0
1896–97	2–1	1935–36	0–0
1897–98	3–0	1936–37	2–0
1898–99	1–2	1937–38	1–3
1899–1900	3–1	1938–39	2–1
1900–01	1–1	1946–47	1–0
1901–02	4–0	1947–48	0–3
1902–03	3–1	1948–49	1–1
1903–04	5–2	1949–50	0–0
1905–06	4–2	1950–51	1–3
1906–07	0–0	1962–63	2–2
1907–08	2–4	1963–64	3–1
1908–09	5–0	1964–65	2–1
1909–10	2–3	1965–66	0–0
1910–11	0–1	1966–67	3–1
1911–12	2–1	1967–68	1–0
1912–13	0–2	1968–69	0–0
1913–14	1–2	1969–70	0–3
1914–15	1–3	1970–71	0–0
1919–20	0–0	1971–72	1–0
1920–21	0–3	1972–73	0–2
1921–22	1–1	1973–74	0–1
1922–23	0–1	1974–75	0–0
1923–24	1–0	1975–76	0–0
1924–25	0–1	1976–77	0–0
1925–26	3–3	1977–78	0–1
1926–27	1–0	1978–79	1–0
1927–28	1–1	1979–80	1–2
1928–29	1–0	1980–81	2–2
1929–30	3–3	1981–82	1–3
1931–32	2–1	1982–83	0–5
1932–33	3–1	1983–84	1–1
1933–34	0–0	1984–85	1–0

League results at Anfield (Liverpool's score first)

Season	Score	Season	Score
1894–95	2–2	1925–26	5–1
1896–97	0–0	1926–27	1–0
1897–98	3–1	1927–28	3–3
1898–99	2–0	1928–29	1–2
1899–1900	1–2	1929–30	0–3
1900–01	1–2	1931–32	1–3
1901–02	2–2	1932–33	7–4
1902–03	0–0	1933–34	3–2
1903–04	2–2	1934–35	2–1
1905–06	1–1	1935–36	6–0
1906–07	1–2	1936–37	3–2
1907–08	0–0	1937–38	1–2
1908–09	0–1	1938–39	0–3
1909–10	0–1	1946–47	0–0
1910–11	0–2	1947–48	4–0
1911–12	1–3	1948–49	0–0
1912–13	0–2	1949–50	3–1
1913–14	1–2	1950–51	0–2
1914–15	0–5	1962–63	0–0
1919–20	3–1	1963–64	2–1
1920–21	1–0	1964–65	0–4
1921–22	1–1	1965–66	5–0
1922–23	5–1	1966–67	0–0
1923–24	1–2	1967–68	1–0
1924–25	3–1	1968–69	1–1

Season	Score	Season	Score
1969–70	0–2	1977–78	0–0
1970–71	3–2	1978–79	1–1
1971–72	4–0	1979–80	2–2
1972–73	1–0	1980–81	1–0
1973–74	0–0	1981–82	3–1
1974–75	0–0	1982–83	0–0
1975–76	1–0	1983–84	3–0
1976–77	3–1	1984–85	

The two Manchesters — Manchester City v Manchester United

City were founded in 1887 as Ardwick FC and became Manchester City in 1894. United were formed a few years earlier in 1878 as Newton Heath and became Manchester United in 1902.

Of the 106 League matches played between the sides City won 31, United 38 and 37 were drawn.

League results at Maine Road (City's score first)

Season	Score	Season	Score
1894–95	2–5	1953–54	2–0
1895–96	2–1	1954–55	3–2
1896–97	0–0	1955–56	1–0
1897–98	0–1	1956–57	2–4
1898–99	4–0	1957–58	2–2
1902–03	0–2	1958–59	1–1
1906–07	3–0	1959–60	3–0
1907–08	0–0	1960–61	1–3
1908–09	1–2	1961–62	0–2
1910–11	1–1	1962–63	1–1
1911–12	0–0	1966–67	1–1
1912–13	0–2	1967–68	1–2
1913–14	0–2	1968–69	0–0
1914–15	1–1	1969–70	4–0
1919–20	3–3	1970–71	3–4
1920–21	3–0	1971–72	3–3
1921–22	4–1	1972–73	3–0
1925–26	1–1	1973–74	0–0
1928–29	2–2	1975–76	2–2
1929–30	0–1	1976–77	1–3
1930–31	4–1	1977–78	3–1
1936–37	1–0	1978–79	0–3
1947–48	0–0	1979–80	2–0
1948–49	0–0	1980–81	1–0
1949–50	1–2	1981–82	0–0
1951–52	1–2	1982–83	1–2
1952–53	2–1		

League results at Old Trafford (United's score first)

Season	Score	Season	Score
1894–95	4–1	1953–54	1–1
1895–96	1–1	1954–55	0–5
1896–97	2–1	1955–56	2–1
1897–98	1–1	1956–57	2–0
1898–99	3–0	1957–58	4–1
1902–03	1–1	1958–59	4–1
1906–07	1–1	1959–60	0–0
1907–08	3–1	1960–61	5–1
1908–09	3–1	1961–62	3–2
1910–11	2–1	1962–63	2–3
1911–12	0–0	1966–67	1–0
1912–13	0–1	1967–68	1–3
1913–14	0–1	1968–69	0–1
1914–15	0–0	1969–70	1–2
1919–20	1–0	1970–71	1–4
1920–21	1–1	1971–72	1–3
1921–22	3–1	1972–73	0–0
1925–26	1–6	1973–74	0–1
1928–29	1–2	1975–76	2–0
1929–30	1–3	1976–77	3–1
1930–31	1–3	1977–78	2–2
1936–37	3–2	1978–79	1–0
1947–48	1–1*	1979–80	1–0
1948–49	0–0*	1980–81	2–2
1949–50	2–1	1981–82	1–1
1951–52	1–1	1982–83	2–2
1952–53	1–1		

* United played at Maine Road

Rivalry in the North-East — Newcastle United v Sunderland

Sunderland were founded in 1879 as Sunderland and District Teachers AFC and became known under their present title in 1881. Newcastle were founded in 1882 as Newcastle East End and changed to Newcastle United in 1892.

Of the 108 League matches played between the two sides, Sunderland have won 38, Newcastle 39 and 31 have been drawn.

League results at Roker Park (Sunderland's score first)

Season	Score	Season	Score
1898–99	2–3	1929–30	1–0
1899–1900	1–2	1930–31	5–0
1900–01	1–1	1931–32	1–4
1901–02	0–0	1932–33	0–2
1902–03	0–0	1933–34	2–0
1903–04	1–1	1948–49	1–1
1904–05	3–1	1949–50	2–2
1905–06	3–2	1950–51	2–1
1906–07	2–0	1951–52	1–4
1907–08	2–4	1952–53	0–2
1908–09	3–1	1953–54	1–1
1909–10	0–2	1954–55	4–2
1910–11	2–1	1955–56	1–6
1911–12	1–2	1956–57	1–2
1912–13	2–0	1957–58	2–0
1913–14	1–2	1961–62	3–0
1914–15	2–4	1962–63	0–0
1919–20	2–0	1963–64	2–1
1920–21	0–2	1965–66	2–0
1921–22	0–0	1966–67	3–0
1922–23	2–0	1967–68	3–3
1923–24	3–2	1968–69	1–1
1924–25	1–1	1969–70	1–1
1925–26	2–2	1976–77	2–2
1926–27	2–0	1978–79	1–1
1927–28	1–1	1979–80	1–0
1928–29	5–2	1984–85	0–0

Bryan 'Pop' Robson (striped shirt) playing for Sunderland in the game with Newcastle United. (Sunderland Echo). BELOW: Sammy McIlroy (United) darts between Dave Watson, left, and Colin Bell (both City) in the Manchester derby. (Manchester Evening News).

League results at St James's Park (Newcastle's score first)

Season	Score	Season	Score
1898–99	0–1	1929–30	3–0
1899–1900	2–4	1930–31	2–0
1900–01	0–2	1931–32	1–2
1901–02	0–1	1932–33	0–1
1902–03	1–0	1933–34	2–1
1903–04	1–3	1948–49	2–1
1904–05	1–3	1949–50	2–2
1905–06	1–1	1950–51	2–2
1906–07	4–2	1951–52	2–2
1907–08	1–3	1952–53	2–2
1908–09	1–9	1953–54	2–1
1909–10	1–0	1954–55	1–2
1910–11	1–1	1955–56	3–1
1911–12	3–1	1956–57	6–2
1912–13	1–1	1957–58	2–2
1913–14	2–1	1961–62	2–2
1914–15	2–5	1962–63	1–1
1919–20	2–3	1963–64	1–0
1920–21	6–1	1965–66	2–0
1921–22	2–2	1966–67	0–3
1922–23	2–1	1967–68	2–1
1923–24	0–2	1968–69	1–1
1924–25	2–0	1969–70	3–0
1925–26	0–0	1976–77	2–0
1926–27	1–0	1978–79	1–4
1927–28	3–1	1979–80	3–1
1928–29	4–3	1984–85	3–1

North London encounters — Arsenal v Tottenham Hotspur

Arsenal were founded in 1886 as Royal Arsenal, becoming Woolwich Arsenal in 1891 and Arsenal from 1914. Tottenham Hotspur were founded four years earlier in 1882 and were known as the Hotspur Football Club before becoming Tottenham Hotspur in 1885.

Of the 96 League matches played between the two sides, Tottenham have won 38, Arsenal 39, and 19 have been drawn.

League results at Highbury (Arsenal's score first)

Season	Score	Season	Score
1909–10	1–0	1960–61	2–3
1910–11	2–0	1961–62	2–1
1911–12	3–1	1962–63	2–3
1912–13	0–3	1963–64	4–4
1920–21	3–2	1964–65	3–1
1921–22	1–0	1965–66	1–1
1922–23	0–2	1966–67	0–2
1923–24	1–1	1967–68	4–0
1924–25	1–0	1968–69	1–0
1925–26	0–1	1969–70	2–3
1926–27	2–4	1970–71	2–0
1927–28	1–1	1971–72	0–2
1933–34	1–3	1972–73	1–1
1934–35	5–1	1973–74	0–1
1950–51	2–2	1974–75	1–0
1951–52	1–1	1975–76	0–2
1952–53	4–0	1976–77	1–0
1953–54	0–3	1978–79	1–0
1954–55	2–0	1979–80	1–0
1955–56	0–1	1980–81	2–0
1956–57	3–1	1981–82	1–3
1957–58	4–4	1982–83	2–0
1958–59	3–1	1983–84	3–2
1959–60	1–1	1984–85	1–2

League results at White Hart Lane (Tottenham's score first)

Season	Score	Season	Score
1909–10	1–1	1933–34	1–1
1910–11	3–1	1934–35	0–6
1911–12	5–0	1950–51	1–0
1912–13	1–1	1951–52	1–2
1920–21	2–1	1952–53	1–3
1921–22	2–0	1953–54	1–4
1922–23	1–2	1954–55	0–1

Season	Score	Season	Score
1923–24	3–0	1955–56	3–1
1924–25	2–0	1956–57	1–3
1925–26	1–1	1957–58	3–1
1926–27	0–4	1958–59	1–4
1927–28	2–0	1959–60	3–0
1960–61	4–2	1972–73	1–2
1961–62	4–3	1973–74	2–0
1962–63	4–4	1974–75	2–0
1963–64	3–1	1975–76	0–0
1964–65	3–1	1976–77	2–2
1965–66	2–2	1978–79	0–5
1966–67	3–1	1979–80	1–2
1967–68	1–0	1980–81	2–0
1968–69	1–2	1981–82	2–2
1969–70	1–0	1982–83	5–0
1970–71	0–1	1983–84	2–4
1971–72	1–1	1984–85	0–2

Duels of the Nottinghams — Notts County v Nottingham Forest

Notts County were founded in 1872 and are the oldest club in the Football League. Nottingham Forest came into being in 1865, but did not enter the League until 1882, four years after Notts County had become a founder member.

Of the 82 League matches played between the two sides, Forest have won 33, County 27, and 22 have been drawn.

League results at Meadow Lane (Notts County score first)

Season	Score	Season	Score
1892–93	3–0	1928–29	1–1
1897–98	1–3	1929–30	0–0
1898–99	2–2	1931–32	2–6
1899–1900	1–2	1932–33	2–4
1900–01	1–0	1933–34	1–0
1901–02	3–0	1934–35	3–5
1902–03	1–1	1949–50	2–0
1903–04	1–3	1951–52	2–2
1904–05	1–2	1952–53	3–2
1905–06	1–1	1953–54	1–1
1907–08	2–0	1954–55	4–1
1908–09	3–0	1955–56	1–3
1909–10	4–1	1956–57	1–2
1910–11	1–1	1973–74	0–1
1913–14	2–2	1974–75	2–2
1920–21	2–0	1975–76	0–0
1921–22	1–1	1976–77	1–1
1923–24	2–1	1981–82	1–2
1924–25	0–0	1982–83	3–2
1926–27	1–2	1983–84	0–0
1927–28	1–2		

League results at the City Ground (Forest's score first)

Season	Score	Season	Score
1892–93	3–1	1928–29	1–2
1897–98	1–1	1929–30	1–1
1898–99	0–0	1931–32	2–1
1899–1900	0–3	1932–33	3–0
1900–01	5–0	1933–34	2–0
1901–02	1–0	1934–35	2–3
1902–03	0–0	1949–50	1–2
1903–04	0–1	1951–52	3–2
1904–05	2–1	1952–53	1–0
1905–06	1–2	1953–54	5–0
1907–08	2–0	1954–55	0–1
1908–09	1–0	1955–56	0–2
1909–10	2–1	1956–57	2–4
1910–11	0–2	1973–74	0–0
1913–14	1–0	1974–75	0–2
1920–21	1–0	1975–76	0–1
1921–22	0–0	1976–77	1–2
1923–24	1–0	1981–82	0–2
1924–25	0–0	1982–83	2–1
1926–27	2–0	1983–84	3–1
1927–28	2–1		

Bryan Robson

A product of the fertile North-East, born at Chester-le-Street on 11 January 1957, he wanted to play for Newcastle United but joined West Bromwich Albion upon leaving school at 16 in 1973 to serve as an apprentice at The Hawthorns.

His League debut came towards the end of the 1974–75 season against York City on 12 April 1975. There were only two more League games left that season and Robson scored a goal in each of them.

Robson slowly established himself during the following season, but in 1976–77 had the extreme misfortune to break his left leg three times during a period of six months.

His first unlucky break came on 2 October against Tottenham Hotspur. After eight weeks out he returned to play for the reserves but suffered a refracture against Stoke.

He regained his place in the League side but shortly after being selected for the England Under-21 team he broke his leg for a third time playing against Manchester City on 16 April 1977; his leg was in plaster for 14 weeks.

Ron Atkinson – the manager who paid the record fee for Bryan Robson. (ASP).

Bryan Robson, who became the most expensive British footballer at £1½ million, emerged before the 1982 World Cup finals in Spain as the most consistent player in the England team, a midfield player of strategic influence and unmatched industry.

LEFT: No lack of effort on Robson's part in this League encounter against Leicester City. (ASP). BELOW: Less frenzied, the England captain in action against France. (ASP).

Robson recovered again and apart from re-establishing himself in Albion's first team gained full international recognition with his debut against the Republic of Ireland in February 1980. This added to the honours he had gained at Youth, Under–21 and 'B' level.

In the World Cup finals in Spain he had the distinction of scoring the fastest goal recorded in any tournament: just 27 seconds after the kick-off against France on 16 June 1982.

In October 1981, Manchester United's manager, Ron Atkinson, paid a record fee to reunite the player with him at Old Trafford, having been his manager previously at The Hawthorns. Despite tempting offers from Italy, the club have resisted efforts to lure him abroad and he has signed a seven-year contract with United.

In an age when work-rate has become a sour phrase for mindless running, Robson's contribution has been purposeful, and the strength in his legs has enabled him to give cover in defence, prompt attacks and finish them with equal voracity.

Jimmy McGrory

Jimmy McGrory was unique among goalscorers, averaging just over a goal per game in his career. Nobody scored more goals for one British club let alone a Scottish one. His tally from his League debut on 20 January 1923 until his last game on 16 October 1937 was 410 League goals in 408 matches.

With cup ties and international games he reached 550 goals, yet amazingly he played only seven times for Scotland scoring six goals. Unfortunately for him he was a contemporary of Hughie Gallacher and in fact he might well have been given fewer opportunities for his country as four of his caps were awarded against Northern Ireland because of his Celtic connection.

Jimmy McGrory pictured in the front row above with Celtic colleagues and below by the near post having beaten Harry Hibbs in the England goal.

James Edward McGrory was born in the Garngad district of Glasgow on 26 April 1904. He first came to prominence with St Roch's as an inside-forward and actually appeared as a left-winger upon joining Celtic in August 1922.

He was loaned to Clydebank for a season in 1923–24 and after being recalled had another short spell on the wing before being converted to centre-forward. The transformation was remarkable.

Despite his success he always maintained that he was scared of being dropped and this constant nagging fear kept him well on his toes throughout his illustrious career.

Short and rather stocky with broad shoulders and a barrel chest, he was brave, quick off the mark and an expert at converting half chances. More than a third of his goals were scored with his head though none of them in his best individual performance on 14 January 1928 against Dunfermline Athletic when he scored eight times including three goals in nine minutes. However, his horizontal headers and ability to direct the ball downward with his head became the scourge of goalkeepers.

McGrory was on the winning side in four of six Scottish Cup finals and he also won two championship medals. Three times he was the leading League marksman with 49 goals in 1926–27, 47 the following season and 50 in 1935–36, celebrating this half-century season with four goals in five minutes against Motherwell which included his hat-trick in three minutes. For Celtic alone he scored 397 in 378 League games.

In 1937, he became manager of Kilmarnock and immediately led them to Scottish Cup success over Celtic. In 1945, he became manager at Parkhead and remained there even after relinquishing the position to Jock Stein in 1965. Then as Public Relations Officer he continued to be the finest ambassador ever possessed by Celtic.

Arsenal in the 30s

Before the 1930–31 season no club outside the North and Midlands had succeeded in winning the First Division championship. Arsenal became the first southern-based side to achieve this honour. They quickly established themselves as the country's leading club winning five titles in eight years and their fame spread around the world. In 1930, they had won the FA Cup and were to finish as runners-up in it in 1932 before winning again in 1936.

Tactically Arsenal had developed under the shrewd managership of Herbert Chapman who had fashioned his reputation at Huddersfield in the 1920s, putting them well on the way to a hat-trick of championship successes, a feat for which he was also able to lay foundations at Highbury.

In 1930–31, Arsenal scored a club record 127 League goals and amassed 66 points, half of them gained from away games. But the following season the Gunners had to be content with runners-up position in both League and Cup.

And it was a shock 2–0 FA Cup defeat at Walsall in 1932–33 which acted as a timely nudge to their over-confidence. Despite being chased by Aston Villa and Sheffield Wednesday they won the championship scoring an unmatched 118 goals.

The following season they retained the title although it was the defence which earned it for them. Midway through the campaign Chapman died and Arsenal suffered three successive defeats. But they recovered and the attendance record was twice broken at Highbury with first 68 828 and then 69 070 spectators cramming into the ground.

George Allison became manager, and seven of the Arsenal players were selected for England against Italy in November 1934. Crowds soared higher, the gate record was smashed twice more with first 70 544 and then 73 295, and Arsenal lost only twice in the second half of the season to make it a hat-trick of championships.

The Football League presented Arsenal with a silver shield and an illuminated address to commemorate it. Their last title of the decade came in 1937–38 from the comparatively small total of 52 points and was achieved by a one point margin, the outcome being in doubt until the last day.

Arsenal were at home to Bolton Wanderers while close rivals Wolverhampton Wanderers had the more difficult task at Sunderland. In the event Arsenal won 5–0 in championship style while Wolves were losing by the only goal at Roker Park.

TOP: Eddie Hapgood, Arsenal's stalwart full-back and captain during their period of domination. ABOVE: Ted Drake, whose goalscoring achievements powered the club towards many of its successful targets.

PICTURES LEFT: Cliff Bastin, Arsenal's goalscoring winger of the years between the wars. BELOW: Arsenal's Underground station, formerly Gillespie Road, christened in the 1930s.

During much of this period an undeserved tag of 'Lucky Arsenal' was grafted to the Gunners from the tactics they employed. Their fast counter-attacking after soaking up pressure with a resolute and well marshalled defence often made nonsense of territorial inferiority.

Real Madrid

Real Madrid accomplished the feat of winning the first five European Cup competitions, reaching their peak in the last of them when they defeated Eintracht Frankfurt 7–3 at Hampden Park, Glasgow, on 18 May 1960 before a record final crowd of 127 621.

Yet they had come close to being forced into a replay in only the second tie in which they were involved against Partizan Belgrade (Yugoslavia) during the second leg of their quarter-final match on 29 January 1956.

The first leg, played in Madrid on Christmas Day, had resulted in a 4–0 win for Real but freezing conditions in the return game were not to their liking.

Partizan scored first then Real missed a penalty. The Yugoslavs converted a spot kick themselves and added a third goal near the end. Real, holding on for a 4–3 aggregate win, were relieved to hear the whistle.

In the Paris final against Reims, the Spaniards began disastrously and were two goals down in 12 minutes. But within half an hour they had asserted themselves to

The Real Madrid team which captured successive League honours in Spain from 1961–62 to 1963–64 inclusive, following triumphs in Europe.

equalize with goals from Alfredo di Stefano and Hector Rial.

Yet after Real had a goal disallowed for offside, Reims took the lead again only for the Spaniards to equalize with a fortunate deflection. Ten minutes from the end Real went ahead for the first time in the game and won 4–3.

The following year, Real successfully defended their title and with the benefit of home advantage in the final defeated Fiorentina (Italy) 2–0. But another Italian club, AC Milan, pushed them to extra time in 1958 in Brussels, Real, again twice behind, scored the winner through Francisco Gento. Real's fourth victims were again Reims when they won 2–0 in Stuttgart. It was a West German side, Eintracht Frankfurt, which bravely tried to emulate Real's devastating attacking skills in 1960. Frankfurt also scored first but Real were well on the way to a crushing victory leading 3–1 at the interval.

In a team which neatly blended individualism and team work, Di Stefano maintained his record of scoring in every final, Ferenc Puskas scored the other four goals, including a penalty, and Real almost became an immortal legend.

Ferenc Puskas after (above) and before (below) – 20 years and a few stones heavier. (ASP). LEFT: Alfredo di Stefano, who maintained a remarkable record in European Cup finals.

Celtic Cup wins

Danny McGrain has skippered Celtic in recent years. (ASP).

By 1980, Celtic had won the Scottish Cup for a record 26 times appearing in 41 finals, almost half the total number played. Their most effective period in the competition had come between 1969 and 1975 when they appeared in seven consecutive finals, winning five of them.

The first trophy had been obtained in 1892 in unusual circumstances. The original game with Queen's Park was disrupted by crowd trouble, with Celtic leading 1–0, but after both clubs protested about the game a replay gave Celtic an emphatic 5–1 win.

Only six Scottish Cup successes have come Celtic's way against close rivals Rangers and, these came near to each other. In 1899, a 2–0 win over the Ibrox club was followed by one in 1904, the year that Jimmy McMenemy gained the first of the six cup medals he won with Celtic. He added a seventh later with Partick Thistle.

In 1909, the cup was withheld after two games with Rangers had ended in 2–2 and 1–1 draws because of a riot by spectators. Protests began with the crowd thinking extra time should be played after the second drawn game and trouble ensued with pay-boxes being burned and hundreds of supporters being injured.

Jimmy Johnstone, Celtic's flying winger of the 1960s and 1970s. (GMcC).

Both Rangers and Celtic refused to play a third game.

It was not until 1969 that Celtic beat Rangers again in a final this time 4–0. In 1971, they repeated the success 2–1 after a 1–1 draw. And Celtic's last two victories in the competition were also at Rangers expense 1–0 in 1977 and by the same score in 1980.

Probably the nearest that Celtic had come to losing a Scottish Cup final before succeeding in snatching victory came in 1931. Motherwell were beating Celtic 2–0 with eight minutes left. First Jimmy McGrory reduce the arrears and then in the last minute a Motherwell defender turned a harmless shot past his own goal-keeper for the equalizer. Celtic won the replay 4–2.

Celtic centre-half Billy McNeill won seven Scottish Cup winner's medals in 1965, 1967, 1969, 1971, 1972, 1974 and 1975 to equal McMenemy's overall record, but he took the lead with one more gained in Celtic's green and white hoops. His medal in 1972 had been won after Celtic gained their biggest Scottish Cup final victory, a 6–1 success over Hibernian.

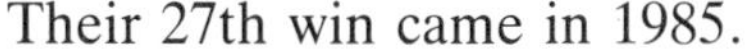

Their 27th win came in 1985.

Billy McNeill was Celtic's captain on numerous cup occasions. BELOW: The Celtic team in the early 1960s before emerging as almost untouchable in the cup.

10

Zico

Artur Antunes Coimbra, known as Zico, literally enjoyed a rags to riches career between the time of his debut for Flamengo and his transfer to the Italian club Udinese in 1983 for £2.5 million. As a boy in his native Rio de Janeiro, he had played with a ball made of rags on the beaches.

Born on 3 March 1953 into a footballing family — his three brothers were professionals and his father formerly a goalkeeper — he joined Flamengo as a frail 15-year-old.

The club immediately put him on a body-building course and a year later the elderly Paraguayan coach of the club Fleitas Solich gave him a chance in the first team. He scored twice in 15 games but was often out of his depth.

He went back to the youth team where he had scored his first goal on 18 March 1970 against Sao Cristobal, and proceeded to score 20 goals in 22 games.

His next appearance in the senior side was the start of a permanent place and he appeared in the Brazilian Olympic side. Then he scored the winner on his full debut against Uruguay.

A quick, unselfish midfield attacker with fine control, precision passing and tireless application, much was expected of a player who had become the latest in the line of those known as the 'White Pelé'.

But he disappointed in the 1978 World Cup finals, carrying one niggling injury into the finals, losing confidence after having a goal disallowed in the dying seconds against Sweden and coming back only to be injured again.

But the following year he returned to his best, scoring 89 goals, 65 of them in the League, 16 in friendlies, 7 for Brazil and 1 for the Rest of Europe. The same year he set up a new scoring record in the Rio 'Carioca' League with his 245th goal for Flamengo. A dead ball expert, he was able to add many more goals to his haul from free-kicks and penalties.

Having been elected South American Footballer of the Year in 1977, he added two more honours in 1981 and 1982. That year he starred for Brazil in the World Cup and a year later after 630 goals, three Brazilian championships, six Rio State titles and South American and World Cup Championship honours he went to Italy.

In his first season with Udinese he finished second highest scorer with 19 goals despite missing half a dozen League games. In June 1985 he returned to Flamengo.

Ian Rush

Ian Rush became the first British player to win the Golden Boot award for finishing as the leading League scorer in Europe in 1983–84 with 32 goals.

His total included five goals in a 6–0 victory over Luton Town on 29 October 1983 and four including a penalty against Coventry City who were beaten 5–0 on 7 May 1984. Rush also scored all three goals against Aston Villa on 20 January 1984.

He had previously established himself as the youngest forward to appear in a full international for Wales when he came on as substitute in the 15th minute of the match against Scotland at Hampden Park on 21 May 1980. He was then aged 18 years, 214 days.

Born in Flint, he had been the youngest of six brothers. The others all played for Flint Town in the Clwyd League. Ian Rush played for Flint Boys and during one season of primary school football at Sir Richard Gwyn's he scored 73 goals in 34 games.

He subsequently turned professional for Chester and was transferred to Liverpool for £300 000 in May 1980 before his debut in the colour of Wales.

Like most undergraduates at the Anfield academy, he had to serve a lengthy examination of his ability in the reserve side in the Central League. Indeed in 1980–81 he made only seven appearances in their First Division side.

Ian Rush became the first Welshman to head the goalscoring charts in European football during 1983–84. (ASP).

But he made an immediate impact when returning to senior League duty in 1981–82 scoring twice against Leeds United in a 3–0 win on 10 October 1981, missed just two other League games and finished with 17 goals.

The following season his tally increased to 24 and in 1983–84 he was absent from League duty just once in scoring his European award-winning 32 goals.

A direct type of central spearhead, his uncanny knack of being in the right position in front of goal at the pertinent moment is allied to his accuracy in finishing with the minimum of fuss with head or feet; a combination of qualities which underline a first class leader.

As a talisman he has few rivals. From the date of his first goals for Liverpool he has never finished on the losing side after scoring in a game for them.

Among Rush's milestones there was a fine individual effort of four goals in the 127th Merseyside derby against Everton in November 1982. Here he is on target in a cup-tie with Barnsley in March 1985. (ASP).

Rangers' championships

Rangers are the most successful club in Scottish League history having won 37 championships. They were concerned in the first championship but had to share the honour with Dumbarton after drawing 2–2 in a play-off.

The club had to wait until 1898–99 for their next success, but achieved it in devastating form, winning all 18 League games and becoming the only club to win every away game and take maximum points in a season. The programme lasted from August to January and Rangers finished ten points clear of Hearts.

Rangers then made it four successive titles, and following three on the trot from 1910–11 to 1912–13 had a narrow lead of a point over Celtic in 1917–18. In 1904–05 they had lost 2–1 to Celtic in another play-off which launched their victors on a successful run until 1910–11.

They were champions again in 1919–20, but in 1920–21 amassed a record number of points with 76 from 42 games. They had 35 wins that season, 16 of which and five draws were away from home.

Rangers began with a 4–1 win over Airdrieonians and were unbeaten in their first 23 games, dropping only two points at Aberdeen and Ayr before losing 2–0 at home to Celtic on New Year's Day when weakened by injuries. It was their only defeat. Between September and mid-December they had had a winning run of 12 games. They finished 10 points ahead of Celtic, the runners-up, and 26 in front of Hearts in third place.

In the previous season they had led by seven points and in these two seasons they lost only 3 out of 84 League games. They had a run of 56 consecutive games in which only one defeat was suffered and that was 2–1 at home by Clydebank.

Rangers lost only one game in 1928–29 when they had a 16 points winning margin, but in 1952–53 it was merely goal average which gave them the title. In 1948–49, they became the first Scottish club to win the treble of League, League Cup and Scottish Cup. William Struth, manager from August 1920 to April 1953, watched over 15 championships.

Other contrasts included an 11-point lead over Celtic in 1938–39 and just one in front of Kilmarnock in 1960–61. Rangers also won the last of the old style Division 1 titles in 1974–75 and the first of the Premier Division honours the following season.

Jock Wallace in his second spell as Manager of Rangers. BELOW: Jim Baxter invents a new Scottish pastime, tossing the trophy.

LEFT: The Glasgow Rangers team in the middle of a hat-trick of League titles in 1911–12. BELOW: Derek Johnstone, who made an impact as a teenager in the early 1970s. (ASP).

Bob Paisley

Bob Paisley became the most successful manager in the history of the Football League between 1974 and 1983 during which time Liverpool won 13 major honours at home and on the continent. With the European Super Cup in 1977 and six Charity Shield honours the total was 20.

Although he had been born in the North-East at Hetton-le-Hole on 23 January 1919, he had been at Anfield since joining them as a professional in 1939 after winning an FA Amateur Cup winners' medal with Bishop Auckland.

As a wing-half he made his first appearances on Merseyside in the trial games prior to the 1939–40 season. In the second of these a *Liverpool Daily Post* report commented: 'Paisley is one of those sturdy never-say-die half-backs. On this display he at least commended himself as being an honest worker with some of the necessary attributes for the rigours of the game.'

War came and he made his senior debut later that season, but Army service took him overseas and it was not until the first peacetime season of 1946–47 that he was able to command a regular place at left-half. But he quickly made his presence felt helping Liverpool to the championship. He was an industrious player, strong in the tackle and noted for his long throw-ins.

Upon retiring in 1954, he went onto the training staff at Anfield, becoming first team trainer in 1959 as Bill Shankly's assistant. Few would have imagined him being able to match and surpass the latter's fine record on Merseywide, but Paisley did.

In 1975–76 Liverpool achieved a double of League and UEFA Cup success. The following year it was the championship and the European Cup. While they had to be content with being runners-up in Division 1 in 1977–78, they retained the European Cup.

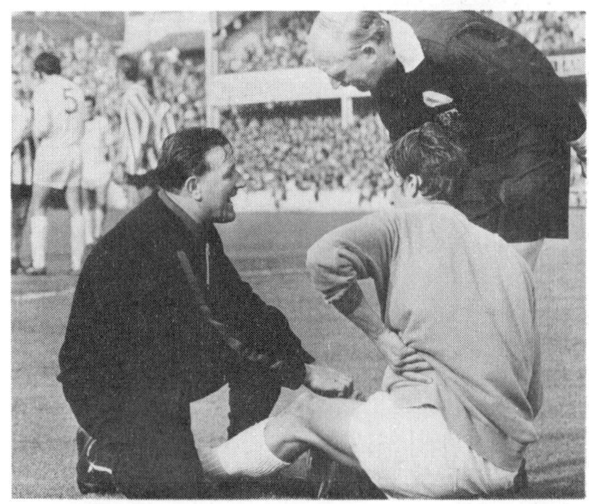

Bob Paisley with the European Cup in 1981 and above tending to goalkeeper Ray Clemence as trainer in 1970. (ASP).

The 1978–79 season brought Paisley's third championship and the fourth arrived the next year. The first League Cup honour came to Anfield in 1980–81, plus another European Cup. In 1981–82 it was a League and League Cup double. Later that year in December 1982, he won his 19th Manager of the Month award in seven years. And honours did not end there, as both the League and Milk Cup trophies remained in the trophy room at Anfield as Paisley retired.

Paisley the player had been noted as a tactician of some maturity and he was able to bring these exceptional qualities into his quiet but firm approach as a manager. His understanding of the essential requirements for a successful team in an environment which had been home to him for almost half a century proved ideal.

Spurs' Cup finals

Tottenham Hotspur have an exemplary record in FA Cup finals; their seven appearances have resulted in seven victories although on three occasions they were forced to a replay before winning.

They are the last non-league club to win the trophy, a feat which they accomplished in 1901 while still members of the Southern League. They were the first London professional team to have won the competition and the first southern side to break the northern and Midland monopoly since 1882.

With the final staged at the Crystal Palace, interest was such that a world record crowd at the time of 110 820 crammed into the ground to bask on a sun-lit afternoon, with many spectators climbing trees for a better view. They had to be content with a 2–2 draw with Sheffield United, but Spurs finished the task at Bolton in the replay winning 3–1.

At the celebration dinner afterwards, blue and white ribbons were tied to the handles of the trophy and this started a tradition. Twenty years later Mrs Morton Cadman, wife of one of the directors, took them to the 1921 final. At the subsequent banquet all the 1901 team were in attendance except goalkeeper George Clawley who had died the year before. Again Spurs with a classical display, despite a cloudburst during the game which turned the pitch into a quagmire, fully deserved victory over Wolverhampton Wanderers. Arthur Grimsdell, Fanny Walden and the scorer Jimmy Dimmock inspired their success.

John White masterminded Spurs in the early 1960s from inside-forward.

Forty years on and it was a year of League and Cup double triumph for the inhabitants of White Hart Lane. The outcome was more memorable than the event itself at Wembley where Leicester City were handicapped by early injury and lost 2–0. But the varied contributions of players like Danny Blanchflower, Dave Mackay, John White and Cliffe Jones — guile, strength, artistry and speed — were conclusive and just as evident a year later when Burnley were defeated 3–1. Mackay collected his third cup winners' medal in the 2–1 victory in the all-London final against Chelsea in 1967.

In the 100th final in 1981, Manchester City forced a replay after a 1–1 draw. Argentine-born Ricardo Villa, substituted in the original game, scored twice in the 3–2 replay win. The following year they made it seven out of seven despite plucky Queen's Park Rangers drawing 1–1 and forcing another Wembley replay before Spurs secured it with a Glenn Hoddle penalty.

The successful Spurs team of 1921 including Arthur Grimsdell, third from left front row.

Delighted 1981 vintage: LEFT TO RIGHT: Chris Hughton, Tony Galvin and Garth Crooks. (Syndication International).

Manchester United attendances

Manchester United have been the best supported team in the British Isles for more than a decade. The origin of this trend came in the days of the Busby Babes in the 1950s and mushroomed after the Munich air disaster in 1958.

The average crowd at Old Trafford in 1957–58 was 46 000, while the following season in a wave of sympathy and affection following the tragic loss, attendances increased to average 53 000.

But after a slump in the early 1960s there was a steady improvement in the following years and United's average home gate of almost 58 000 in 1967–68 is an all-time Football League record. They celebrated that year by winning the European Cup at Wembley. The actual average crowd was 57 758.

Individually, the club has had many similar records. Yet oddly enough the highest attendance ever recorded for a League game involving Manchester United was against Arsenal and played in the city but at Maine Road not Old Trafford. United were then still using their wartime home at Manchester City's headquarters after the resumption of peacetime football and 83 260 watched this Division 1 game.

United's biggest home crowd occurred on 27 December 1930 when 70 504 were present for a Division 1 match with Aston Villa. The same ground held the biggest crowd gathered outside a final for the League Cup when their local derby with City on 17 December 1969 attracted 63 418.

United's legendary support has been all the more remarkable since major honours have been scarce. They last won the League championship in 1966–67. In the 1970s there was only one FA Cup success in 1977, although they won the Cup in 1983 and again in 1985.

Their 1985 Cup run was watched by an average of more than 48 000 spectators at home and away matches including the Final at Wembley. In the Milk Cup and UEFA Cup home games produced an aggregate of over 235 000.

Not even a season in Division 2 appeared to dent the enthusiasm. In 1974–75 the average gate was 48 000, an increase of five thousand per game on the season in which they were relegated.

Since the 1946–47 season, Manchester United have averaged 43 000 spectators each season. Healthy clicks at the turnstiles have resulted in huge gate receipts. They were the first British club to record a six-figure profit when they announced a surplus of £100 000 in 1958. Yet receipts from the Cup Winners' Cup semi-final with Juventus on 11 April 1984 were £192 956!

ABOVE: The aerial view of Old Trafford which in 1984–85 housed the highest average crowds in the Canon League at 43 000 per game – exactly the club's level of support over the post-war period. (Courtesy Manchester United FC) RIGHT: Just two of the many youthful supporters of Manchester United who have shown their allegience to the club from various areas of this country and abroad. Oddly enough the largest attendance at the ground was for a match not involving the club: 76 962 for Wolves v Grimsby Town in a FA Cup semi-final on 25 March 1939.

Mark Hateley

Mark Hateley made an immediate impact upon the Italian scene in 1984–85 and his association with AC Milan revived memories of other British strikers who had trodden a similarly successful path in earlier times including John Charles, Denis Law and Gerry Hitchens.

The son of Tony Hateley, a goalscoring centre-forward in his own right, Mark made his first impression in the Midlands with Coventry City who introduced him, after his apprenticeship, in the 1978–79 season while still a teenager. By the time he had reached his 20th birthday he was a

England's exports to Italy 1984 vintage included Mark Hateley (left) and Ray Wilkins who successfully linked up with each other in the colours of AC Milan. (Allsport Photographic).

regular choice. Then in 1981–82 he won the first of ten Under–21 caps for England.

However, after an unhappy 1982–83 season for the club there was a dramatic changeover of personnel at Highfield Road and rather surprisingly Hateley was allowed to leave for Portsmouth at the relatively small fee of £180 000. There he enjoyed his best domestic season, scoring 22 goals in 38 games as the Hampshire club tried to obtain promotion from Division 2.

Though Pompey were not quite able to make the step up, Hateley's reputation soared to such a degree that he was given his first full outing for England as substitute against the USSR after Italian scouts had been chasing him. AC Milan paid nearly £1 million for his signature in June 1984, the actual fee being £915 000.

The ban on foreign players which had been lifted in Italy previously had seen the Republic of Ireland's Liam Brady move to Juventus from Arsenal in 1980. The success of this midfield player there prompted others to undertake a similar trek. Trevor Francis joined Sampdoria and was himself later united there with Brady. Last summer Brady moved again, this time to Internazionale, AC's rivals, and Graeme Souness arrived from Liverpool in his place.

Hateley's qualities have not only mirrored his father's prodigious heading prowess but have produced a far more potent rate of scoring on the ground. His bustling style which had upset defences has been an important asset, but his presence alone in the attack unsettled the opposition and created inspiration among his colleagues.

After finding a few more international opportunities in England's 1984 tour of South America, Hateley showed how much he had learned in the tight marking cauldrons of the Italian arena. This was never better illustrated than against Ireland in Belfast in February 1985 when he took advantage of a rare chance in the game to score the only goal of this vital World Cup qualifier for England.

ABOVE: The successful England Under-21 team which carried off the European Championship at this level in May 1984 and gave Mark Hateley his first taste of achievement at international level. BELOW: Hateley in AC Milan colours. (Associated Sports Photography).

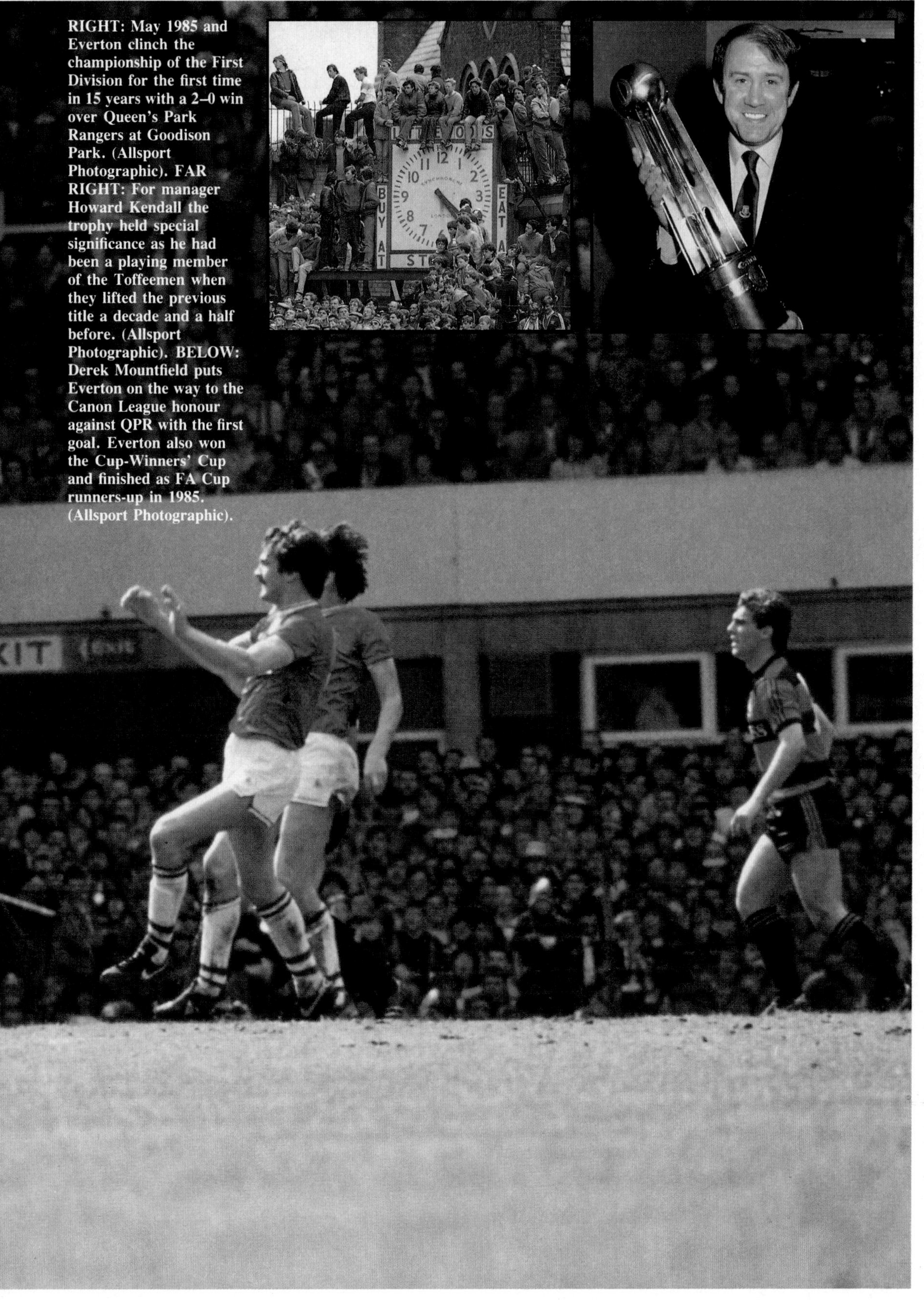

RIGHT: May 1985 and Everton clinch the championship of the First Division for the first time in 15 years with a 2–0 win over Queen's Park Rangers at Goodison Park. (Allsport Photographic). FAR RIGHT: For manager Howard Kendall the trophy held special significance as he had been a playing member of the Toffeemen when they lifted the previous title a decade and a half before. (Allsport Photographic). BELOW: Derek Mountfield puts Everton on the way to the Canon League honour against QPR with the first goal. Everton also won the Cup-Winners' Cup and finished as FA Cup runners-up in 1985. (Allsport Photographic).

Mark Hughes, the Manchester United and Welsh International striker, established himself as one of the most dangerous forwards in the British game in 1984–85. His memorable volley for Wales against Spain in a World Cup qualifying match was the best goal of the season. (Allsport Photographic).

ABOVE: John Barnes scores one of England's eight goals in their World Cup qualifying win over luckless Turkey. It was the fourth goal against Yasar, the Turks' helpless goalkeeper. (Associated Sports Photography). RIGHT: England manager Bobby Robson's shrewd guidance of the national team made a place in the Mexico finals appear an early likelihood in the qualifying series for 1986. (Associated Sports Photography). BELOW: Tony Woodcock catches the Turkish custodian off-balance as he scores the second of England's eight in their rout of the opposition. It was England's highest score abroad since beating Portugal 10–0 in 1947. (Associated Sports Photography).

Pelé

The most rewarding tribute to Pelé came when he was past 40 years of age and was offered £3 million to come out of retirement for a second time to play again for New York Cosmos.

LEFT: Two of the most outstanding individuals produced by the game in the last 40 years—George Best and Pelé. (Duncan Raban). Both found that late exposure in the USA added to their reputations and their laurels. BELOW: Pelé in the familiar yellow shirt of Brazil in which he produced many of those unforgettable touches which arguably made him the best known name in football around the world. (Duncan Raban).

His earlier presence in the USA had kindled interest in professional soccer to an unprecedented degree, often attracting crowds of more then 70 000 to New York even though he had retired previously after more than a decade of brilliance in Brazilian football. Gifted with wide peripheral vision as perhaps no other player in the history of the game, his all-round ability was unmatched.

Born Edson Arantes do Nascimento in Tres Coracoes on 23 October 1940, his first football was played in Bauru in the state of São Paulo. Careful handling by Waldemar de Brito, a former Brazilian World Cup player and coach of the local Second Division club, proved crucial.

Waldemar never once attempted to curb Pelé's obvious natural ability, but concen-

Pele (left) turns in delight after scoring the first Brazilian goal in the 1970 World Cup final in Mexico. Below he is assisted in being projected by Jairzinho. (Syndication International).

trated on his faults and continually encouraged him. At the age of 15 he suggested that Pelé should join Santos. Here he progressed rapidly and was appearing for the Brazilian national team at 17 and outstandingly in their 1958 World Cup winning team in Sweden.

He became the only player to appear for three World Cup winning teams, though he missed the final of the 1962 competition through injury. He made four appearances in the 1958 final tournament, two in 1962 before injury and six in 1970. He also appeared in two matches in 1966 for a total of 14 appearances.

Pelé's best scoring year was 1959, when he totalled 126 goals and his 1000th goal came ten years later in his 909th game.

In all he played 111 times for Brazil, scoring 97 goals. His last international was on 18 July 1971. He played his final game for Santos against Ponte Preta on 2 October 1974, but a year later was persuaded to come back for Cosmos with a three-year contract.

Pelé played his last match in New Jersey on 1 October 1977, before a crowd of 75 646. During it he appeared for both sides — Cosmos and Santos. It was his 1363rd match and in it he scored his 1281st goal. He later added two more goals in special appearances.

Frequently the victim of unscrupulous defenders, Pelé rarely retaliated and in later years invariably humiliated his opponents with feints and footwork, achieving it with consummate ease.

Bobby Moore

Bobby Moore is the most capped player in the history of English international football. His career spanned 11 years and he was absent on only 12 occasions during his entire international career, which lasted from 20 May 1962 to 14 November 1973 and embraced 108 appearances.

Bobby Moore (England) and Eusebio (Portugal) with the BBC International Sports Personality of the Year trophy in 1966. (ASP).

He was never absent on more than two occasions in succession and his zenith was reached when he captained England superbly to victory in the 1966 World Cup.

The stability which was reflected in his games for England mirrored the lengthy settled period he enjoyed with West Ham United where he spent most of his career before moving to finish it at Fulham.

Before leaving Craven Cottage he managed to record his 1000th appearance overall in all games at club and national level.

Moore acted as the sweeper, and as one of the twin centre-backs whose role was not restricted to the tight-marking of his opposing striker he suited it perfectly. His impeccable positioning enabled him to give the extra cover and depth required by the role.

His other outstanding capabilities concerned his expert reading of the game, vision and constructive prowess in quickly switching defence into attack with precision and accuracy.

These characteristics and his strong physique more than compensated for deficiencies in his make-up which included not being the best header of a ball for a key defender and lacking pace and the ability to turn quickly. But his tackling was well judged and measured and he was rarely caught off balance. For over a decade he was truly a world class player.

He played a record 18 times for England at youth level before graduating to full status through the Under-23 side. At West Ham, though honours were scarce, he helped them win the 1964 FA Cup and then the 1965 Cup Winners' Cup.

When he retired from playing he coached Oxford City and then had a spell in Hong Kong before accepting the chance of an administrative post with Southend United. Then in May 1984 he achieved his cherished ambition of becoming the manager of a League team with the same club.

Bobby Moore in his West Ham United days playing against Derby County for whom Roy McFarland is in the background. (JB).

Brazil

When Brazil achieved their third World Cup success in 1970 in Mexico they did it with arguably the finest team ever seen in the competition before or since. But it was the presence of several outstanding individuals which produced such a formidable blend.

The measure of their strengths was greater than the problems which surrounded them. The Brazilian goalkeeper Felix was uncertain and their four-man zonal defence was particularly vulnerable to attacks down the flanks, but when moving forward the team was almost irresistible.

While the deceptively languid Gerson was the master of midfield control and direction, he had the perfect foil alongside in the industrious Clodoaldo. In attack, the unselfishness of Tostao, playing despite an eye injury which prevented him from heading the ball, and the penetration on the wings of the speedy Jairzinho were matched by the explosive dead ball shooting of Rivelino.

Yet the indelible ingredient was the genius of Pelé who brought an entirely new dimension to the performance of the team as a whole.

Pelé had also graced the first Brazilian side to win the World Cup in 1958 which to date is the only team to be acclaimed winners in the competition outside its own continent.

Their style was immensely attractive; players stole the ball rather than tackled for it, only then to unleash plundering attacks on their opponents' defence. Three of them stood out: Pelé, then a teenage prodigy, Garrincha, a devastating right-winger and Didi, a midfield player of rare delicacy.

LEFT: Carlos Alberto the Brazilian captain lifts the 1970 World Cup. BELOW: Brazilian officials reflect their disappointment after the 1966 World Cup dismissal. (Syndication International).

ABOVE: Rivelino wards off a challenge from Aldo Maldera (Italy) in the 1978 match for third place in the World Cup. BELOW: Gerson is congratulated by officials after the 1970 success in Mexico. (Syndication International).

Brazil decisively won the final 5–2 despite Sweden's brave fight but four years later in Chile, the Brazilians were not as impressive, having adopted the caution that was creeping over the game as a whole and pulling winger Mario Zagalo into midfield for a 4–3–3 formation.

Brazil used only 12 players throughout this tournament, Amarildo replacing the injured Pelé in the final in which they defeated Czechoslovakia, 3–1.

But in Mexico, in 1970, they crushed Italy, the architects of defensive football, in buccaneering fashion, fully deserving their 4–1 victory.

Kenny Dalglish

Kenny Dalglish is the most capped player in Scottish history. He also equalled the previous record number of goals scored in Scotland's international matches in 1984. In the European Cup in 1983–84 he overtook Denis Law's total of 14 goals to become the highest scoring British player in this competition.

He developed with Celtic and was transferred to Liverpool in August 1977 as a replacement for Kevin Keegan for £440 000, then a record fee for British clubs. But he might have cost the Anfield club much less at an earlier age.

Born in Glasgow on 4 March 1951, he played for Glasgow Schools before joining Drumchapel Amateurs, then Glasgow United. He went to Celtic shortly afterwards and while on their books had a two-week trial with Liverpool!

While at Anfield he played in their 'B' team on 20 August 1966 in the No. 8 shirt in a match lost 1–0 to Southport. Afterwards he returned to Celtic who farmed him out to Cumbernauld to help his skills to develop.

Dalglish won Scottish honours at schools and youth level and became a professional with Celtic in August 1967. He established himself in the early 1970s and added Scottish Under-23 caps to his list of honours.

He won his first full cap as substitute against Belgium on 10 November 1971, and having become a regular choice had a run of 43 consecutive games for Scotland between 1976 and 1981.

Upon moving to Liverpool, he had scored 112 goals in 204 League games, adding a further 34 Scottish League Cup goals in 60 matches and 11 in 28 Scottish Cup ties, plus 9 in European competitions. In 1978, he overtook Law's record of 55 caps.

In his first season on Merseyside he played at Wembley three times in Charity Shield, League Cup and European Cup finals and was not once on the losing side. He completed 177 consecutive League and Cup appearances before missing a League Cup game at Bradford City on 27 August 1980.

Top Scot

On 26 November 1983 he scored his 100th League goal for Liverpool, becoming only the third player to achieve a century of such goals on either side of the border. He reached his 90th cap in March of that year against Switzerland.

A compact forward with sharp awareness in the penalty area, he has fine-edged reflexes and the close control to make space and finish in clinical style.

In May 1985, Dalglish was appointed player-manager.

LEFT: Kenny Dalglish chases after John Wark, then of Ipswich Town but shortly afterwards to become a colleague in the Liverpool attack at Anfield. (ASP).
BELOW: As Scotland's most capped international, Dalglish was expected to reach a century of appearances in the national colours. (ASP).

Italy

In 1982, Italy emulated Brazil's feat of winning the World Cup three times, although they had to wait more than 40 years before achieving their third success.

Home advantage when staging the 1934 finals helped considerably towards the Italians' first title. Their manager, Vittorio Pozzo, was a shrewd leader, admirably controlling his temperamental team which included three former Argentine internationals.

Their most fiery game, which disintegrated because of weak refereeing, was against Spain. Seven Spaniards and four Italians were injured, one of the Italians suffering a broken leg. The replay was mercifully quieter and Italy reached the final against Czechoslovakia despite having to play three matches in four days. Moreover, they managed to beat the Czechs 2–1 in extra time.

With only two survivors from their successful side, Italy retained their title four years later when the finals were held in France. They might have had a tougher semi-final against Brazil but their over-confident opponents rested key players and Italy won 2–1. In the final Italy deservedly beat Hungary 4–2.

Oddly enough the Italians owed their success in 1982 to another convincing victory against the Brazilians. The Italian defence held the Brazilian attack and a hat-trick by Paolo Rossi gave them a memorable 3–2 victory. In the semi-final, Rossi hit both goals against Poland to produce a classic confrontation for the final against West Germany.

To have reached the final after a miserable performance in the opening group in which they succeeded in drawing all three games and scoring just twice was remarkable. In fact they had only reached the final stage by scoring one more goal than Cameroon, who also drew their trio of games. If there were reservations about their overall performance there was no denying that they were the most improved team over the tournament.

Paolo Rossi of Juventus became Italy's goalscoring hero in the 1982 World Cup finals in Spain. (Trevor Jones). RIGHT: Dino Zoff who captained his country at the ripe old age of 40. (ASP).

Rossi, the prodigal son of Italy, returned from a two-year suspension following a bribes scandal and struggled at first to find his form, but was lethal when he did so.

In the final he scored again in the 3–1 win. Italy shrugged off injury problems and showed themselves technically correct, professional and clinical in their finishing. In doing so the strictures of Italian domestic football were firmly put aside.

ITALIA

Maradona
CIRIO

Diego Armando Maradona is the most expensive player in the history of the game. His transfer to Napoli from Barcelona in the summer of 1984 was at the cost of £6.9 million.

Within hours of signing him, Napoli sold 40 000 season tickets at £150 each and recouped almost the entire sum they had paid out.

Two years earlier he had been signed by the Spanish club from Boca Juniors for a then world record fee of £4 235 000, although he had an unhappy spell in Spain suffering a bout of hepatitis which kept him out of action for three months and then a particularly severe ankle injury, the result of a blatant foul, one of many he received.

Born in Buenos Aires on 30 October 1960, he emerged originally with Argentinos Juniors, making his debut in the championship on 20 October 1976 in a 1–0 defeat against Talleres Cordoba.

His first appearance for the Argentine national team came on 27 February 1977 in a 4–1 win over Hungary, but the manager Luis Cesar Menotti wisely decided to leave him out of the 1978 World Cup squad so that he could mature at a steadier pace.

Voted South American Footballer of the Year in 1979 and 1980, he was transferred to Boca Juniors the following year after reaching a century of goals in the championship in just over 150 games while still only 20.

He scored 144 goals in 206 games for his two Argentine clubs before being transferred to Barcelona, where he added 45 goals in 74 competitive matches and friendlies. It was estimated that his £831 000 income from signing-on fees, wages and bonuses in two seasons cost £18 467 per goal!

Once established in the Argentine national team, Maradona scored 15 goals in 40 matches, but found it continually difficult not to retaliate against defenders anxious to challenge his ability and was sent off against Brazil in the World Cup in 1982.

An attacking midfield player of exceptional quality, vision, as well as supreme control and confidence, problems of weight and proneness to injury have hampered his further progress.

LEFT: Diego Maradona in the colours of Napoli during the 1984–85 season. (Dave Cannon). BELOW: An earlier view of the Argentine international wearing his country's blue and white stripes at Hampden Park in a match against Scotland. (Glasgow Herald).

Aberdeen

Aberdeen achieved a treble of honours in 1983–84, winning the League Championship, Scottish League Cup and European Super Cup. It was the culmination of several outstanding seasons which began in the late 1970s under Alex Ferguson's managership.

Architect of Aberdeen's recent successes has been Manager Alex Ferguson. In 1984–85 the club again carried off the championship and set fresh records for the Premier Division, despite the loss of key players to clubs abroad from the previous campaign. (Dave Cannon).

After success in the League Cup in 1976–77, they were runners-up in both League and Scottish Cup in 1977–78. Then the club won its first Premier Division honour in 1979–80 after twice finishing as beaten finalists in the League Cup.

In 1980–81, they were in second place again in the championship and repeated their near miss the following season, though they also beat Rangers in the Scottish Cup final 4–1 after extra time.

With a place in the Cup Winners' Cup in 1982–83, Aberdeen found themselves having to play in the preliminary round of the competition. But they made light of their first test despatching the Swiss club Sion 11–1 on aggregate.

Dinamo Tirana from Albania proved more difficult opposition in the first round proper, but again Aberdeen were successful by the only goal of the tie. Lech Poznan (Poland) were dismissed 3–0 over the two legs in the second round and Bayern Munich (West Germany) were edged out 3–2 after a courageous quarter-final win in the away leg.

Although Waterschei (Belgium) became the first team in the Cup Winners' Cup to defeat them, Aberdeen had enough goals to spare from the first leg to win through 5–2 on aggregate, earning a final place in Gothenburg against Spain's Real Madrid.

Victory here by the odd goal in three gave the club its first major European honour and was the second cup to come to Pittodrie that season after Aberdeen had again beaten Rangers 1–0 in extra time to retain the Scottish Cup.

In 1983–84, the strength and depth of Aberdeen's squad was underlined when the championship was won despite using 23 players, only one of whom appeared in every game. From 22 October to 3 March they went 16 games unbeaten in the League, dropping only two points. Postponed games in the winter called for them to play nine League games alone in three weeks at the season's end but they had clinched the title long before the finale. They conceded only 21 goals and amassed a record 57 points. Their four defeats equalled the previous record.

Earlier they had beaten Hamburg 2–0 for the Super Cup and retained the Scottish Cup for a third season by defeating Celtic 2–1 after extra time.

In 1985 Aberdeen won the League with a record 27 wins and 59 points, losing only 4 times.

Before his move to Manchester United in 1984, Gordon Strachan was an influential player in the Aberdeen midfield and contributed considerable strategy to their performances. (ASP).

Michel Platini

Michel Platini, the French international midfield player and captain, became European Footballer of the Year for the second year in succession in 1984. His first such honour had come in 1982–83 after his first season playing in Italian football with Juventus.

Born on 21 June 1955, he played seven seasons for Nancy in his native France, scoring 98 goals in 175 League appearances before moving to St Etienne. There he scored 58 goals in 107 appearances before being transferred to the Italian club in 1982 at the cost of £1.2 million. Despite the defensive prowess of Italian football, he was able to score 16 League goals and finished top of the First Division marksmen.

Juventus finished second that season, but won the championship in 1983–84 when Platini was again leading scorer with 20 goals. It proved a double triumph for Platini that summer as he captained France to a memorable European Championship title.

He scored nine times in the five games they played in the final series including two hat-tricks. He has scored more goals for France than any other player in the country's history and overtook Just Fontaine's previous record of 31 goals.

Platini came to national prominence in the 1976 Montreal Olympics and later played in both the 1978 and 1982 World Cup final competitions.

In earlier times he would have been described as a goalscoring inside-forward. Today, he is a mercurial midfield master wearing the No. 10 shirt, initiating and finishing attacks with skilled understanding and control. He is a free-kick expert and adept at eluding marking defenders, patiently waiting for just one lapse to steal away into space to produce either an opening for a colleague or for himself.

Platini is France's most accomplished marksman in three areas. Up to 1984 his 22 goals in World Cup and European Championship games were over half of the 41 overall for his country and in addition he had scored 19 goals in the European Cup for St Etienne and Juventus.

His ability to direct the ball with precision either for other players or for himself has made him unique in present football, where specialists are uncommon and individual accomplishment rarer.

LEFT: Michel Platini is held back by several Porto players in the 1984 Cup Winners Cup Final. (Dave Cannon). ABOVE: The master invites opposition. (Trevor Jones).

Liverpool's

Liverpool are the most successful club in English League football having won 15 Division 1 titles. Eight of these championships have been achieved in the last 13 seasons, 5 of them in the last 7 campaigns.

TOP: Ian St John (right) gets the better of this heading duel with Dave Mackay (Spurs). (ASP). ABOVE: Emlyn Hughes who led Liverpool on many of their triumphs in the 1970s. (ASP).

The club's first title came in 1900–01 when they won by two points from the early leaders Sunderland after remaining unbeaten in 12 games. Five seasons later and after relegation to Division 2 they finished four points in front of Preston North End, thus becoming the first team to win the championship of both Second and First Divisions.

They won the Division 1 championship again in 1921–22 and 1922–23, winning on both occasions by a margin of six points against Tottenham Hotspur and Sunderland respectively.

But the Anfield club had to wait until after the Second World War for their fifth championship in what proved their closest struggle for Division 1. Many postponements due to the weather led to the season being extended to 14 June and Liverpool had to wait two weeks after completing their programme before realizing their ambitions.

A spell of eight years in Division 2 from 1954 prevented further honours until 1963–64. The impact of manager Bill Shankly who arrived in December 1959 was now beginning to take shape.

In 1964, as champions again, Liverpool had four points to spare over Manchester United and two seasons later it was a margin of six over Leeds. Liverpool used only 14 players during that entire League campaign.

Title number eight arrived in 1973 with Arsenal three points behind, but in

championships

LEFT: Phil Neal succeeded to the Anfield captaincy and revealed a remarkable record of consistency at full-back. (ASP). ABOVE: Peter Thompson seen in action as a winger in the 1971 FA Cup Final against Arsenal. (ASP).

successive seasons 1975–76 and 1976–77 it was just a one point gap over first Queen's Park Rangers then Manchester City.

Liverpool with 68 points and conceding just 16 goals — both records — turned the tables on Nottingham Forest in 1978–79 by eight points having been runners-up to them previously. In 1979–80, the Reds retained the honour and in 1981–82 were 12th at the turn of the year but still gained the crown.

They lost twice in succession in early October 1982 and dropped to fifth, but they were never headed and became champions again with five games to go, although they actually took only one point from their last half dozen games!

In 1983–84 they had a similar lapse around October but were only once briefly caught from then on in winning their 15th championship, equalling the record of winning three successive titles.

Arthur Rowley

Arthur Rowley's aggregate total of 434 League goals has never been bettered in the history of the competition, yet the player himself missed several years of official scoring through starting his career during the Second World War.

In addition, he was never capped at full level, played most of his career in Division 2 and an England 'B' cap became his highest honour apart from playing for the Football League representative team.

Like his older brother, Jack, with whom he made his first senior appearance for Manchester United in the war years, George Arthur Rowley had a particularly strong left foot shot and his heavily built frame made him extremely difficult to shake off the ball.

He played chiefly in what was the inside-left position before becoming one of the twin strikers in the latter stages of his career, and his readiness to shoot on sight of goal made him a dangerous attacker.

While still an amateur he also assisted Wolverhampton Wanderers, his home town team, before joining West Bromwich Albion as a professional in 1944. He had been born on 21 April 1926.

Rowley showed his versatility by guesting for Brighton at left-back before going overseas in the Armed Forces. However, it was not until he moved to Fulham that his full potential as a marksman was revealed. And he came to their notice during 1948–49 on a day when he was given a rare first team outing for West Bromwich as deputy for Davy Walsh who was on international duty for the Republic of Ireland.

Having starred in Albion's win over Fulham he was eventually signed by the Craven Cottage club in exchange for winger Ernie Shepherd, having scored 4 goals in 24 games. But his 19 goals in 22 games pushed Fulham to promotion in Division 1.

He was less effective the following season scoring 8 times in 34 games and in the following close season was transferred to Leicester City where he also assisted them to two promotion campaigns into Division 1 in 1953–54 and 1956–57, the second of these seasons producing a personal best total of 44 goals.

Having scored 251 League goals for Leicester in 303 games he moved to Shrewsbury Town as player-manager in 1958 and in seven seasons there added a further 152 goals in 236 matches. At the end of his first season he maintained his record by guiding them to promotion from Divison 3.

After retiring, Rowley carried on as manager until taking charge of Sheffield United in 1968 and later Southend United who he also piloted to Division 3 in 1972.

More Great Derbies

Sheffield steel — Sheffield United v Sheffield Wednesday

United were founded in 1889, Wednesday in 1867. Of the 92 matches played between the clubs United have won 35, Wednesday 30, and 27 have been drawn.

League results at Bramall Lane (United's score first)

Season	Score	Season	Score
1893–94	1–1	1927–28	1–1
1894–95	1–0	1928–29	1–1
1895–96	1–1	1929–30	2–2
1896–97	2–0	1930–31	1–1
1897–98	1–1	1931–32	1–1
1898–99	2–1	1932–33	2–3
1900–01	1–0	1933–34	5–1
1901–02	3–0	1937–38	2–1
1902–03	2–3	1938–39	0–0
1903–04	1–1	1949–50	2–0
1904–05	4–2	1951–52	7–3
1905–06	0–2	1953–54	2–0
1906–07	2–1	1954–55	1–0
1907–08	1–3	1958–59	1–0
1908–09	2–1	1961–62	1–0
1909–10	3–3	1962–63	2–2
1910–11	0–1	1963–64	1–1
1911–12	1–1	1964–65	2–3
1912–13	0–2	1965–66	1–0
1913–14	0–1	1966–67	1–0
1914–15	0–1	1967–68	0–1
1919–20	3–0	1970–71	3–2
1926–27	2–0	1979–80	1–1

League results at Hillsborough (Wednesday's score first)

Season	Score	Season	Score
1893–94	1–2	1927–28	3–3
1894–95	2–3	1928–29	5–2
1895–96	1–0	1929–30	1–1
1896–97	1–1	1930–31	1–3
1897–98	0–1	1931–32	2–1
1898–99	1–1	1932–33	3–3
1900–01	1–0	1933–34	0–1
1901–02	1–0	1937–38	0–1
1902–03	0–1	1938–39	1–0
1903–04	3–0	1949–50	2–1
1904–05	1–3	1951–52	1–3
1905–06	1–0	1953–54	3–2
1906–07	2–2	1954–55	1–2
1907–08	2–0	1958–59	2–0
1908–09	1–0	1961–62	1–2
1909–10	1–3	1962–63	3–1
1910–11	2–0	1963–64	3–0
1911–12	1–1	1964–65	0–2
1912–13	1–0	1965–66	2–2
1913–14	2–1	1966–67	2–2
1914–15	1–1	1967–68	1–1
1919–20	2–1	1970–71	0–0
1926–27	2–3	1979–80	4–0

West Country clashes — Bristol City v Bristol Rovers

Bristol City were founded in 1894 as Bristol South End and became known under their present title in 1897. Bristol Rovers were founded in 1883 as Black Arabs, changed to Eastville Rovers in 1884, Bristol Eastville Rovers in 1897 and became known as Bristol Rovers in 1898. The 62 League meetings between the two clubs have resulted in Bristol City winning 25 matches, Rovers 14, with the other 22 drawn.

League results at Ashton Gate (City's score first)

Season	Score	Season	Score
1922–23	0–1	1951–52	1–1
1924–25	2–0	1952–53	0–0
1925–26	0–0	1955–56	1–1
1926–27	3–1	1956–57	5–3
1932–33	3–1	1957–58	3–2
1933–34	0–3	1958–59	1–1
1934–35	1–1	1959–60	2–1
1935–36	0–2	1962–63	4–1
1936–37	4–1	1963–64	3–0
1937–38	0–0	1964–65	2–1
1938–39	2–1	1974–75	1–1
1946–47	4–0	1975–76	1–1
1947–48	5–2	1980–81	0–0
1948–49	1–1	1981–82	1–2
1949–50	1–2	1984–85	3–0
1950–51	1–0		

League results at Eastville (Rovers' score first)

Season	Score	Season	Score
1922–23	1–2	1951–52	2–0
1924–25	0–0	1952–53	0–0
1925–26	0–1	1955–56	0–3
1926–27	0–5	1956–57	0–0
1932–33	1–1	1957–58	3–3
1933–34	5–1	1958–59	1–2
1934–35	2–2	1959–60	2–1
1935–36	1–1	1962–63	1–2
1936–37	3–1	1963–64	4–0
1937–38	1–0	1964–65	1–1
1938–39	1–1	1974–75	1–4
1946–47	0–3	1975–76	0–0
1947–48	0–2	1980–81	0–0
1948–49	3–1	1981–82	1–0
1949–50	2–3	1984–85	1–0
1950–51	2–1		

Glasgow divided — Rangers v Celtic

Rangers were founded in 1873, Celtic in 1888. Of the 196 Scottish League matches played between the clubs, Rangers have won 75, Celtic 62 and 59 have been drawn.

League results at Ibrox Park (Rangers' score first)

Season	Score	Season	Score
1890–91	1–2	1929–30	1–0
1891–92	1–1	1930–31	1–0
1892–93	2–2	1931–32	0–0
1893–94	5–0	1932–33	0–0
1894–95	1–1	1933–34	2–2
1895–96	2–4	1934–35	2–1
1896–97	2–0	1935–36	1–2
1897–98	0–4	1936–37	1–0
1898–99	4–1	1937–38	3–1
1899–1900	3–3	1938–39	2–1
1900–01	2–1	1946–47	1–1
1901–02	2–2	1947–48	2–0
1902–03	3–3	1948–49	4–0
1903–04	0–0	1949–50	4–0
1904–05	1–4	1950–51	1–0
1905–06	3–2	1951–52	1–1
1906–07	2–1	1952–53	1–0
1907–08	0–1	1953–54	1–1
1908–09	1–3	1954–55	4–1
1909–10	0–0	1955–56	0–0
1910–11	1–1	1956–57	2–0
1911–12	3–1	1957–58	2–3
1912–13	0–1	1958–59	2–1
1913–14	0–2	1959–60	3–1
1914–15	2–1	1960–61	2–1
1915–16	3–0	1961–62	2–2
1916–17	0–0	1962–63	4–0
1917–18	1–2	1963–64	2–1
1918–19	1–1	1964–65	1–0
1919–20	3–0	1965–66	2–1
1920–21	0–2	1966–67	2–2
1921–22	1–1	1967–68	1–0
1922–23	2–0	1968–69	1–0
1923–24	0–0	1969–70	0–1
1924–25	4–1	1970–71	1–1
1925–26	1–0	1971–72	2–3
1926–27	2–1	1972–73	2–1
1927–28	1–0	1973–74	0–1
1928–29	3–0		

1974–75	3–0	1980–81	3–0
1975–76	2–1		0–1
	1–0	1981–82	0–2
1976–77	0–1		1–0
	2–2	1982–83	1–2
1977–78	3–2		2–4
	3–1	1983–84	1–2
1978–79	1–1		1–0
	1–0	1984–85	0–0
1979–80	2–2		1–2
	1–1		

League results at Parkhead (Celtic's score first)

Season	Score	Season	Score
1890–91	2–2	1946–47	2–3
1891–92	3–0	1947–48	0–4
1892–93	3–0	1948–49	0–1
1893–94	3–2	1949–50	1–1
1894–95	5–3	1950–51	3–2
1895–96	6–2	1951–52	1–4
1896–97	1–1	1952–53	2–1
1897–98	0–0	1953–54	1–0
1898–99	0–4	1954–55	2–0
1899–1900	3–2	1955–56	0–1
1900–01	2–1	1956–57	0–2
1901–02	2–4	1957–58	0–1
1902–03	1–1	1958–59	2–2
1903–04	2–2	1959–60	0–1
1904–05	2–2	1960–61	1–5
1905–06	1–0	1961–62	1–1
1906–07	2–1	1962–63	0–1
1907–08	2–1	1963–64	0–1
1908–09	2–3	1964–65	3–1
1909–10	1–1	1965–66	5–1
1910–11	0–1	1966–67	2–0
1911–12	3–0	1967–68	2–2
1912–13	3–2	1968–69	2–4
1913–14	4–0	1969–70	0–0
1914–15	2–1	1970–71	2–0
1915–16	2–2	1971–72	2–1
1916–17	0–0	1972–73	3–1
1917–18	0–0	1973–74	1–0
1918–19	0–3	1974–75	1–2
1919–20	1–1	1975–76	1–1
1920–21	1–2		0–0
1921–22	0–0	1976–77	2–2
1922–23	1–3		1–0
1923–24	2–2	1977–78	1–1
1924–25	0–1		2–0
1925–26	2–2	1978–79	3–1
1926–27	0–1		4–2
1927–28	1–0	1979–80	1–0
1928–29	1–2		1–0
1929–30	1–2	1980–81	1–2
1930–31	2–0		3–1
1931–32	1–2	1981–82	3–3
1932–33	1–1		2–1
1933–34	2–2	1982–83	3–2
1934–35	1–1		0–0
1935–36	3–4	1983–84	2–1
1936–37	1–1		3–0
1937–38	3–0	1984–85	1–1
1938–39	6–2		1–1

Dundee v Dundee United

Dundee were founded in 1893 while Dundee United were formed in 1909 as Dundee Hibernians; they became known as Dundee United in 1923.
The 66 League meetings between the two clubs have resulted in Dundee United winning 32 times to Dundee's 23 with 11 drawn matches.

League results at Dens Park (Dundee's score first)

Season	Score	Season	Score
1925–26	0–0	1971–72	6–4
1926–27	5–0	1972–73	3–0
1929–30	1–0	1973–74	0–1
1931–32	1–1	1974–75	2–0
1938–39	2–0	1975–76	0–0
1946–47	2–0		2–1
1960–61	3–0	1979–80	1–0
1961–62	4–1		1–1
1962–63	1–2	1981–82	1–3
1963–64	1–1		0–2
1964–65	2–4	1982–83	0–2
1965–66	0–5		1–2
1966–67	2–3	1983–84	1–4
1967–68	2–2		2–5
1968–69	1–2	1984–85	0–2
1969–70	1–2		1–0
1970–71	2–3		

League results at Tannadice Park (Dundee United's score first)

Season	Score	Season	Score
1925–26	0–1	1971–72	1–1
1926–27	1–0	1972–73	2–1
1929–30	0–1	1973–74	1–2
1931–32	0–3	1974–75	3–0
1938–39	3–0	1975–76	1–2
1946–47	1–2		1–0
1960–61	3–1	1979–80	3–0
1961–62	1–2		2–0
1962–63	1–1	1981–82	5–2
1963–64	2–1		1–1
1964–65	1–4	1982–83	1–0
1965–66	2–1		5–3
1966–67	1–4	1983–84	0–1
1967–68	0–0		1–1
1968–69	3–1	1984–85	3–4
1969–70	4–1		4–0
1970–71	3–2		

The homes of Dundee United (left) and Dundee are close indeed. (D. C. Thomson). BELOW: Hearts and Hibs battle it out. (Scotsman Publications).

Capital clashes — Heart of Midlothian v Hibernian

Heart of Midlothian were founded in 1874 and Hibernian in 1875. The two clubs have played each other 162 times in the League; Hearts have won 69 matches, Hibs 49 and 44 have been drawn.

League results at Tynecastle (Hearts' score first)

Season	Score	Season	Score
1895–96	4–3	1938–39	0–1
1896–97	1–0	1946–47	2–3
1897–98	3–2	1947–48	2–1
1898–99	4–0	1948–49	3–2
1899–1900	1–3	1949–50	5–2
1900–01	0–3	1950–51	2–1
1901–02	2–1	1951–52	1–1
1902–03	1–1	1952–53	1–2
1903–04	2–0	1953–54	4–0
1904–05	1–0	1954–55	5–1
1905–06	1–0	1955–56	0–1
1906–07	4–1	1956–57	0–2
1907–08	1–2	1957–58	3–1
1908–09	1–1	1958–59	1–3
1909–10	1–0	1959–60	2–2
1910–11	2–0	1960–61	1–2
1911–12	3–0	1961–62	4–2
1912–13	1–0	1962–63	3–3
1913–14	3–1	1963–64	4–2
1914–15	3–1	1964–65	0–1
1915–16	1–3	1965–66	0–4
1916–17	2–1	1966–67	0–0
1917–18	1–0	1967–68	1–4
1918–19	3–1	1968–69	0–0
1919–20	1–3	1969–70	0–2
1920–21	5–1	1970–71	0–0
1921–22	0–2	1971–72	0–2
1922–23	2–2	1972–73	0–7
1923–24	1–1	1973–74	4–1
1924–25	2–0	1974–75	0–0
1925–26	1–4	1975–76	1–1
1926–27	2–2		0–1
1927–28	2–2	1976–77	0–1
1928–29	1–1		2–2
1929–30	1–1	1978–79	1–1
1930–31	4–1		1–2
1933–34	0–0	1983–84	3–2
1934–35	5–2		1–1
1935–36	8–3	1984–85	0–0
1936–37	3–2		2–2
1937–38	3–2		

League results at Easter Road (Hibs score first)

Season	Score	Season	Score
1895–96	3–2	1938–39	4–0
1896–97	2–0	1946–47	0–1
1897–98	1–1	1947–48	3–1
1898–99	5–1	1948–49	3–1
1899–1900	1–0	1949–50	1–2
1900–01	0–0	1950–51	0–1
1901–02	1–2	1951–52	2–3
1902–03	0–0	1952–53	3–1
1903–04	4–2	1953–54	1–2
1904–05	3–0	1954–55	2–3
1905–06	0–3	1955–56	2–2
1906–07	0–0	1956–57	2–3
1907–08	2–3	1957–58	0–2
1908–09	0–1	1958–59	0–4
1909–10	1–4	1959–60	1–5
1910–11	1–0	1960–61	1–4
1911–12	0–4	1961–62	1–4
1912–13	0–3	1962–63	0–4
1913–14	1–2	1963–64	1–1
1914–15	2–2	1964–65	3–5
1915–16	1–2	1965–66	2–3
1916–17	0–2	1966–67	3–1
1917–18	1–3	1967–68	1–0
1918–19	1–3	1968–69	1–3
1919–20	2–4	1969–70	0–0
1920–21	3–0	1970–71	0–0
1921–22	2–1	1971–72	0–0
1922–23	2–1	1972–73	2–0
1923–24	1–1	1973–74	3–1
1924–25	2–1	1974–75	2–1
1925–26	0–0	1975–76	3–0
1926–27	2–2		1–0
1927–28	2–1	1976–77	3–1
1928–29	1–0		1–1
1929–30	1–1	1978–79	1–1
1930–31	2–2		1–2
1933–34	1–4	1983–84	1–1
1934–35	1–0		0–0
1935–36	1–1	1984–85	1–2
1936–37	3–3		1–2
1937–38	2–2		

Teams who have scored eight or more goals in post-war Football League matches

Season	Match				Other 10-goal games not shown on left			
1946–47	Newcastle United	13	Newport County	0	Liverpool	7	Chelsea	4
	Reading	10	Crystal Palace	2	Wolverhampton W	6	Chelsea	4
	Bristol City	9	Aldershot	0				
	Doncaster Rovers	5	Carlisle United	2				
	Doncaster Rovers	8	Barrow	0				
	Accrington Stanley	8	Lincoln City	4				
	Northampton Town	0	Walsall	8				
	Rotherham United	8	Oldham Athletic	0				
1947–48	Arsenal	8	Grimsby Town	0	Preston North End	7	Derby County	4
	Wolverhampton W	8	Grimsby Town	1	Port Vale	6	Aldershot	4
1948–49	Notts County	11	Newport County	1	Walsall	5	Millwall	6
	Notts County	9	Exeter City	0				
	Notts County	9	Ipswich Town	2				
	Brentford	8	Bury	2				
	Carlisle United	1	Rotherham United	8				

Season								
1949–50					Newport County	6	Bristol City	4
1950–51	Gillingham	9	Exeter City	4	Derby County	6	Sunderland	5
	Nottingham Forest	9	Gillingham	2	Middlesbrough	7	Charlton Athletic	3
	Brighton & Hove Albion	9	Newport County	1				
	Lincoln City	9	Accrington Stanley	1				
	Middlesbrough	8	Huddersfield Town	0				
	Southend United	8	Swindon	2				
1951–52	Oldham Athletic	11	Chester	2	Sheffield United	7	Sheffield Wednesday	3
	Lincoln City	11	Crewe Alexandra	1	Leicester City	5	Sheffield United	5
	Torquay United	9	Swindon Town	0				
	Bury	8	Southampton	2				
	Grimsby Town	8	Halifax Town	1				
	Norwich City	8	Walsall	0				
1952–53	Blackpool	8	Charlton Athletic	4	Wolverhampton W	7	Manchester City	3
	Huddersfield Town	8	Everton	2	Fulham	4	Leicester City	6
	Carlisle United	8	Scunthorpe United	0	Nottingham Forest	6	Swansea City	4
	Shrewsbury Town	1	Norwich City	8	Bolton Wanderers	4	Arsenal	2
1953–54	Leicester City	9	Lincoln City	2	Newcastle United	3	West Bromwich Albion	7
	Lincoln City	8	Blackburn Rovers	0	Bradford City	6	Accrington Stanley	4
	Everton	8	Plymouth Argyle	4	Shrewsbury	6	Watford	4
	Charlton Athletic	8	Middlesbrough	1				
	Wolverhampton W	8	Chelsea	1				
	Hull	8	Oldham Athletic	0				
	Wrexham	8	Workington Town	0				
1954–55	Birmingham City	9	Liverpool	1	Chelsea	5	Manchester United	6
	Blackburn Rovers	9	Middlesbrough	0	Luton Town	7	Blackburn Rovers	3
	Blackburn Rovers	8	Bristol Rovers	3	West Bromwich Albion	6	Leicester City	4
					Chesterfield	3	Stockport County	7
					Southampton	6	Brentford	4
					Wolverhampton W	6	Huddersfield Town	4
1955–56	Cardiff City	1	Wolverhampton W	9	Blackpool	7	Sunderland	3
	Leyton Orient	8	Aldershot	3	Blackburn Rovers	4	Bristol City	6
	Leyton Orient	8	Crystal Palace	0				
	Luton Town	8	Sunderland	2				
	Chesterfield	8	Crewe Alexandra	0				
	Stockport County	8	Carlisle United	1				
1956–57	York City	9	Southport	1	Wolverhampton W	7	Charlton Athletic	3
	Sunderland	8	Charlton Athletic	1	Arsenal	7	Manchester City	3
	Stoke City	8	Lincoln City	0	Fulham	7	Swansea City	3
					Mansfield Town	7	Darlington	3
					Shrewsbury Town	7	Swindon Town	3
					Crewe Alexandra	6	Mansfield Town	4
					Wrexham	6	Carlisle United	4
1957–58	West Bromwich Albion	9	Manchester City	2	Charlton Atheltic	7	Huddersfield Town	6
	Chester	9	York City	2	Chelsea	7	Portsmouth	4
	Northampton Town	9	Exeter City	0	Burnley	7	Leicester City	3
	Hull	9	Oldham Athletic	0	Southampton	7	Norwich City	3
	Leicester City	8	Manchester City	4	Mansfield Town	6	Bury	4
	Bury	8	Tranmere Rovers	2	Swansea City	6	Bristol Rovers	4
	Preston North End	8	Birmingham City	0				
	West Ham United	8	Rotherham United	0				
1958–59	Tottenham Hotspur	10	Everton	4	Bristol Rovers	7	Grimsby Town	3
	Hartlepool United	10	Barrow	1	Chelsea	6	Newcastle United	5
	Middlesbrough	9	Brighton & Hove Albion	0	Barnsley	4	Bristol City	7
	Tranmere Rovers	9	Accrington Stanley	0	Brighton & Hove Albion	4	Middlesbrough	6
	Plymouth Argyle	8	Mansfield Town	3	Doncaster Rovers	4	Plymouth Argyle	6
	Colchester United	8	Stockport County	2				
	Aldershot	8	Gateshead	1				
	Port Vale	8	Gateshead	0				
1959–60	Aston Villa	11	Charlton Athletic	1	Newcastle United	7	Manchester United	3
	Wolverhampton W	9	Fulham	0	Manchester City	4	Wolverhampton W	6
	Crystal Palace	9	Barrow	0	Plymouth Argyle	6	Charlton Athletic	4
	Crystal Palace	8	Watford	1				
	Newcastle United	8	Everton	2				
	Burnley	8	Nottingham Forest	0				
	Northampton Town	8	Oldham Athletic	1				
	Walsall	8	Southport	0				
1960–61	Stoke City	9	Plymouth Argyle	0	Charlton Athletic	6	Middlesbrough	6
	Queen's Park Rangers	9	Tranmere Rovers	2	Charlton Athletic	7	Portsmouth	4
	Crystal Palace	9	Accrington Stanley	2	Charlton Athletic	6	Plymouth	4
					Plymouth Argyle	6	Charlton Athletic	4
					Newcastle United	5	West Ham United	5

1961–62	Wrexham	10	Hartlepool United	1	Barnsley	7	Bristol City	3
	Colchester United	9	Bradford City	1	Southampton	6	Scunthorpe United	4
	Aston Villa	8	Leicester City	3				
	Everton	8	Cardiff City	3				
	Notts County	8	Newport County	1				
1962–63	Oldham Athletic	11	Southport	0	Blackburn Rovers	5	Arsenal	5
	Tottenham Hotspur	9	Nottingham Forest	2				
	Wolverhampton W	8	Manchester City	1				
1963–64	Fulham	10	Ipswich Town	1	Southampton	6	Derby County	4
	Stoke City	9	Ipswich Town	1				
	West Ham United	2	Blackburn Rovers	8				
	Doncaster Rovers	10	Darlington	0				
	Brentford	9	Wrexham	0				
	Torquay United	8	Newport County	3				
	Aldershot	8	Barrow	2				
	Manchester City	8	Scunthorpe United	1				
	Coventry City	8	Shrewsbury Town	1				
1964–65	Mansfield Town	8	Queen's Park Rangers	1	Birmingham City	5	Blackburn	5
	Scunthorpe United	8	Luton Town	1	Tottenham Hotspur	7	Wolverhampton W	4
					Oldham Athletic	7	Bristol City	3
1965–66	Southampton	9	Wolverhampton W	3	Tottenham Hotspur	5	Aston Villa	5
	Preston North End	9	Cardiff City	0	Birmingham City	5	Derby County	5
	Brighton & Hove Albion	9	Southend United	1	Rotherham United	6	Cardiff City	4
					Brighton & Hove Albion	6	Mansfield Town	4
1966–67	Lincoln City	8	Luton Town	1	Chelsea	5	West Ham United	5
					Doncaster Rovers	4	Mansfield Town	6
1967–68	West Bromwich Albion	8	Burnley	1	West Ham United	7	Manchester City	3
1968–69	Manchester United	8	Queen's Park Rangers	1				
	West Ham United	8	Sunderland	0				
1969–70	Bradford City	8	Bournemouth	1	Bolton Wanderers	6	Queen's Park Rangers	4
	Preston North End	8	Oldham Athletic	1				
	Halifax Town	0	Fulham	8				
	Reading	8	Southport	0				
1970–71					Shrewsbury Town	7	Port Vale	3
					Brentford	6	York City	4
1971–72	Everton	8	Southampton	0				
1972–73	Chester	8	Peterborough United	2				
1973–74	Brighton & Hove Albion	2	Bristol Rovers	8				
	Crewe Alexandra	1	Rotherham United	8				
1974–75					Shrewsbury Town	7	Doncaster Rovers	4
					Bournemouth	3	Plymouth Argyle	7
1976–77	Derby County	8	Tottenham Hotspur	2				
1977–78	Tottenham Hotspur	9	Bristol Rovers	0	Crewe Alexandra	4	Brentford	6
	Swansea City	8	Hartlepool United	0				
1978–79					Bristol Rovers	5	Charlton Athletic	5
1979–80	Swindon Town	8	Bury	0	Orient	3	Chelsea	7
1980–81	Lincoln City	8	Northampton Town	0				
1981–82					Southampton	5	Coventry City	5
					Sheffield United	7	Northampton Town	3
1982–83	Watford	8	Sunderland	0	Doncaster Rovers	7	Reading	5
					Aldershot	6	Rochdale	4
1983–84	Southampton	8	Coventry City	2				
	Bolton Wanderers	8	Walsall	1				
1984–85					Queen's Park Rangers	5	Newcastle United	5
					Plymouth Argyle	6	Preston North End	4

Football League goalscorers

Division 1 from 1888–89, other divisions since 1919–20 because of the difficulty in checking earlier scorers.

1888–1915

Season	Leading scorer	Team	Goals
1888–89	John Goodall	Preston North End	21
1889–90	Jimmy Ross	Preston North End	24
1890–91	Jack Southworth	Blackburn Rovers	26
1891–92	John Campbell	Sunderland	32
1892–93	John Campbell	Sunderland	31
1893–94	Jack Southworth	Everton	27
1894–95	John Campbell	Sunderland	22
1895–96	Johnny Campbell	Aston Villa	20
1895–96	Steve Bloomer	Derby County	20
1896–97	Steve Bloomer	Derby County	22
1897–98	Fred Wheldon	Aston Villa	21
1898–99	Steve Bloomer	Derby County	23
1899–1900	Bill Garratt	Aston Villa	27
1900–01	Steve Bloomer	Derby County	24
1901–02	James Settle	Everton	18
1901–02	Fred Priest	Sheffield United	18
1902–03	Alec Raybould	Liverpool	31
1903–04	Steve Bloomer	Derby County	20
1904–05	Arthur Brown	Sheffield United	23
1905–06	Bullet Jones	Birmingham City	26
1905–06	Albert Shepherd	Bolton Wanderers	26
1906–07	Alec Young	Everton	30
1907–08	Enoch West	Nottingham Forest	27
1908–09	Bert Freeman	Everton	38
1909–10	John Parkinson	Liverpool	29
1910–11	Albert Shepherd	Newcastle United	25
1911–12	Harold Hampton	Aston Villa	25
1911–12	Dave McLean	Sheffield Wednesday	25
1911–12	George Holley	Sunderland	35
1912–13	David McLean	Sheffield Wednesday	30
1913–14	George Elliot	Middlesbrough	31
1914–15	Bobby Parker	Everton	35

Division 1 1919–39

Season	Leading scorer	Team	Goals
1919–20	Fred Morris	West Bromwich Albion	37
1920–21	Joe Smith	Bolton Wanderers	38
1921–22	Andy Wilson	Middlesbrough	31
1922–23	Charlie Buchan	Sunderland	30
1923–24	Wilf Chadwick	Everton	28
1924–25	Fred Roberts	Manchester City	31
1925–26	Ted Harper	Blackburn Rovers	43
1926–27	Jimmy Trotter	Sheffield Wednesday	37
1927–28	Dixie Dean	Everton	60
1928–29	Dave Halliday	Sunderland	43
1929–30	Vic Watson	West Ham United	41
1930–31	Pongo Waring	Aston Villa	49
1931–32	Dixie Dean	Everton	44
1932–33	Jack Bowers	Derby County	35
1933–34	Jack Bowers	Derby County	35
1934–35	Ted Drake	Arsenal	42
1935–36	Ginger Richardson	West Bromwich Albion	39
1936–37	Freddie Steele	Stoke City	33
1937–38	Tommy Lawton	Everton	28
1938–39	Tommy Lawton	Everton	35

Division 1 1946–85

Season	Leading scorer	Team	Goals
1946–47	Dennis Westcott	Wolverhampton Wanderers	37
1947–48	Ronnie Rooke	Arsenal	33
1948–49	Willie Moir	Bolton Wanderers	25
1949–50	Dickie Davis	Sunderland	25
1950–51	Stan Mortensen	Blackpool	30
1951–52	George Robledo	Newcastle United	33
1952–53	Charlie Wayman	Preston North End	24
1953–54	Jimmy Glazzard	Huddersfield Town	29
1953–54	Johnny Nicholls	West Bromwich Albion	29
1954–55	Ronnie Allen	West Bromwich Albion	27
1955–56	Nat Lofthouse	Bolton Wanderers	33
1956–57	John Charles	Leeds United	38
1957–58	Bobby Smith	Tottenham Hotspur	36
1958–59	Jimmy Greaves	Chelsea	32
1959–60	Dennis Viollet	Manchester United	32
1960–61	Jimmy Greaves	Chelsea	41
1961–62	Ray Crawford	Ipswich Town	33
1961–62	Derek Kevan	West Bromwich Albion	33
1962–63	Jimmy Greaves	Tottenham Hotspur	37
1963–64	Jimmy Greaves	Tottenham Hotspur	35
1964–65	Jimmy Greaves	Tottenham Hotspur	29
1964–65	Andy McEvoy	Blackburn Rovers	29
1965–66	Roger Hunt	Liverpool	30
1966–67	Ron Davies	Southampton	37
1967–68	George Best	Manchester United	28
1967–68	Ron Davies	Southampton	28
1968–69	Jimmy Greaves	Tottenham Hotspur	27
1969–70	Jeff Astle	West Bromwich Albion	25
1970–71	Tony Brown	West Bromwich Albion	28
1971–72	Francis Lee	Manchester City	33
1972–73	Bryan Robson	West Ham United	28
1973–74	Mick Channon	Southampton	21
1974–75	Malcolm Macdonald	Newcastle United	21
1975–76	Ted MacDougall	Norwich City	23
1976–77	Malcolm Macdonald	Arsenal	25
1976–77	Andy Gray	Aston Villa	25
1977–78	Bob Latchford	Everton	30
1978–79	Frank Worthington	Bolton Wanderers	24
1979–80	Phil Boyer	Southampton	23
1980–81	Steve Archibald	Tottenham Hotspur	20
1980–81	Peter Withe	Aston Villa	20
1981–82	Kevin Keegan	Southampton	26
1982–83	Luther Blissett	Watford	27
1983–84	Ian Rush	Liverpool	32
1984–85	Kerry Dixon	Chelsea	24
	Gary Lineker	Leicester City	24

Vic Watson, who holds the scoring record for West Ham United with 41 goals in 1929–30. (Colorsport).

Division 2 1919–39

Season	Leading scorer	Team	Goals
1919–20	Sam Taylor	Huddersfield Town	35
1920–21	Syd Puddefoot	West Ham United	29
1921–22	Jimmy Broad	Stoke City	25
1922–23	Harry Bedford	Blackpool	32
1923–24	Harry Bedford	Blackpool	34
1924–25	Arthur Chandler	Leicester City	33
1925–26	Bob Turnbull	Chelsea	39
1926–27	George Camsell	Middlesbrough	59
1927–28	Jimmy Cookson	West Bromwich Albion	38
1928–29	Jimmy Hampson	Blackpool	40
1929–30	Jimmy Hampson	Blackpool	45
1930–31	Dixie Dean	Everton	39
1931–32	Cyril Pearce	Swansea Town	35
1932–33	Ted Harper	Preston North End	37
1933–34	Pat Glover	Grimsby Town	42
1934–35	Jack Milsom	Bolton Wanderers	31
1935–36	Jack Dodds	Sheffield United	34
1935–36	Bob Finan	Blackpool	34
1936–37	Jack Bowers	Leicester City	33
1937–38	George Henson	Bradford Park Avenue	27
1938–39	Hugh Billington	Luton Town	28

Division 2 1946–85

Season	Leading scorer	Team	Goals
1946–47	Charlie Waymen	Newcastle United	30
1947–48	Eddie Quigley	Sheffield Wednesday	23
1948–49	Charlie Wayman	Southampton	32
1949–50	Tommy Briggs	Grimsby Town	35
1950–51	Cecil McCormack	Barnsley	33
1951–52	Derek Dooley	Sheffield Wednesday	46
1952–53	Arthur Rowley	Leicester City	39
1953–54	John Charles	Leeds United	42
1954–55	Tommy Briggs	Blackburn Rovers	33
1955–56	Bill Gardiner	Leicester City	34
1956–57	Arthur Rowley	Leicester City	44
1957–58	Tom Johnston	Leyton Orient (35) and Blackburn Rovers (8)	43
1958–59	Brian Clough	Middlesbrough	42
1959–60	Brian Clough	Middlesbrough	39
1960–61	Ray Crawford	Ipswich Town	39
1961–62	Roger Hunt	Liverpool	41
1962–63	Bobby Tambling	Chelsea	35
1963–64	Ron Saunders	Portsmouth	33
1964–65	George O'Brien	Southampton	34
1965–66	Martin Chivers	Southampton	30
1966–67	Bobby Gould	Coventry City	24
1967–68	John Hickton	Middlesbrough	24
1968–69	John Toshack	Cardiff City	22
1969–70	John Hickton	Middlesbrough	24
1970–71	John Hickton	Middlesbrough	25
1971–72	Bob Latchford	Birmigham City	23
1972–73	Don Givens	Queen's Park Rangers	23
1973–74	Duncan McKenzie	Nottingham Forest	26
1974–75	Brian Little	Aston Villa	20
1975–76	Derek Hales	Charlton Athletic	28
1976–77	Mickey Walsh	Blackpool	26
1977–78	Bob Hatton	Blackpool	22
1978–79	Bryan Robson	West Ham United	24
1979–80	Clive Allen	Queen's Park Rangers	28
1980–81	David Cross	West Ham United	22
1981–82	Ronnie Moore	Rotherham United	22
1982–83	Gary Lineker	Leicester City	26
1983–84	Kerry Dixon	Chelsea	28
1984–85	John Aldridge	Oxford United	30

Division 3 (South) 1920–39

Season	Leading scorer	Team	Goals
1920–21	John Connor	Crystal Palace	28
1920–21	Ernie Simms	Luton Town	28
1920–21	George Whitworth	Northampton Town	28
1921–22	Frank Richardson	Plymouth Argyle	31
1922–23	Fred Pagnam	Watford	30
1923–24	Billy Haines	Portsmouth	28
1924–25	Jack Fowler	Swansea Town	28
1925–26	Jack Cock	Plymouth Argyle	32
1926–27	Harry Morris	Swindon Town	47
1927–28	Harry Morris	Swindon Town	38
1928–29	Andrew Rennie	Luton Town	43
1929–30	George Goddard	Queen's Park Rangers	37
1930–31	Peter Simpson	Crystal Palace	46
1931–32	Clarrie Bourton	Coventry City	49
1932–33	Clarrie Bourton	Coventry City	40
1933–34	Albert Dawes	Northampton Town (11) and Crystal Palace (16)	27
1934–35	Ralph Allen	Charlton Athletic	32
1935–36	Albert Dawes	Crystal Palace	38
1936–37	Joe Payne	Luton Town	55
1937–38	Harry Crawshaw	Mansfield Town	25
1938–39	Ben Morton	Swindon Town	28

Jimmy Glazzard (Huddersfield Town) bears down on the opposing goalkeeper. He was joint top Division

Division 3 (South) 1946–58

Season	Leading scorer	Team	Goals
1946–47	Don Clark	Bristol City	36
1947–48	Len Townsend	Bristol City	29
1948–49	Don McGibbon	Bournemouth	30
1949–50	Tommy Lawton	Notts County	31
1950–51	Wally Ardron	Nottingham Forest	35
1951–52	Ronnie Blackman	Reading	39
1952–53	Geoff Bradford	Bristol Rovers	33
1953–54	Jack English	Northampton Town	28
1954–55	Ernie Morgan	Gillingham	31
1955–56	Sammy Collins	Torquay United	40
1956–57	Ted Phillips	Ipswich Town	41
1957–58	Sam McCrory	Southend United	31
1957–58	Derek Reeves	Southampton	31

Division 3 (North) 1921–39

Season	Leading scorer	Team	Goals
1921–22	Jim Carmichael	Grimsby Town	37
1922–23	George Beel	Chesterfield	23
1922–23	Jim Carmichael	Grimsby Town	23
1923–24	David Brown	Darlington	27
1924–25	David Brown	Darlington	39
1925–26	Jimmy Cookson	Chesterfield	44
1926–27	Albert Whitehurst	Rochdale	44
1927–28	Joe Smith	Stockport County	38
1928–29	Jimmy McConnell	Carlisle United	43
1929–30	Frank Newton	Stockport County	36
1930–31	Jimmy McConnell	Carlisle United	37
1931–32	Alan Hall	Lincoln City	42
1932–33	Bill McNaughton	Hull City	39
1933–34	Alf Lythgoe	Stockport County	46
1934–35	Gilbert Alsop	Walsall	40
1935–36	Bunny Bell	Tranmere Rovers	33
1936–37	Ted Harston	Mansfield Town	55
1937–38	John Roberts	Port Vale	28
1938–39	Sam Hunt	Carlisle United	32

Division 3 (North) 1946–58

Season	Leading scorer	Team	Goals
1946–47	Clarrie Jordan	Doncaster Rovers	42
1947–48	Jimmy Hutchinson	Lincoln City	32
1948–49	Wally Ardron	Rotherham United	29
1949–50	Peter Doherty	Doncaster Rovers	26
1949–50	Reg Phillips	Crewe Alexandra	26
1950–51	Jack Shaw	Rotherham United	37
1951–52	Andy Graver	Lincoln City	36
1952–53	Jimmy Whitehouse	Carlisle United	29
1953–54	Jack Connor	Stockport County	31
1954–55	Jack Connor	Stockport County	30
1954–55	Arthur Bottom	York City	30
1954–55	Don Travis	Oldham Athletic	30
1955–56	Bob Crosbie	Grimsby Town	36
1956–57	Ray Straw	Derby County	37
1957–58	Alf Ackerman	Carlisle United	35

Division 3 1958–85

Season	Leading scorer	Team	Goals
1958–59	Jim Towers	Brentford	32
1959–60	Derek Reeves	Southampton	39
1960–61	Tony Richards	Walsall	36
1961–62	Cliff Holton	Northampton Town (36) and Walsall (1)	37
1962–63	George Hudson	Coventry City	30
1963–64	Alf Biggs	Bristol Rovers	30
1964–65	Ken Wagstaff	Mansfield Town (8) and Hull City (23)	31
1965–66	Les Allen	Queen's Park Rangers	30
1966–67	Rodney Marsh	Queen's Park Rangers	30
1967–68	Don Rogers	Swindon Town	25
1967–68	Bobby Owen	Bury	25
1968–69	Brian Lewis	Luton Town	22
1968–69	Don Rogers	Swindon Town	22
1969–70	George Jones	Bury	26
1970–71	Gerry Ingram	Preston North End	22
1970–71	Dudley Roberts	Mansfield Town	22
1971–72	Ted MacDougall	Bournemouth	35
1971–72	Alf Wood	Shrewsbury Town	35
1972–73	Bruce Bannister	Bristol Rovers	25
1972–73	Arthur Horsfield	Charlton Athletic	25
1973–74	Billy Jennings	Watford	26
1974–75	Dixie McNeil	Hereford United	31
1975–76	Dixie McNeil	Hereford United	35
1976–77	Peter Ward	Brighton & Hove Albion	32
1977–78	Alex Bruce	Preston North End	27
1978–79	Ross Jenkins	Watford	29
1979–80	Terry Curran	Sheffield Wednesday	22
1980–81	Tony Kellow	Exeter City	25
1981–82	Gordon Davies	Fulham	24
1982–83	Kerry Dixon	Reading	26
1983–84	Keith Edwards	Sheffield United	33
1984–85	Tommy Tynan	Plymouth Argyle	31

Division 4 1958–85

Season	Leading scorer	Team	Goals
1958–59	Arthur Rowley	Shrewsbury Town	37
1959–60	Cliff Holton	Watford	42
1960–61	Terry Bly	Peterborough United	52
1961–62	Bobby Hunt	Colchester United	41
1962–63	Ken Wagstaff	Mansfield Town	34
1962–63	Colin Booth	Doncaster Rovers	34
1963–64	Hugh McIlmoyle	Carlisle United	39
1964–65	Alick Jeffrey	Doncaster Rovers	36
1965–66	Kevin Hector	Bradford Park Avenue	44
1966–67	Ernie Phythian	Hartlepool United	23
1967–68	Roy Chapman	Port Vale	25
1967–68	Les Massie	Halifax Town	25
1968–69	Gary Talbot	Chester	22
1969–70	Albert Kinsey	Wrexham	27
1970–71	Ted MacDougall	Bournemouth	42
1971–72	Peter Price	Peterborough United	28
1972–73	Fred Binney	Exeter City	28
1973–74	Brian Yeo	Gillingham	31
1974–75	Ray Clarke	Mansfield Town	28
1975–76	Ronnie Moore	Tranmere Rovers	34
1976–77	Brian Joicey	Barnsley	25
1977–78	Steve Phillips	Brentford	32
1977–78	Alan Curtis	Swansea City	32
1978–79	John Dungworth	Aldershot	26
1979–80	Colin Garwood	Portsmouth (17) and Aldershot (10)	27
1980–81	Alan Cork	Wimbledon	23
1981–82	Keith Edwards	Sheffield United	36
1982–83	Steve Cammack	Scunthorpe United	25
1983–84	Trevor Senior	Reading	36
1984–85	John Clayton	Tranmere Rovers	31

LEFT: Peter Withe, joint top scorer in Division 1 in 1980–81. (ASP). **INSET:** Bill Hartill who holds a Wolves scoring record. (Colorsport). **BELOW:** George Camsell, a Middlesbrough marksman of repute. (Colorsport).

Arthur Chandler (Leicester City), the Second Division's leading scorer in 1924–25. (Colorsport).

Andy Gray in Aston Villa colours. (ASP).

Bob Latchford in Everton's strip. (ASP).

Phil Boyer (Southampton). (ASP).

Jack Connor (Stockport County).

Kerry Dixon (Chelsea). (ASP).

Leading goalscorer for each Football League Championship-winning team

Season	Player and team	Goals
1888–89	J. Goodall, Preston North End	21
1889–90	J. Ross, Preston North End	24
1890–91	F. Geary, Everton	20
1891–92	J. M. Campbell, Sunderland	32
1892–93	J. M. Campbell, Sunderland	31
1893–94	J. H. G. Devey, Aston Villa	21
1894–95	J. M. Campbell, Sunderland	25
1895–96	J. Campbell, Aston Villa	20
1896–97	G. F. Wheldon, Aston Villa	17
1897–98	W. Bennett, Sheffield United	12
1898–99	J. H. G. Devey, Aston Villa	22
1899–1900	W. Garratty, Aston Villa	27
1900–01	S. A. Raybould, Liverpool	16
1901–02	W. Hogg, Sunderland	10
1902–03	H. Davis, Sheffield Wednesday	14
1903–04	H. Chapman, Sheffield Wednesday	16
1904–05	W. Appleyard, Newcastle United	14
1905–06	J. Hewitt, Liverpool	22
1906–07	W. Appleyard, Newcastle United	17
1907–08	A. Turnbull, Manchester United	25
1908–09	A. Shepherd, Newcastle United	12
1909–10	H. Hampton, Aston Villa	26
1910–11	E. West, Manchester United	19
1911–12	W. Aitkenhead, Blackburn Rovers	16
1912–13	C. M. Buchan, Sunderand	27
1913–14	D. Shea, Blackburn Rovers	27
1914–15	R. N. Parker, Everton	35
1919–20	F. Morris, West Bromwich Albion	37
1920–21	J. Anderson, Burnley	25
1921–22	H. Chambers, Liverpool	19
1922–23	H. Chambers, Liverpool	23
1923–24	C. Wilson, Huddersfield Town	18
1924–25	C. Wilson, Huddersfield Town	24
1925–26	G. Brown, Huddersfield Town	35
1926–27	H. Gallacher, Newcastle United	36
1927–28	W. R. Dean, Everton	60
1928–29	J. D. W. Allen, Sheffield Wednesday	33
1929–30	J. D. W. Allen, Sheffield Wednesday	34
1930–31	J. Lambert, Arsenal	38
1931–32	W. R. Dean, Everton	44
1932–33	C. S. Bastin, Arsenal	33
1933–34	C. S. Bastin and E. R. Bowden, Arsenal	13
1934–35	E. J. Drake, Arsenal	42
1935–36	H. S. Carter, Sunderland	31
1936–37	P. D. Doherty, Manchester City	30
1937–38	E. J. Drake, Arsenal	17
1938–39	T. Lawton, Everton	35
1946–47	J. Balmer, Liverpool	24
1947–48	R. L. Rooke, Arsenal	33
1948–49	P. P. Harris, Portsmouth	17
1949–50	I. Clarke, Portsmouth	17
1950–51	L. S. Duquemin, Tottenham Hotspur	15
1951–52	J. F. Rowley, Manchester United	30
1952–53	D. Lishman, Arsenal	22
1953–54	J. Hancocks, Wolverhampton Wanderers	25
1954–55	R. T. F. Bentley, Chelsea	21
1955–56	T. Taylor, Manchester United	25
1956–57	W. Whelan, Manchester United	26
1957–58	J. Murray, Wolverhampton Wanderers	29
1958–59	J. Murray, Wolverhampton Wanderers	21
1959–60	J. Connelly, Burnley	20
1960–61	R. A. Smith, Tottenham Hotspur	28
1961–62	R. Crawford, Ipswich Town	33
1962–63	T. R. Vernon, Everton	24
1963–64	R. Hunt, Liverpool	31
1964–65	D. Law, Manchester United	28
1965–66	R. Hunt, Liverpool	30
1966–67	D. Law, Manchester United	23
1967–68	N. J. Young, Manchester City	19
1968–69	M. D. Jones, Leeds United	14
1969–70	J. Royle, Everton	23
1970–71	R. Kennedy, Arsenal	20
1971–72	A. Hinton, Derby County	15
1972–73	J. B. Toshack and J. K. Keegan, Liverpool	13
1973–74	M. D. Jones, Leeds United	14
1974–75	B. D. Rioch, Derby County	15
1975–76	J. B. Toshack, Liverpool	16
1976–77	J. K. Keegan, Liverpool	12
1977–78	P. Withe and J. M. Robertson, Nottingham Forest	12
1978–79	K. M. Dalglish, Liverpool	21
1979–80	D. E. Johnson, Liverpool	21
1980–81	P. Withe, Aston Villa	20
1981–82	I. J. Rush, Liverpool	17
1982–83	I. J. Rush, Liverpool	24
1983–84	I. J. Rush, Liverpool	32
1984–85	G. Sharp, Everton	21

Frank Worthington in Bolton Wanderers colours. (ASP).

Bob Hatton (Birmingham City) with initials on shorts. (ASP).

Highest aggregate goalscorers for each Football League club, in descending order

Goals	Player	Club	Years
349	Dixie Dean	Everton	1925–37
326	George Camsell	Middlesbrough	1925–39
315	John Atyeo	Bristol City	1951–66
306	Vic Watson	West Ham United	1920–35
291	Steve Bloomer	Derby County	1892–1906 1910–14
262	Arthur Chandler	Leicester City	1923–35
255	Nat Lofthouse	Bolton Wanderers	1946–61
249	Joe Bradford	Birmingham City	1920–35
247	Jimmy Hampson	Blackpool	1927–38
245	Geoff Bradford	Bristol Rovers	1949–64
245	Roger Hunt	Liverpool	1959–69
243	Gordon Turner	Luton Town	1949–64
220	Jimmy Greaves	Tottenham Hotspur	1961–70
218	Tony Brown	West Bromwich Albion	1963–79
216	Harry Morris	Swindon Town	1926–33
213	Harry Hampton	Aston Villa	1904–20
213	Billy Walker	Aston Villa	1919–34
209	Charlie Buchan	Sunderland	1911–25
205	Harry Johnson	Sheffield United	1919–30
204	Sammy Collins	Torquay United	1948–58
203	Ray Crawford	Ipswich Town	1958–63 1966–69
202	Ron Eyre	Bournemouth	1924–33
200	Andy Wilson	Sheffield Wednesday	1900–20
199	Grenville Morris	Nottingham Forest	1898–1913
198	Bobby Charlton	Manchester United	1956–73
195	Chris Chilton	Hull City	1960–71
194	Peter Harris	Portsmouth	1946–60
187	Tom Finney	Preston North End	1946–60
184	Tony Richards	Walsall	1954–63
184	Colin Taylor	Walsall	1958–63 1964–68 1969–73
182	Pat Glover	Grimsby Town	1930–39
182	Mike Channon	Southampton	1966–77 1979–82
180	Sammy Black	Plymouth Argyle	1924–38
180	Tom Keetley	Doncaster Rovers	1923–29
178	George Beel	Burnley	1923–32
178	Jackie Milburn	Newcastle United	1946–57
175	Tom Bamford	Wrexham	1928–34
172	George Goddard	Queen's Park Rangers	1926–34
171	Jack Howarth	Aldershot	1965–71 1972–77
171	Clarrie Bourton	Coventry City	1931–37
166	Ivor Allchurch	Swansea City	1949–58 1965–68
164	Bobby Tambling	Chelsea	1958–70
164	Bill Hartill	Wolverhampton Wanderers	1928–35
158	Tommy Johnson	Manchester City	1919–30
156	Ronnie Blackman	Reading	1947–54
155	Peter Lorimer	Leeds United	1965–79 1983–
154	Peter Simpson	Crystal Palace	1930–36
154	Bedford Jezzard	Fulham	1948–56
154	Wilf Kirkham	Port Vale	1923–29 1931–33
153	Stuart Leary	Charlton Athletic	1953–62
153	Jim Towers	Brentford	1954–61
152	Arthur Rowley	Shrewsbury Town	1958–65
150	Cliff Bastin	Arsenal	1930–47
144	Andy Graver	Lincoln City	1950–55 1958–61
144	Tom Barnett	Watford	1928–39
142	George Brown	Huddersfield Town	1921–29
142	Jimmy Glazzard	Huddersfield Town	1946–56
142	Freddie Steele	Stoke City	1934–39
140	Tommy Briggs	Blackburn Rovers	1952–58

RIGHT: Ron Eyre (Bournemouth). (Colorsport). INSET TOP: Billy Walker (Aston Villa). (Colorsport). INSET CENTRE: Harry Morris (Swindon Town). (Colorsport). INSET BELOW: Harry Johnson (Sheffield United). (Colorsport).

Joe Bradford (Birmingham City). (Colorsport).

139	Ernie Moss	Chesterfield	1969–76, 1979–81 1984–
135	Brian Yeo	Gillingham	1963–75
135	Jack English	Northampton Town	1947–60
132	Jack Connor	Stockport County	1951–56
131	Martyn King	Colchester United	1959–65
130	Gladstone Guest	Rotherham United	1946–56
129	Ernest Dixon	Halifax Town	1922–30
127	Len Davies	Cardiff City	1921–29
126	Jimmy McConnell	Carlisle United	1928–32
126	Bert Swindells	Crewe Alexandra	1928–37
125	Les Bradd	Notts County	1967–78
125	Norman Wilkinson	York City	1954–66
124	Norman Bullock	Bury	1920–35
123	Ernest Hine	Barnsley	1921–26 1934–38
122	Johnny Gavin	Norwich City	1946–54 1955–58
122	Roy Hollis	Southend United	1953–60
122	Jim Hall	Peterborough United	1967–75
121	Tom Johnston	Orient	1956–58 1959–61
119	Reg Jenkins	Rochdale	1964–73
113	Tommy Cook	Brighton & Hove Albion	1922–29
110	Eric Gemmell	Oldham Athletic	1947–54
108	Bobby Campbell	Bradford City	1981–84, and 1984–
106	Alan Cork	Wimbledon	1977–
105	Alan Banks	Exeter City	1963–66 1967–73
104	Harry Johnson	Mansfield Town	1931–36
104	Bunny Bell	Tranmere Rovers	1931–36
99	Reg Parker	Newport County	1948–54
98	Ken Johnson	Hartlepool United	1949–64
97	Steve Cammack	Scunthorpe United	1979–81, and 1981
90	Alan Walsh	Darlington	1978–84
85	Dixie McNeil	Hereford United	1974–77
83	Gary Talbot	Chester	1963–67 1968–70
79	Derek Possee	Millwall	1967–73
74	Alan Biley	Cambridge United	1975–80
73	Graham Atkinson	Oxford United	1962–73
62	Peter Houghton	Wigan Athletic	1978–84

Jack Howarth (Aldershot).

Alan Biley in Everton colours but with a Cambridge United record for goals. (ASP).

Players who, since the 1914–18 War, have scored as many as half of a team's Football League goals in a completed season

Player	Team	Division	Season	Goals	Out of
George Elliott	Middlesbrough	1	1919–20	31	61
Bob Blood	Port Vale	2	1919–20	24	42
Dave McLean	Bradford Park Avenue	1	1920–21	22	43
John McIntyre	Sheffield Wednesday	2	1920–21	27	48
Sid Puddefoot	West Ham United	2	1920–21	29	51
Jack Doran	Brighton & Hove Albion	3S	1920–21	22	42
Jack Doran	Brighton & Hove Albion	3S	1921–22	23	45
Jim Carmichael	Grimsby Town	3N	1921–22	37	72
Harry Bedford	Blackpool	2	1922–23	32	60
Fred Pagnam	Watford	3S	1922–23	30	57
Joe Bradford	Birmingham	1	1923–24	24	41
Tommy Roberts	Preston North End	1	1923–24	26	52
Hugh Davey	Bournemouth	3S	1923–24	20	40
Bertie Mills	Hull City	2	1924–25	25	50
Wilf Kirkham	Port Vale	2	1924–25	26	48
David Brown	Darlington	3N	1924–25	39	78
Tom Jennings	Leeds United	1	1926–27	35	69
Dixie Dean	Everton	1	1927–28	60	120
Tom Keetley	Doncaster Rovers	3N	1928–29	40	76
Jim McConnell	Carlisle United	3N	1928–29	43	86
Jimmy Dunne	Sheffield United	1	1930–31	41	78
Leopold Stevens	New Brighton	3N	1931–32	20	38
Ted Harper	Preston North End	2	1932–33	37	74
Jack Bowers	Derby County	1	1933–34	35	68
Albert Valentine	Halifax Town	3N	1935–36	29	57
Joe Payne	Luton Town	3S	1936–37	55	103
Ted Harston	Mansfield Town	3N	1936–37	55	91
John Charles	Leeds United	1	1956–57	38	72
Gordon Turner	Luton Town	1	1956–57	30	58
Colin Booth	Doncaster Rovers	4	1962–63	34	64
Ron Davies	Southampton	1	1966–67	37	74
Ted MacDougall	Bournemouth	4	1970–71	42	81

Note: Jack Doran, Irish international centre-forward, is the only player to have achieved this feat twice, and he did it in successive seasons.

Players scoring five goals or more in a Football League post-war match

Division 1

Player	For	Goals	Against	Home or away	Date
J. McIntosh	Blackpool	5	Preston North End	away	1.5.48
E. R. Firmani	Charlton Athletic	5	Aston Villa	home	5.2.55
A. Stokes	Tottenham Hotspur	5	Birmingham City	home	18.9.57
R. Smith	Tottenham Hotspur	5	Aston Villa	home	29.3.58
J. Greaves	Chelsea	5	Wolverhampton Wanderers	home	30.8.58
P. Harris	Portsmouth	5	Aston Villa	home	3.9.58
J. Robson	Burnley	5	Nottingham Forest	home	21.11.59
J. Greaves	Chelsea	5	Preston North End	away	19.12.59
D. T. Kevan	West Bromwich Albion	5	Everton	home	19.3.60
J. Greaves	Chelsea	5	West Bromwich Albion	home	3.12.60
B. Dear	West Ham United	5	West Bromwich Albion	home	16.3.65
A. Lochhead	Burnley	5	Chelsea	home	24.4.65
R. Tambling	Chelsea	5	Aston Villa	away	17.9.66
G. Hurst	West Ham United	6	Sunderland	home	19.10.68
R. Davies	Derby County	5	Luton Town	home	29.3.75
A. Brazil	Ipswich Town	5	Southampton	home	16.2.82
I. Rush	Liverpool	5	Luton Town	home	29.10.83
T. Woodcock	Arsenal	5	Aston Villa	away	29.10.83

Division 2

Players	For	Goals	Against	Home or Away	Date
L. F. Shackleton	Newcastle United	6	Newport County	home	5.10.46
E. Quigley	Bury	5	Millwall	home	15.2.47
G. Smith	Manchester City	5	Newport County	home	14.6.47
J. Dailey	Sheffield Wednesday	5	Barnsley	home	6.9.47
C. Wayman	Southampton	5	Leicester City	home	23.10.48
P. McKennan	Brentford	5	Bury	home	19.2.49
C. McCormack	Barnsley	5	Luton Town	home	9.9.50
D. Dooley	Sheffield Wednesday	5	Notts County	home	3.11.51
T. J. Eglington	Everton	5	Doncaster Rovers	home	27.9.52
D. Hines	Leicester City	5	Lincoln City	home	21.11.53
J. Evans	Liverpool	5	Bristol Rovers	home	15.9.54
T. H. Briggs	Blackburn Rovers	7	Bristol Rovers	home	5.2.55
B. Jezzard	Fulham	5	Hull City	home	8.10.55
N. Coleman	Stoke City	7	Lincoln City	home	23.2.57

Player	For	Goals	Against	Home or Away	Date
J. Summers	Charlton Athletic	5	Huddersfield	home	21.12.57
J. Hill	Fulham	5	Doncaster Rovers	away	15.3.58
B. Clough	Middlesbrough	5	Brighton & Hove Albion	home	23.8.58
G. Hitchens	Aston Villa	5	Charlton Athletic	home	14.11.59
J. Summers	Charlton Athletic	5	Portsmouth	home	1.10.60
W. Carter	Plymouth Argyle	5	Charlton Athletic	home	27.12.60
D. Sharkey	Sunderland	5	Norwich City	home	20.3.63
R. Pointer	Bury	5	Rotherham United	home	2.10.65
S. Garner	Blackburn Rovers	5	Derby County	home	10.9.83

Division 3 (Southern section)

Player	For	Goals	Against	Home or Away	Date
J. Devlin	Walsall	5	Torquay United	home	1.9.49
C. Mortimore	Aldershot	5	Leyton Orient	away	25.2.50
R. H. Blackman	Reading	5	Brighton & Hove Albion	home	11.11.50
R. W. Hollis	Norwich City	5	Walsall	home	29.12.51
R. H. Blackman	Reading	5	Southend United	home	14.4.52
A. Thorne	Brighton & Hove Albion	5	Watford	home	30.4.58

Division 3 (Northern section)

Player	For	Goals	Against	Home or Away	Date
A. Patrick	York City	5	Rotherham United	home	20.11.48
E. Passmore	Gateshead	5	Hartlepool United	away	5.9.49
A. Graver	Lincoln City	6	Crewe Alexandra	home	29.9.51
E. Gemmell	Oldham Athletic	7	Chester	home	19.1.52
J. T. Connor	Stockport County	5	Workington	home	8.11.52
J. E. Whitehouse	Carlisle United	5	Scunthorpe United	home	25.12.52
G. T. S. Stewart	Accrington Stanley	5	Gateshead	home	27.11.54
J. T. Connor	Stockport County	5	Carlisle United	home	7.4.56
J. Dailey	Rochdale	5	Hartlepool United	home	2.11.57
B. Jepson	Chester	5	York City	home	8.2.58

Division 3

Player	For	Goals	Against	Home or Away	Date
B. Thomas	Scunthorpe United	5	Luton Town	home	24.4.65
K. East	Swindon Town	5	Mansfield Town	home	20.11.65
S. Earle	Fulham	5	Halifax Town	away	16.9.69
A. Wood	Shrewsbury	5	Blackburn Rovers	home	2.10.71
T. Caldwell	Bolton Wanderers	5	Walsall	home	10.9.83

Division 4

Player	For	Goals	Against	Home or Away	Date
R. Folland	Hartlepool United	5	Oldham Athletic	home	1.4.61
R. Lister	Oldham Athletic	6	Southport	home	26.12.62
R. Stubbs	Torquay United	5	Newport County	home	19.10.63
K. Hector	Bradford	5	Barnsley	home	20.11.65
D. Banton	Aldershot	5	Halifax Town	home	7.5.83

Football League post-war hat-tricks from three penalty-kicks

Player	For	Against	Date
George Milburn	Chesterfield	Sheffield Wednesday	June 1947
Charlie Mitten	Manchester United	Aston Villa	March 1950
Joe Willetts	Hartlepool United	Darlington	March 1951
Ken Barnes	Manchester City	Everton	December 1957
Trevor Anderson	Swindon Town	Walsall	April 1976
Alan Slough	Peterborough	Chester	April 1978
Andy Blair	Sheffield Wednesday	Luton Town	November 1984

Players scoring hat-tricks in the Football League against their former clubs during the last 20 years.

Player	For	Against	Date
Ivor Allchurch	Cardiff City	Swansea Town	April 1965
Barry Hutchinson	Darlington	Chesterfield	April 1966
Derek Dougan	Leicester City	Aston Villa	September 1966
Harry Burrows	Stoke City	Aston Villa	December 1966
Ray Smith	Wrexham	Southend United	October 1967
Terry Harkin	Shrewsbury Town	Southport	May 1969
John Fairbrother	Mansfield Town	Peterborough United	October 1972
Peter Noble	Burnley	Newcastle United	November 1974
Derek Hales	Charlton Athletic	Luton Town	September 1976
Malcolm Macdonald	Arsenal	Newcastle United	December 1976
*Edward Woods	Newport County	Scunthorpe United	October 1977
Phil Boyer	Southampton	Derby County	September 1979
David Kemp	Plymouth Argyle	Carlisle United	September 1980
Leighton James	Swansea City	Derby County	October 1980
Paul Goddard	West Ham United	Queen's Park Rangers	April 1981
Trevor Christie	Notts County	Leicester City	August 1983
Wayne Biggins	Burnley	Lincoln City	February 1984

* Woods had been on loan to Scunthorpe

Post-war instances of two Football League hat-tricks scored by a player against the same opponents in the same season

Player	For		Division	Season
+L. F. Shackleton	Newcastle United	Newport County	2	1946–47
H. Billington	Luton Town	Brentford	2	1947–48
G. B. Sutherland	Leyton Orient	Ipswich Town	3S	1949–50
W. Ardron	Nottingham Forest	Gillingham	3S	1950–51
*J. Shaw	Rotherham United	New Brighton	3N	1950–51
E. Gemmell	Oldham Athletic	Chester	3N	1951–52
*G. A. Rowley	Leicester City	Fulham	2	1952–53
E. Carr	Bradford City	Carlisle United	3N	1952–53
W. J. Charles	Leeds United	Rotherham United	2	1953–54
+T. Briggs	Blackburn Rovers	Bristol Rovers	2	1954–55
W. Grant	Ipswich Town	Millwall	3S	1955–56
R. Dwight	Fulham	Swansea Town	2	1956–57
+N. Coleman	Stoke City	Lincoln City	2	1956–57
B. Clough	Middlesbrough	Brighton & Hove Albion	2	1958–59
B. Clough	Middlesbrough	Scunthorpe United	2	1958–59
J. Rogers	Coventry City	Aldershot	4	1958–59
B. Frear	Chesterfield	Southend United	3	1958–59
J. Greaves	Chelsea	Preston North End	1	1959–60
D. Viollet	Manchester United	Burnley	1	1960–61
T. Bly	Peterborough United	Exeter City	4	1960–61
P. Dobing	Manchester City	West Ham United	1	1961–62
K. Havenhand	Derby County	Bristol Rovers	2	1961–62
R. Saunders	Portsmouth	Leyton Orient	2	1963–64
C. Napier	Workington	Swansea Town	3	1965–66
+G. Hurst	West Ham United	Sunderland	1	1968–69

* Against his former club
\+ Two hat-tricks in one game

Len Shackleton (Sunderland) with Newcastle United scoring records previously.

Andy Blair (Sheffield Wednesday) with a unique penalty hat-trick in recent years. (ASP).

Post-war Football League matches in which players on both sides scored hat-tricks

(Home team given first)

Division	Player	For	Against	Date	Result
1	Fenton Steele	Middlesbrough Stoke City	Stoke City Middlesbrough	7.9.46	5–4
3N	Mercer Cheetham	Accrington Stanley Lincoln City	Lincoln City Accrington Stanley	31.5.47	8–4
3S	Allen Jones McNicol	Port Vale Port Vale Aldershot	Aldershot Aldershot Port Vale	6.9.47	6–4
2	Carter Milburn	Bury Newcastle United	Newcastle United Bury	18.10.47	3–5
2	Jezzard Allchurch, I.	Fulham Swansea Town	Swansea Town Fulham	19.4.54	4–3
1	O'Connell, S. Viollet	Chelsea Manchester United	Manchester United Chelsea	16.10.54	5–6
2	Chappell Atyeo	Barnsley Bristol City	Bristol City Barnsley	27.8.58	4–7
1	Smith Harris, J.	Tottenham Hotspur Everton	Everton Tottenham Hotspur	11.10.58	10–4
1	Thompson Greaves	Preston North End Chelsea	Chelsea Preston North End	19.12.59	4–5
2	Edwards Clough	Charlton Athletic Middlesbrough	Middlesbrough Charton Athletic	22.10.60	6–6
3	Bly Beesley	Coventry City Southend United	Southend United Coventry City	1.9.62	3–4
1	Keyworth Law	Leicester City Manchester United	Manchester United Leicester City	16.4.63	4–3
1	Kevan Lee	West Bromwich Albion Bolton Wanderers	Bolton Wanderers West Bromwich Albion	22.9.62	5–4
1	Jones Baker	Tottenham Hotspur Ipswich Town	Ipswich Town Tottenham Hotspur	4.4.64	6–3
3	McKinven Hamilton	Southend United Bristol Rovers	Bristol Rovers Southend United	24.10.64	6–3
3	Large Mabbutt	Northampton Town Bristol Rovers	Bristol Rovers Northampton Town	28.10.67	4–5
1	Francis MacDonald	Birmingham City Arsenal	Arsenal Birmingham City	18.1.77	3–3
4	Ingram Daniels	Bradford City Stockport County	Stockport County Bradford City	11.9.76	3–3
4	Cooke Houchen	Peterborough United Hartlepool United	Hartlepool United Peterborough United	27.2.82	4–4
3	Snodin, G. Dixon	Doncaster Reading	Reading Doncaster	25.9.82	7–5
3	White Neville	Gillingham Exeter City	Exeter City Gillingham	8.1.83	4–4

Players scoring three or more Division 1 hat-tricks in one post-war season

Six hat-tricks		
Jimmy Greaves	Chelsea	1960–61
Four hat-tricks		
Doug Lishman	Arsenal	1951–52
Jack Rowley	Manchester United	1951–52
Eddie Firmani	Charlton Athletic	1954–55
Alex Govan	Birmingham City	1956–57
Gordon Turner	Luton Town	1956–57
Bobby Smith	Tottenham Hotspur	1957–58
Jimmy Greaves	Tottenham Hotspur	1962–63
Andy McEvoy	Blackburn Rovers	1963–64
Fred Pickering	Blackburn Rovers and Everton	1963–64
Jimmy Greaves	Tottenham Hotspur	1963–64
Three hat-tricks		
Jack Balmer	Liverpool	1946–47
Freddie Steele	Stoke City	1946–47

Jack Rowley	Manchester United	1947–48
Willie Moir	Bolton Wanderers	1948–49
Doug Reid	Portsmouth	1949–50
Jack Lee	Derby County	1950–51
Alex McCrae	Middlesbrough	1950–51
Nat Lofthouse	Bolton Wanderers	1952–53
Ronnie Allen	West Bromwich Albion	1953–54
Jimmy Glazzard	Huddersfield Town	1953–54
Nat Lofthouse	Bolton Wanderers	1955–56
Roy Swinbourne	Wolverhampton Wanderers	1955–56
Gordon Turner	Luton Town	1957–58
Jimmy Greaves	Chelsea	1959–60
Billy McAdams	Manchester City	1959–60
Jimmy Robson	Burnley	1960–61
Peter Dobing	Manchester City	1961–62
Derek Kevan	West Bromwich Albion	1962–63
Denis Law	Manchester United	1963–64
Willie Irvine	Burnley	1965–66
Ron Davies	Southampton	1966–67
Jeff Astle	West Bromwich Albion	1967–68
Jimmy Greaves	Tottenham Hotspur	1968–69
Kevin Hector	Derby County	1973–74
Mick Ferguson	Coventry City	1977–78
Phil Boyer	Southampton	1979–80
Ian Rush	Liverpool	1982–83
Paul Walsh	Luton Town	1982–83
Ian Rush	Liverpool	1983–84

Total Football League attendances since 1946–47

Season	Matches	Total	Division 1	Division 2	Division 3S	Division 3N
1946–47	1 848	35 604 606	15 005 316	11 071 572	5 664 004	3 863 714
1947–48	1 848	40 259 130	16 732 341	12 286 350	6 653 610	4 586 829
1948–49	1 848	41 271 414	17 914 667	11 353 237	6 998 429	5 005 081
1949–50	1 848	40 517 865	17 278 625	11 694 158	7 104 155	4 440 927
1950–51	2 028	39 584 967	16 679 454	10 780 580	7 367 884	4 757 109
1951–52	2 028	39 015 866	16 110 322	11 066 189	6 958 927	4 880 428
1952–53	2 028	37 149 966	16 050 278	9 686 654	6 704 299	4 708 735
1953–54	2 028	36 174 590	16 154 915	9 510 053	6 311 508	4 198 114
1954–55	2 028	34 133 103	15 087 221	8 988 794	5 996 017	4 051 071
1955–56	2 028	33 150 809	14 108 961	9 080 002	5 692 479	4 269 367
1956–57	2 028	32 744 405	13 803 037	8 718 162	5 622 189	4 691 017
1957–58	2 028	33 562 208	14 468 652	8 663 712	6 097 183	4 332 661
					Division 3	**Division 4**
1958–59	2 028	33 610 985	14 727 691	8 641 997	5 946 600	4 276 697
1959–60	2 028	32 538 611	14 391 227	8 399 627	5 739 707	4 008 050
1960–61	2 028	28 619 754	12 926 948	7 033 936	4 784 256	3 874 614
1961–62	2 015	27 979 902	12 061 194	7 453 089	5 199 106	3 266 513
1962–63	2 028	28 885 852	12 490 239	7 792 770	5 341 362	3 261 481
1963–64	2 028	28 535 022	12 486 626	7 594 158	5 419 157	3 035 081
1964–65	2 028	27 641 168	12 708 752	6 984 104	4 436 245	3 512 067
1965–66	2 028	27 206 980	12 480 644	6 914 757	4 779 150	3 032 429
1966–67	2 028	28 902 596	14 242 957	7 253 819	4 421 172	2 984 648
1967–68	2 028	30 107 298	15 289 410	7 450 410	4 013 087	3 354 391
1968–69	2 028	29 382 172	14 584 851	7 382 390	4 339 656	3 075 275
1969–70	2 028	29 600 972	14 868 754	7 581 728	4 223 761	2 926 729
1970–71	2 028	28 194 146	13 954 337	7 098 265	4 377 213	2 764 331
1971–72	2 028	28 700 729	14 484 603	6 769 308	4 697 392	2 749 426
1972–73	2 028	25 448 642	13 998 154	5 631 730	3 737 252	2 081 506
1973–74	2 027	24 982 203	13 070 991	6 326 108	3 421 624	2 163 480
1974–75	2 028	25 577 977	12 613 178	6 955 970	4 086 145	1 992 684
1975–76	2 028	24 896 053	13 089 861	5 798 405	3 948 449	2 059 338
1976–77	2 028	26 182 800	13 647 585	6 250 597	4 152 218	2 132 400
1977–78	2 028	25 392 872	13 255 677	6 474 763	3 332 042	2 330 390
1978–79	2 028	24 540 627	12 704 549	6 153 223	3 374 558	2 308 297
1979–80	2 028	24 623 975	12 163 002	6 112 025	3 999 328	2 349 620
1980–81	2 028	21 907 569	11 392 894	5 175 442	3 637 854	1 701 379
1981–82	2 028	20 006 961	10 420 793	4 750 463	2 836 915	1 998 790
1982–83	2 028	18 766 158	9 295 613	4 974 937	2 943 568	1 552 040
1983–84	2 028	18 342 116	8 701 230	5 359 757	2 726 062	1 555 067
1984–85	2 028	17 895 847	(official figures not available)			

Highest attendances

At each Football League club's current ground, listed in descending order

Team	Attendance	Opponents	Match	Date
Manchester City	84 569	Stoke City	FA Cup 6th rd	3.3.34
Chelsea	82 905	Arsenal	Division 1	12.10.35
Everton	78 299	Liverpool	Division 1	18.9.48
Aston Villa	76 588	Derby County	FA Cup 6th rd	2.3.46
Sunderland	75 118	Derby County	FA Cup 6th rd replay	8.3.33
Tottenham Hotspur	75 038	Sunderland	FA Cup 6th rd	5.3.38
Charlton Athletic	75 031	Aston Villa	FA Cup 5th rd	12.2.38
Arsenal	73 295	Sunderland	Division 1	9.3.35
Sheffield Wednesday	72 841	Manchester City	FA Cup 5th rd	17.2.34
Manchester United	70 504	Aston Villa	Division 1	27.12.20
Bolton Wanderers	69 912	Manchester City	FA Cup 5th rd	18.2.33
Newcastle United	68 386	Chelsea	Division 1	3.9.30
Sheffield United	68 287	Leeds United	FA Cup 5th rd	15.2.36
Huddersfield Town	67 037	Arsenal	FA Cup 6th rd	27.2.32
Birmingham City	66 844	Everton	FA Cup 5th rd	11.2.39
West Bromwich Albion	64 815	Arsenal	FA Cup 6th rd	6.3.37
Liverpool	61 905	Wolverhampton Wanderers	FA Cup 4th rd	2.2.52
Blackburn Rovers	61 783	Bolton Wanderers	FA Cup 6th rd	2.3.29
Wolverhampton Wanderers	61 315	Liverpool	FA Cup 5th rd	11.2.39
Leeds United	57 892	Sunderland	FA Cup 5th rd replay	15.3.67
Cardiff City	57 800	Arsenal	Division 1	22.4.53
Hull City	55 019	Manchester United	FA Cup 6th rd	26.2.49
Burnley	54 775	Huddersfield Town	FA Cup 3rd rd	23.2.24
Middlesbrough	53 596	Newcastle United	Division 1	27.12.49
Crystal Palace	51 801	Burnley	Division 2	11.5.79
Coventry City	51 457	Wolverhampton Wanderers	Division 2	29.4.67
Portsmouth	51 385	Derby County	FA Cup 6th rd	26.2.49
Stoke City	51 380	Arsenal	Division 1	29.3.37
Port Vale	50 000	Aston Villa	FA Cup 5th rd	20.2.60
Nottingham Forest	49 945	Manchester United	Division 1	28.10.67
Fulham	49 335	Millwall	Division 2	8.10.38
Millwall	48 672	Derby County	FA Cup 5th rd	20.2.37
Oldham Athletic	47 671	Sheffield Wednesday	FA Cup 4th rd	25.1.30
Notts County	47 310	York City	FA Cup 6th rd	12.3.55
Leicester City	47 298	Tottenham Hotspur	FA Cup 5th rd	18.2.58
Norwich City	43 984	Leicester City	FA Cup 6th rd	30.3.63
Plymouth Argyle	43 596	Aston Villa	Division 2	10.10.36
Bristol City	43 335	Preston North End	FA Cup 5th rd	16.2.35
Preston North End	42 684	Arsenal	Division 1	23.4.68
West Ham United	42 322	Tottenham Hotspur	Division 1	17.10.70
Derby County	41,826	Tottenham Hotspur	Division 1	20.9.69
Barnsley	40 255	Stoke City	FA Cup 5th rd	15.2.36
Brentford	39 626	Preston North End	FA Cup 6th rd	5.3.38
Bradford City	39 146	Burnley	FA Cup 4th rd	11.3.11
Blackpool	39 118	Manchester United	Division 1	19.4.52
Bristol Rovers	38 472	Preston North End	FA Cup 4th rd	30.1.60
Ipswich Town	38 010	Leeds United	FA Cup 6th rd	8.3.75
Doncaster Rovers	37 149	Hull City	Division 3N	2.10.48
Halifax Town	36 885	Tottenham Hotspur	FA Cup 5th rd	14.2.53
Brighton & Hove Albion	36 747	Fulham	Division 2	27.12.58
Queen's Park Rangers	35 353	Leeds United	Division 1	28.4.74
Bury	35 000	Bolton Wanderers	FA Cup 3rd rd	9.1.60
Wrexham	34 445	Manchester United	FA Cup 4th rd	26.1.57

Arsenal score against Huddersfield Town in the 1930 Cup Final at Wembley. Arsenal figure prominently in many highest attendances. (PA).

Orient	34 345	West Ham United	FA Cup 4th rd	25.1.64
Watford	34 099	Manchester United	FA Cup 4th rd	3.2.69
Reading	33 042	Brentford	FA Cup 5th rd	19.2.27
Swansea City	32 796	Arsenal	FA Cup 4th rd	17.2.68
Swindon Town	32 000	Arsenal	FA Cup 3rd rd	15.1.72
Grimsby Town	31 657	Wolverhampton Wanderers	FA Cup 5th rd	20.2.37
Southampton	31 044	Manchester United	Division 1	8.10.69
Southend United	31 036	Liverpool	FA Cup 3rd rd	10.1.79
Chesterfield	30 968	Newcastle United	Division 2	7.4.39
Peterborough United	30 096	Swansea Town	FA Cup 5th rd	20.2.65
Luton Town	30 069	Blackpool	FA Cup 6th rd replay	4.3.59
Bournemouth	28.799	Manchester United	FA Cup 6th rd	2.3.57
York City	28 123	Huddersfield Town	FA Cup 6th rd	5.3.38
Stockport County	27 833	Liverpool	FA Cup 5th rd	11.2.50
Carlisle United	27 500	Birmingham City	FA Cup 3rd rd	5.1.57
Carlisle United	27 500	Middlesbrough	FA Cup 5th rd	7.2.70
Wigan Athletic	27 500	Hereford United	FA Cup 2nd rd	12.12.53
Walsall	25 453	Newcastle United	Division 2	29.8.61
Rotherham United	25 000	Sheffield United	Division 2	13.12.52
Rotherham United	25 000	Sheffield Wednesday	Division 2	26.1.52
Northampton Town	24 523	Fulham	Division 1	23.4.66
Mansfield Town	24 467	Nottingham Forest	FA Cup 3rd rd	10.1.53
Tranmere Rovers	24 424	Stoke City	FA Cup 4th rd	5.2.72
Newport County	24 268	Cardiff City	Division 3S	16.10.37
Rochdale	24 231	Notts County	FA Cup 2nd rd	10.12.49
Scunthorpe United	23 935	Portsmouth	FA Cup 4th rd	30.1.54
Lincoln City	23 196	Derby County	League Cup 4th rd	15.11.67
Gillingham	23 002	Queen's Park Rangers	FA Cup 3rd rd	10.1.48
Oxford United	22 730	Preston North End	FA Cup 6th rd	29.2.64
Torquay United	21 908	Huddersfield Town	FA Cup 4th rd	29.1.55
Darlington	21 023	Bolton Wanderers	Lge Cup 3rd rd	14.11.60
Exeter City	20 984	Sunderland	FA Cup 6th rd replay	4.3.31
Chester City	20 500	Chelsea	FA Cup 3rd rd replay	16.1.52
Crewe Alexandra	20 000	Tottenham Hotspur	FA Cup 4th rd	30.1.60
Aldershot	19 138	Carlisle United	FA Cup 4th rd replay	28.1.70
Colchester United	19 072	Reading	FA Cup 1st rd	27.11.48
Shrewsbury Town	18 917	Walsall	Division 2	26.4.61
Hereford United	18 114	Sheffield Wednesday	FA Cup 3rd rd	4.1.58
Wimbledon	18 000	HMS Victory	Amateur Cup 3rd rd	23.2.35
Hartlepool United	17 426	Manchester United	FA Cup 3rd rd	5.1.57
Cambridge United	14 000	Chelsea	Friendly	1.5.70

At each Scottish League club's current ground, in descending order

Team	Attendance	Opponents	Match	Date
Rangers	118 567	Celtic	Division 1	2.1.39
Queen's Park	95 722	Rangers	Scottish Cup 1st rd	18.11.30
Celtic	92 000	Rangers	Division 1	1.1.38
Hibernian	66 840	Heart of Midlothian	Division 1	2.1.50
Heart of Midlothian	53 496	Rangers	Scottish Cup 3rd 4d	13.2.32
Partick Thistle	49 838	Rangers	Division 1	18.2.22
Clyde	52 000	Rangers	Division 1	21.11.28
St Mirren	47 428	Celtic	Scottish Cup 4th rd	7.3.25
Aberdeen	45 061	Heart of Midlothian	Scottish Cup 4th rd	13.3.54
Dundee	43 024	Rangers	Scottish Cup 2nd rd	7.2.53
Motherwell	35 632	Rangers	Scottish Cup 4th rd replay	12.3.52
Kilmarnock	34 246	Rangers	League Cup	20.8.63
Raith Rovers	31 306	Heart of Midlothian	Scottish Cup 2nd rd	7.2.53
St Johnstone	29 972	Dundee	Scottish Cup 2nd rd	10.2.52
Hamilton Academical	28 690	Heart of Midlothian	Scottish Cup 3rd rd	3.3.37
Dundee United	28 000	Barcelona	Fairs Cup 2nd rd	16.11.66
Dunfermline Athletic	27 816	Celtic	Division 1	30.4.68
Albion Rovers	27 381	Rangers	Scottish Cup 2nd rd	8.2.36
Stirling Albion	26 400	Celtic	Scottish Cup 4th rd	14.3.59
Cowdenbeath	25 586	Rangers	League Cup quarter final	21.9.49
Ayr United	25 225	Rangers	Division 1	13.9.69
Queen of the South	24 500	Heart of Midlothian	Scottish Cup 3rd rd	23.2.52
Airdrieonians	24 000	Heart of Midlothian	Scottish Cup 4th rd	8.3.52
Morton	23 500	Rangers	Scottish Cup 3rd rd	21.2.53
Falkirk	23 100	Celtic	Scottish Cup 3rd rd	21.2.53
East Fife	22 515	Raith Rovers	Division 1	2.1.50
Dumbarton	18 000	Faith Rovers	Scottish Cup quarter final	2.3.57
Alloa	15 467	Celtic	Scottish Cup 5th rd	5.2.55
Clydebank	14 900	Hibernian	Scottish Cup 1st rd	10.2.65
Arbroath	13 510	Rangers	Scottish Cup 3rd rd	23.2.52
Berwick Rangers	13 365	Rangers	Scottish Cup 1st rd	28.1.67
Stenhousemuir	12 500	East Fife	Scottish Cup 4th rd	11.3.50
East Stirling	11 500	Hibernian	Scottish Cup 2nd rd	10.2.60
Forfar Athletic	10 780	Rangers	Scottish Cup 2nd 4d	2.2.70
Montrose	8 983	Dundee	Scottish Cup 3rd rd	17.3.73
Brechin City	8 123	Aberdeen	Scottish Cup 3rd rd	3.2.73
Stranraer	6 500	Rangers	Scottish Cup 1sr rd	24.1.48
Meadowbank Thistle	4 000	Albion Rovers	League Cup	9.8.74

World's largest grounds

Brazil	
Mario Filho (Maracana), Rio de Janeiro	200 000
Morumbi, São Paulo	150 000
Castelao, Fortaleza	130 000
Magalhaes Pinto, Belo Horizonte	110 000
Beira Rio, Porto Alegre	100 000
Olimpico, Porto Alegre	100 000
Egypt	
Nasser Stadium, Cairo	100 000
England	
Wembley Stadium	100 000
India	
Eden Garden Stadium, Calcutta	100 000
Corporation Stadium, Calicur	100 000
Iran	
Azadi, Karadj Auto Band	100 000
Indonesia	
Senayan Main Stadium, Jakarta	110 000
Mexico	
Aztec, Mexico City	*108 499
Universitaria, Monterrey	100 000
Spain	
Nou Camp, Barcelona	120 000
Santiago Bernabeu, Madrid	101 663
USSR	
Central Stadium, Kiev	100 000
Lenin Stadium, Moscow	100 000

* To be increased to 115 000 for the 1986 World Cup.

The giant Maracana Stadium in Rio de Janeiro, venue for the 1950 World Cup and the world's largest ground.

Index of General Subjects

Index to Teams